WOMEN VS FEMINISM

Why We All Need Liberating from the Gender Wars

PREVIOUS BOOKS BY JOANNA WILLIAMS

Consuming Higher Education: Why Learning Can't Be Bought (2012)

Academic Freedom in an Age of Conformity: Confronting the Fear of Knowledge (2016)

WOMEN VS FEMINISM

Why We All Need Liberating from the Gender Wars

BY

JOANNA WILLIAMS
University of Kent, Canterbury, UK

United Kingdom – North America – Japan
India – Malaysia – China

Emerald Publishing Limited
Howard House, Wagon Lane, Bingley BD16 1WA, UK

First edition 2017

Reprints and permissions service
Contact: permissions@emeraldinsight.com

British Library Cataloguing in Publication Data
A catalogue record for this book is available from the British
Library

ISBN: 978-1-78714-476-7 (Print)
ISBN: 978-1-78714-475-0 (Online)
ISBN: 978-1-78714-940-3 (Epub)

ISOQAR certified
Management System,
awarded to Emerald
for adherence to
Environmental
standard
ISO 14001:2004.

ISOQAR
REGISTERED

Certificate Number 1985
ISO 14001

INVESTOR IN PEOPLE

CONTENTS

PART TWO

PRIVATE RELATIONSHIPS, PUBLIC CONCERNS

PART THREE

FEMINISM THEN AND NOW

ACKNOWLEDGEMENTS

So many people have helped and encouraged me to write this book. I am grateful to all of them but perhaps most especially to those who have helped despite disagreeing with the arguments I put forward. It has been a pleasure to work with *Emerald Publishing* and particularly with Philippa Grand. Few publishers nowadays seem willing to take a risk on a book that can't be easily categorized and I was all but ready to give up on this project before I was fortunate enough to meet with Philippa. Another stroke of luck has been my contact with David Snyder, Program Coordinator at the *Charles Koch Foundation*. David helped me to secure the academic grant from the Foundation that has permitted me the huge privilege of uninterrupted time to write. David has shown an interest in my progress without ever once seeking to influence the direction in which I was heading.

The online magazine *Spiked*, where I am education editor, not only provides me with daily inspiration but has given me a platform to test out some of the ideas presented in this book. Articles I have written for *Spiked* on the gender pay gap, rape culture, feminism and the meaning of gender were the impetus for me writing this book. I want to thank everyone at *Spiked* but most especially Viv Regan for her encouragement and faith in me. Claire Fox at the *Institute of Ideas* is one of the very few people I have ever met who I would consider to be a role model. Claire's unwavering support for me and this book has been humbling and I only hope it lives up to her expectations.

David Didau, Gareth Sturdy, Bríd Hehir and Jan Macvarish all not only helped me to make sense of the issues I struggled most to understand but generously permitted me to reproduce their words in this book. Many other people have discussed and debated with me the ideas I put forward. Louise Burton and Kevin Rooney provided me with valuable feedback and examples on the topic of education. I hope the friends, colleagues and comrades who crowded into a caravan in Camber Sands can see the considerable influence their views have had on my thinking over the course of the following pages. I am especially grateful to Ellie Lee, Frank Furedi and Sally Millard for their intellectual and political insights; their impact upon my thinking cannot be overstated. Both Helen Williams and Patrick West proved to be superb draftreaders, urging me to have the courage of my convictions when I showed signs of compromise. I am thankful to them both.

This book simply would not exist as it does without the input of one person in particular. More than anyone else, it is Jennie Bristow who has inspired and encouraged me. Every conversation I have with Jennie challenges me to think through my arguments more clearly, to read and think more deeply and to question my assumptions. The extent to which Jennie has influenced my thinking is evident in all the strengths of this book. Jennie remains streets ahead of me intellectually and I am always running to catch up with her; the weaknesses of this book are evidence of the distance I still have to go.

On a more personal note, I'd like to thank two of my friends in particular: Geraldine Knights and Lucy Abraham. Being able to share the glory messiness of families, work and being a woman with these two wonderful ladies never fails to make me feel better. My own children, George, Harry and Florence, mean more to me than they will ever know. For more than twenty years I have shared my life with Jim Butcher and his love has made me the person I am. Jim — thank you for everything. Finally, while writing every section of this book, I had at the back of my mind women I consider epitomize love, strength and the best type of bloody-minded determination. To my mother-in-law Helen Butcher, my sisters Lesley, Alex and Helen, and my mother Charlotte Williams — this book is for you.

WOMEN VS FEMINISM

This book offers a critique of the new feminism that has become so fashionable today. Its focus is on the lives of women in comparatively wealthy, Western societies, most specifically the United States of America and the United Kingdom. Ardent followers of social media and academic debates will no doubt retort that there is not one type of feminism but many, and nuanced positions can't be lumped together. They have a point, of course. But at the same time there is a dominant feminist narrative that fills newspaper columns, book shelves, speeches at the United Nations and guidance for teachers. This is a feminism that cannot be defined by the sexuality or skin colour of its proponents. Yet it clearly espouses one idea above all others: that women are disadvantaged and oppressed; routine victims of everyday sexism, casual misogyny and the workings of patriarchy. The better women's lives become, the harder it seems that a new generation of feminists must try to justify their purpose through uncovering ever more obscure problems.

This book is in three parts. Part one looks at women's experiences today in education, at work and as mothers.

Although women are doing better than ever before, and often better than men, there is also recognition that life is not as good as it gets — for either women or men. But the problems we face are rarely those identified by feminist campaigners. Part two explores the growing disjuncture that has emerged between the statistical successes women are ratcheting up and the persistent narrative of female disadvantage. We see how a feminism premised upon the notion of women as victims increasingly seeks to regulate not just our behaviour but our innermost thoughts and feelings. The final part of this book considers what feminism once was and what it represents today. The historical gains of feminism provide a context to its current limitations.

PERMISSIONS

Extracts from Chapter 10 were originally published as 'The Prison House of Gender' in *The Spiked Review* (October 2016) and are reprinted here with permission.

PREFACE

Criticising feminism does not come naturally to me. As a child growing up under the shadow of my country's first female prime minister, I knew for certain that feminism was important. I wore a badge given to me by my mother with a picture of a washing line and the slogan 'wages for housework'. I had a postcard stuck to my bedroom wall showing a line drawing of two babies peering earnestly into their nappies. 'Oh! So that explains the difference in our salaries!' read the caption. I even had a T-shirt with a picture of a man and woman having a drink: 'Men's brains are heavier than women's brains,' said the stick man before, in the next picture, falling on to the floor head first. I never once doubted that a woman could do anything a man did – so of course that made me a feminist.

In my first year at university, I helped to make a banner for a 'Take Back the Night' march, although I never actually made it on to the demonstration. I can't ever remember feeling afraid walking alone at night. I'd love now to be able to say that my refusal to march was a protest against being told, for the first time, that I should see myself as a victim. The truth is that I wasn't critical of this new direction in feminism so much as bored with it. As part of my degree in English Literature, I had become far more familiar with work by literary critics like Julia Kristeva, Helene Cixous, Luce Irigaray and Toril Moi than I was with Shakespeare, Chaucer or Dickens. Criticism became reduced to 'sexism spotting' and it didn't seem to matter whether the author was male or female, writing in this century or the seventeenth, our aim was to expose the misogynistic assumptions apparent in the text. Simply appreciating good quality writing was not considered sufficiently academic.

QUESTIONING FEMINISM

The first time I publicly confessed to doubts about feminism, I took myself by surprise. In an attempt at rehabilitating my post-maternity leave teaching career I began a Master's Degree in Education at my local university. One week we learnt about projects to empower girls, to interest them in science and to encourage them to go to university. It was worthy and inspiring stuff but for one issue that was not acknowledged: girls were doing better at school than boys and had been for over a decade. When I raised this with my tutor I was told, 'No one expressed concerns when boys were doing better than girls.' So, I thought, perhaps this is just historical retribution, payback for all those years in which girls lost out. Perhaps that was what feminism now meant.

The following week we learnt about a school initiative to raise awareness of, and ultimately prevent, domestic violence. Children were to take part in various activities such as discussions and role-play exercises, each carrying the same message: women and girls were at risk in their own homes and fathers, husbands and brothers were the violent perpetrators. I thought of my own boys, then aged three and one. I wanted to protect them from knowing about domestic violence; I was devastated by the implication that they somehow carried guilt by association, that their essential maleness, their masculinity, was something dangerous and inherently threatening.

If feminism meant ignoring boys falling behind at school, and telling girls to fear members of their own families as well as half of their classmates, then it wasn't something I wanted anything to do with. I hadn't planned to say this out loud. I didn't even realize it was what I thought until the words left my mouth. But the shock that greeted my outburst was something that I remember vividly. My tutor and my classmates were all equally horrified: 'But you're a woman!' 'You've benefited from feminism!' 'Feminism just means equality and of course you believe in equality!' Although as students we were instructed in the importance of critical thinking, challenging the direction of feminism and its significance to education was clearly a step too far. Being critical meant employing a feminist perspective; it did not mean questioning it. I can't remember what the intended learning outcome was for that particular class but I was clear about my own take home message: when it comes to criticizing feminism, 'You can't say that!'

THE DIFFICULTIES OF WRITING

Since this time I've spoken at public meetings and written articles questioning a feminism that seems to have grown increasingly distant from the reality of many young women's lives. As a result, I'm no stranger to the strength of feeling criticizing feminism evokes. But the more I've been confronted with fourth-wave or intersectional feminism, the more I've become convinced it is detrimental. As I explore in this book, the feminism we have today seems all too often to demonize men and degrade women by imbuing them with a false sense of their own victimhood. My determination to challenge these ideas meant that I began writing this book with relish. As a woman who has always had an interest in feminism, I thought writing a book on the subject would be easy. Perhaps even fun.

My bravado did not last for long. As I soon realized, a critique of feminism cannot be separated from an evaluation of women's lives. On paper, women are doing better than ever before and, particularly when younger, better than men. But in reality it doesn't always feel this way and the popularity of feminism speaks to a sense of dissatisfaction with life as it currently is. The progress women have made can only be understood when seen in relation to the oppression women experienced in the past. Likewise, women's experiences at school, work and in the home today only make sense when viewed alongside men's lives. Writing about this did not prove to be straightforward; one problem was simply knowing where to start and stop.

Neither feminism nor women's lives have developed as one coherent narrative. Different women experience the world very differently. Feminism is, and always has been, fractured and diverse, emphasizing different issues in new eras. What looks like progress in one direction is matched by moves sideways and backwards in other areas. A book must have a beginning, middle and end and this necessity risks sweeping over contradictions and ignoring the nuances of an argument. I am fearfully aware that many feminist scholars, with far more academic credibility than me, have dedicated entire careers to exploring, in detail, issues that I merely prod and poke here.

Over the course of writing this book my bravado has been tempered by humility. What's here is not intended to be a definitive answer to the twenty-first century's 'woman question'. Instead, it's a series of themed essays that I hope might puncture what seems to be the current consensus around women's lives and raise questions about the direction and purpose of feminism today.

PART ONE

—

WOMEN'S LIVES TODAY

CHAPTER ONE

SCHOOLING FOR SUCCESS

Schools are on the front line in the gender wars. St Paul's Girls' School in West London is one of Britain's leading independent schools. Having wealthy parents is not enough to secure entry; potential pupils must also pass a competitive exam. Former students include famous actors, authors, academics and Members of Parliament. In February 2017 St Paul's made the news following the announcement of a new 'gender identity protocol' that would permit pupils to take boys' names and wear boys' clothes. From the age of 16, girls will now be able to request that their teachers refer to them as boys or address them using gender neutral pronouns. One report suggests ten current pupils want to take advantage of the new guidance.[1]

St Paul's is playing catch-up to the more forward-looking Brighton College, another independent boarding school. A full year earlier, Brighton College announced that the distinction between boys' and girls' school uniforms had been abolished in order to accommodate transgender students. A statement issued by the school noted that, 'Public schools are usually seen as bastions of conservatism but Brighton College feels it is time to break ranks.'[2] Meanwhile, delegates at the UK's National Union of Teachers conference passed a motion calling for children as young as 2 to be taught about transgender issues and same sex relationships.[3] In American universities students in some classes are asked to state their preferred gender pronouns when they introduce themselves, and debates about the provision of gender neutral bathrooms have become a national talking point. In Sweden it became a legal requirement for schools to challenge gender stereotyping in 1998.[4] Teachers are encouraged to use 'hen' as a gender neutral pronoun to avoid propagating sexist assumptions.

In the past, a combination of socialization and coercion meant girls were denied access to the same educational opportunities as boys. Girls were less likely to study a full range of academic subjects; they achieved lower exam results and did not carry on to university at the same rate as men. Feminists successfully challenged the low expectations schools and teachers held for girls, and today, as this chapter shows, a very different picture emerges. At every stage of their education, girls are now outperforming boys and yet the influence of feminism on education shows no signs of diminishing.

Education is increasingly viewed by teachers, campaigners and policy makers as a key site for influencing the next generation and shaping society. As such, national governments charge schools with responsibility for an array of economic and political goals such as skills training, entrepreneurship and social mobility. It can seem as if there is no problem that can't be solved by putting it on the curriculum: schools teach children about sex and relationships, healthy eating, internet safety, environmental awareness, budgeting and a whole host of other issues. Teaching subject knowledge is blurred with a more explicit promotion of values, at the forefront of which is feminism. Schooling has taken on board political goals concerned with encouraging children to think about gender and sexuality in new ways. This chapter explores the impact of feminism upon education and asks what girls' educational success means today.

GIRLS ARE OUTPERFORMING BOYS

Girls do better at school than boys. All around the world, irrespective of the status of women or the levels of gender equality within a society, it is girls who are notching up more exam passes in almost every subject and at every level.[5] This is not a recent phenomenon; in both the United States (US) and the United Kingdom (UK), girls have been outperforming boys for well over a quarter of a century. Neither is it the case that girls are doing just a little bit better than boys; they are so far ahead that some British universities now have twice as many female undergraduates than males.[6] Meanwhile, in America, over 60 per cent of all bachelor degrees are awarded to women.[7]

A gender attainment gap emerges almost as soon as children start school. At age seven, British children take national curriculum assessments in reading, writing, speaking and listening, maths and science. Girls do better than boys in every area with the biggest attainment gaps occurring in reading, writing, speaking and listening. Boys do marginally better at reaching the highest levels in maths and science.[8] By the time they are 16, girls perform significantly better than boys in national assessments (in England and Wales, GCSEs). In 2016 the attainment gap between boys and girls at this age was the largest in over a decade at 8.9 per cent. 71.3 per cent of GCSEs taken by girls were awarded at least a C grade, compared to just 62.4 per cent of exams sat by boys.[9] Success aged 16 leads to a greater number of female students continuing along an academic route to take 'A' levels aged 18, the exams still most closely associated with university entry. It's not just in the UK: in the US too girls are more likely to receive a high school diploma. In 2014 in the State of California, 84.7 per cent of girls graduated from high school compared to only 77.1 per cent of boys.[10]

Success at school results in more women than men going on to university.[11] Gender has come to be more closely correlated with the likelihood of attending and graduating from college than family income. Research from the American Brookings Institute suggests that 'the female advantage in college attendance and completion among recent cohorts is about half as large as corresponding gaps between students in the first and second quartiles of the income distribution'.[12]

In Britain, women students first began to outnumber men at university in 1992 and this has remained the case every year since. In 2015 young British women were 35 per cent more likely to go to university than their male peers and 57.5 per cent of students were female.[13] On some courses, such as veterinary science and subjects allied to medicine, over 75 per cent of students are now female. What's more, women are more likely to stay the course, complete their studies, and perform better than men. Whereas 79 per cent of women get at least a 2.1 degree classification, only 70 per cent of men score this highly.[14] Importantly, this attainment gap exists even when comparing the results of students who entered university with exactly the same levels of prior academic achievement. American women are also going to university in greater numbers than men and doing better once there: they are less likely to drop out and more likely to attain a higher degree classification. In 2008, US universities awarded more doctorates to women and this has remained the case every subsequent year.[15] In 2015, American women taking postgraduate degrees outnumbered men by 135 to 100.[16]

A DRAMATIC CHANGE

The educational performance of girls has undergone a phenomenal transformation over a relatively short period. Up until the late 1980s, it was boys who did better at school and men who went on to university in greater numbers. Well into the latter half of the twentieth century, boys and girls rarely received the same education. Assumptions about the lives children would lead as adults meant boys and girls studied different subjects: boys studied woodwork or metalwork, while girls were taught the domestic skills considered necessary for their future role as wives and mothers alongside some academic subjects. There was often little expectation that girls would continue on to higher education or pursue a career.

Women first began to go to university in greater numbers following the expansion of higher education in the decades following the Second World War, although this was limited to predominantly middle-class women. By 1970, women comprised roughly 30 per cent of the UK student population. Some women who were students at this time report 'endless derision' from an older generation of male academics who questioned, sometimes publicly, their right to be at university. This could extend to not marking work completed by women, refusing to allow them to take part in seminar discussions or subjecting them to mockery in the lecture hall. The battle to overturn not just the practical restrictions that limited women's access to education but the attitudes of both male and female family, friends, teachers and lecturers was long and hard fought. Feminist campaigners strove to improve educational opportunities for girls and their success is evident in the improvement in girls' performance we see today.

Nowadays, in most Western countries, it is taken for granted that boys and girls should have the same educational opportunities. Although boys and girls might, on average, perform better in different subjects, or prefer some subjects to others, students tend not to be excluded from particular classes on the basis of their gender. Likewise, although single sex schools still exist, they teach a national curriculum, or the common core in the US, and generally enter pupils for nationally recognized exams. It is mostly accepted that boys and girls can learn the same subjects in the same school, sitting side by side.

It was in the 1980s that girls started outperforming boys at school and increasingly continuing on to higher education. Since this time, the educational landscape has changed very quickly. In America, the proportion of women in work with a college degree trebled between 1970 and 2014, increasing from 11.2 to 40.0 per cent.[17] The pace of change means that commentators and educators alike have been left behind. Having been used to considering girls as the underrepresented and disadvantaged group, the new reality of girls outperforming boys provides an inconvenient challenge to the traditional feminist narrative. In response, many campaigners have either doubled down on their original claims or searched for more specific areas in which girls can still be said to be underperforming in comparison to boys, such as in physical sciences and computer studies. A backlash to this dominant narrative, in the form of a panic about the underachievement of boys, is beginning to emerge. As a result, an honest appraisal of the educational performance of both boys and girls is difficult to establish.

UNDERACHIEVING BOYS

In July 2016 the British charity *Save the Children* published an evocatively-titled report, *The Lost Boys*, in which it sought to lay bare 'the potentially devastating and lifelong

consequences for boys in England who start school significantly trailing girls in basic early language skills'. It
highlighted the fact that 'boys are nearly twice as likely to fall
behind girls by the time they start school'.[18]

One group has attracted particular cause for concern:
white working class boys. In 2016, only 26 per cent of white
British boys on free school meals (shorthand for a family on
a very low income or state benefits) achieved five top GCSE
grades including English and maths – the benchmark for
school success. This compared with 40 per cent of black boys
and 63 per cent of all other pupils on free school meals.
Martin Daubney, a journalist concerned with men's issues
and the founder of the *Men and Boys Coalition*, describes
poor white boys as 'the new educational underclass'.

In America, by contrast, it is black boys who are
getting left behind. According to research carried out
by the American National Education Association (NEA),
42 per cent of black students attend schools that are under-
resourced and performing poorly and black boys are three
times more likely to be suspended or expelled from school
than their white classmates. Black and Hispanic boys make
up almost 80 per cent of those enroled in special education
programmes. Although black males comprise 9 per cent of
the student population, they constitute 20 per cent of all students classified as 'mentally retarded'. The NEA's 2011
report, *Race Against Time: Educating Black Boys* highlights
that 'less than half of black male students graduate from high
school on time' and 'only 11 percent of black males complete
a bachelor's degree'.[19]

For the first couple of decades after girls began to outperform boys at school and go onto higher education in greater
numbers, relatively little attention was paid to the comparative drop in boys' performance. Girls were considered merely
to be correcting a historical injustice and taking advantage of

the opportunities that should have always rightfully been theirs. Worrying about the underachievement of boys was seen as a ploy to detract attention and hard won resources away from girls. Even today the underperformance of boys is often played down. In 2014 the British government noted: 'The problem of white "working class" underachievement is not specific to boys; attention to both sexes is needed'. Daubney notes that 'boys have had few political allies in the corridors of power. Nobody, it seems, cares about our failing boys'.[20] Dr Gijsbert Stoet, professor of cognitive psychology at Leeds Beckett University agrees: 'When it comes to boys falling behind, the real scandal is that this isn't a scandal', he argues. We can only imagine the outcry if girls had been falling behind boys for the past three decades.

Most recently, championed by the likes of Daubney, attention has focused on the need for 'boy friendly' pedagogy and male role models in schools. One project, based in New York and launched in 2015, aims to recruit 1000 male teachers of colour over 3 years. Mary Curnock Cook, the Chief Executive of the UK's university admission service, UCAS, has raised concern about the men apparently 'missing' from higher education. Widening participation initiatives that once focused solely on the educational achievements of girls have slowly begun to shift attention to boys.

In contrast to well-established projects designed to encourage girls to study science, campaigns aimed at boys tend to be piecemeal and underfunded. More worrying are the assumptions driving such initiatives. The University of Edinburgh's *Educated Pass* scheme, for example, aims to get boys 'hooked' on university through links with local football clubs.[21] Not only is there an assumption that all boys are interested in football, there is clearly a view that higher education is not exciting in its own terms and boys need to be 'tricked' into participating through conversations about football.

THE MOST INTELLIGENT GENDER

The growing gender attainment gap has given new impetus to attempts at drawing a connection between gender and intelligence. Biological explanations for intelligence once focused on men's larger brain size but today, in a complete about turn, neuroscientists point to the female brain developing earlier than the male brain. Researchers from Michigan State University have found evidence of superior cognitive ability in girls as young as 2, with girls between 2 and 7 performing better than boys in tests of general intelligence.[22] This early advantage is then said to stick with girls throughout their time in formal education.

This turn to biology presents a view of gender differences as 'hardwired' and intelligence as an innate characteristic that can be measured and recorded, much like height or eye colour. However, whereas no one would seriously seek to make a link between eye colour and intelligence, correlations between gender and intelligence are looked for and then found. Some, like the University of Cambridge psychologist Simon Baron-Cohen, rehabilitate old stereotypes. He argues: 'The female brain is predominantly hardwired for empathy. The male brain is predominantly hardwired for understanding and building systems.'[23]

As Cordelia Fine notes in her excellent debunking of the science behind sex differences, 'The neuroscientific discoveries we read about in magazines, newspaper articles, books and sometimes even journals tell a tale of two brains – essentially different – that create timeless and immutable psychological differences between the sexes.'[24] Unfortunately, as Fine explains, however neat the link between brain differences and gendered ways of thinking and behaving may appear, such claims 'simply reflect – and give scientific authority to' majority opinion. 'When we follow the trail of contemporary science,' Fine counters, 'we discover a surprising number of gaps, assumptions, inconsistencies, poor methodologies, and leaps of faith.' The problem for neuroscientists is that 'the culture in which we develop and function enjoys a "deep reach" into our minds'.[25] The world in which children develop today is one that assumes girls will outperform boys and, unsurprisingly, this is exactly what many researchers then find.

Understanding intelligence as innate and gendered separates an abstract notion of intelligence from, on the one hand, what it is that an individual knows and, on the other, what it is that society formally values and rewards. A baby may be born with the potential to learn but until this potential is nurtured by parents, teachers and eventually the individual themselves, they know little. The neurophysiologist Ruth Bleier argues that when it comes to intelligence, 'Biology can be said to define possibilities but not determine them; it is never irrelevant but it is also not determinant.'[26] In other words, the experiences and circumstances individuals find themselves in, and how they choose to respond to those circumstances, have a huge influence on someone's intelligence.

WHAT GETS MEASURED, COUNTS

Common sense appears to suggest a connection between school success, exam performance and intelligence, but it may be the case that exams measure little more than an ability to answer exam questions. Academic success means different things in different subjects, schools and cultures. It might mean a capacity to comply with expectations, memorize and recall facts, think creatively and independently or solve problems logically. As what is measured by exam success changes, so too will the children deemed to be successful.

The qualities, skills and knowledge that teachers and national education systems value and assess change over time. In the UK, girls began to outperform boys when traditional exams began to be replaced by new forms of assessment that put more emphasis on coursework completed throughout the school year. A belief in intelligence as innate and gendered would lead us to the view that this new 'feminized' approach favoured girls. This was expressed at the time by Masden Pine, writing in *The Spectator*:

> *The old exams – O-levels, A-levels and degree finals – tended to reward the qualities which boys are good at. That is, they favoured risk-taking and grasp of the big picture, rather than the more systematic, consistent, attention-to-detail qualities which favour girls. The old O-level, with its high-risk, swot-it-all-up-for-the-final-throw, and then attempt not more than four out of nine questions, was a boys' exam. The GCSE which replaced it places much more emphasis on systematic preparation in modules, worked on consistently over time. It is not surprising that girls have done better since the change was made, since GCSEs represent the way girls work.*[27]

Interestingly, however, a gender gap in educational attainment began to open up at around the same point in other countries all over the world which had not made such fundamental changes to school assessment methods. As the American philosopher and 'factual feminist' Christina Hoff

Sommers notes in her book *The War Against Boys*, 'In 1985, boys and girls took AP (Advanced Placement) courses at nearly the same rate. Around 1990, the girls moved ahead of boys and never looked back.'[28] We clearly need to look beyond just changes in assessment methods to explain why boys began to fall behind girls.

One explanation for the improvement in the performance of girls might lie in economic changes that happened in the 1980s, in particular, the collapse of many traditionally male-dominant occupations, which began with the recession that hit the UK in 1980 and the US a year later. The new more service-driven economy that was to emerge favoured the skills women had to offer. Perhaps for the first time, many more girls than ever before could see the rewards available to them with school success. Hanna Rosin, writing in *The End of Men*, notes that, 'In 1967, 97 per cent of American men with only a high school diploma were working; in 2010 just 76 per cent were.'[29] Perhaps some girls also realized that marriage and children no longer provided a financially viable future.

Hoff Sommers points to another development that can be traced back to the late 1980s: a new 'therapeutic sensibility' that she describes as rejecting 'almost all forms of competition in favor of a gentle and nurturing climate of co-operation'. This points to a broader shift in the emphasis of schooling and the role of the teacher that occurred at this time: from discipline to care and from the transition of knowledge to the cultivation of skills and values. Rewarding students for caring and co-operating reinforces the behaviour patterns that girls are socialized into demonstrating from a very young age. Meanwhile, Hoff Sommers suggests, this new approach to schooling is 'a sure-fire way to bore and alienate boys'.[30] In this context, England's move away from high stakes exams can best be understood as a reflection of this broader 'therapeutic sensibility' and simply one factor among many that contributed to the growing success of girls.

GENDERED EXPECTATIONS

Measuring intelligence in very young children is likely to tell us far more about the stimulation they have received from family members and their environment since being born than about innate properties of the brain. The expectations of parents, teachers and children themselves will have an impact upon a child's perception of their own intelligence, their confidence and their willingness to put themselves forward for new challenges. Research conducted at the University of Kent suggests that girls see themselves as cleverer, more successful and harder working than boys from the age of just 4. By the age of 7 or 8, boys come to share this view and they also think that girls are more intelligent than boys.[31] On the other hand, a different research project suggests that by age 6, girls believe brilliance is a male trait.[32] Although this research has been used to point to the damning impact of gender stereotypes, it may, ironically, reinforce among girls the view that they need to work hard to achieve success — a virtue which is ultimately rewarded.

Gendered expectations can become a self-fulfilling prophecy as girls live up to the high standards set for them while 'boys will be boys' excuses poor performance. As sociologist Frank Furedi argues, 'Many teachers and parents have internalised the premise that boys are naturally distracted in the classroom and are less focused and less intellectually curious than girls.'[33] Lower expectations of boys are particularly evident when it comes to reading. A former secondary school Head of History recalls attending a parents' meeting in which a literature teacher stressed how important it was for boys to see their fathers enjoying reading. The advice to those present was, 'Dads: just pretend!' The idea that men might genuinely enjoy reading was clearly unimaginable.

Children are very good at confirming the expectations others hold of them and as our expectations of girls have changed so too has their educational success. One illustration of this is recent research showing that in top-level maths the male advantage 'has shrunk to an all-time low'.[34] An analysis of exam results suggests long-held assumptions about girls performing less well than boys in this area can no longer be taken for granted. Mathematician Hannah Fry, commenting on the research, noted: 'We have a cultural tendency to view maths as a male subject, so girls were socialised to think of themselves as mathematically incompetent.' 'However,' she continues, 'the difference in maths performance of boys and girls is not universal. In Asia and the Middle East, girls often outperform boys. It suggests any problems we have in getting girls to perform in maths are cultural rather than an innate difference in ability.'[35] One conclusion is that the original cause of men's superior mathematical ability must have been down to social and cultural factors rather than innate intelligence. This means that the remaining gender attainment gap in maths could eventually disappear altogether. We can see then that gender does have some influence on educational attainment but rather than this being a biological and causal relationship, it has far more to do with cultural factors and is only one of many explanations for academic success.

OVERSTATING GENDER

Explaining educational success and failure through the prism of gender appears to be common sense. All the data about exam passes and university attendance presented in this chapter point to a link between gender and performance but this doesn't necessarily mean that gender is the single factor most likely to determine academic success. As David Didau, a teacher turned author and well-known educational blogger, puts it, 'I'm not suggesting gender has nothing to do with attainment − it probably does have *some* bearing − but maybe a lot less than we're inclined to believe.'[36]

When I spoke to Didau he told me that drawing a link between gender and attainment is tempting 'because it appears so plausible and the data really does seem indisputable. On average, girls are outperforming boys'. He continues, 'The "pattern" of boys' underachievement is compelling because of the way we think about gender: girls are quiet, hard-working and sensible; boys are immature, unruly and easily bored. But as any teacher and every parent could tell you, these are stereotypes − shorthand that saves us from having to think about reality.' Didau explains there may be many reasons for the apparent relationship between gender and attainment that actually have little to do with gender, or more specifically with sex as a biological category. 'When it comes to interpreting data, it is possible to read into statistics what the researcher wants to find. This doesn't mean that a link between gender and attainment is not there, but if the researcher had looked for relationships between left-handedness, or even house number, and attainment they may have found a similar correlation.'[37]

In 1986, the feminist writer Juliet Mitchell noted that, 'When I started working on the topic of women in 1962, it was virtually impossible to get the differential information on the sexes − I remember how particularly hard it was in the field of education. Everything was broken down into socioeconomic groups. Today I find the reverse: it is easy to obtain information on male/female differences but not on social class achievements and positions.'[38] It may well be the case that

the attainment gap that appeared in the late 1980s was not
new at all — but simply that at this point, as a result of pressure from campaigners and researchers such as Mitchell,
school success started being correlated with gender for the
first time.

A closer look at who goes to university also suggests that
perhaps the link between gender and educational success has
been overstated. For example, Subjects Allied to Medicine,
the disciplinary grouping in which the gender participation
gap is widest, is a relatively new category in the university
landscape. Traditionally, nursing and occupational therapy,
careers dominated by women, were not graduate professions.
Taking training out of hospitals and relocating it within
universities meant that, at a stroke, more women became university students. Likewise, in my lifetime primary school teachers did not need a university degree and, when government
policy made this a requirement, women who would have previously attended teacher training colleges became university
students. When Subjects Allied to Medicine and Education
are removed from the higher education statistics then 'the
disparity in the total number of male and female higher
education students' reduces 'from around 281,000 to just
34,000'.[39] Women still outnumber men in traditional academic subjects but the discrepancy is far more modest.

Didau argues that behaviour and attendance are two factors that can predict educational success far more accurately
than gender, and with this we return to expectations. When it
comes to girls' success, he tells me, 'It might not be an innate
difference but rather cultural expectations that are being measured. Whereas teachers and parents expect girls to do well
and set them high standards, they expect boys to struggle.
This becomes a self-fulfilling prophecy and boys meet the low
expectations people have for them.' Girls, meanwhile, might
be highly rewarded for behaviours that have little to do with

intelligence. To illustrate this Didau tells me about a study that showed the extent to which exam markers were influenced by handwriting and disproportionately rewarded candidates with neat handwriting who, in turn, were more likely to be girls. Handwriting, Didau explains, would be a good example of a trait more connected to cultural expectations than biology: 'whereas girls gain kudos with their peers for having neat writing and police each other in this regard, boys are more likely to see messy writing almost as a badge of pride'.

IS GIRLS' SUCCESS WORTH CELEBRATING?

The emphasis on neat handwriting and good behaviour calls into question what girls' achievement at school really represents. Increased attention has focused on girls' schooling at a time when there has been a change in what education is perceived to be for. The founders of the first girls' schools, such as Frances Mary Buss who established the North London Collegiate School in 1850, wanted girls to have the same educational opportunities as boys. They were clear that this meant access to the same subject knowledge. Today, as we will explore in more detail in Chapter Nine, the idea of education as a vehicle for the pursuit and transmission of knowledge has become problematized. The curriculum no longer emerges from a recognized canon of 'great books' but is instead contested as different groups argue for the inclusion of their favoured issues on the syllabus.

Teaching has always been a profession dominated by women and ideas about feminism and women's rights have, over several decades, had an influence upon practice in the classroom. The point at which second-wave feminism began to take off in earnest coincided with a broader move to question the role of education – and particularly of the knowledge taught – in reproducing social class, racial and sexual inequalities. There were moves to make teaching more 'child centred' and progressive; pedagogy became more focused on child development than on direct instruction. Rejecting a traditional curriculum and teaching methods created the space for a more values-driven approach to education with feminist ideas to the fore. Teachers began, rightly, to question the gendered assumptions that prevented girls from achieving their full academic potential. But when girls began to be more successful it was in a different educational context, with different values and standards.

As we noted at the beginning of this chapter, education has come to be concerned with a range of instrumental goals connected to employability and tackling social problems. The achievements of girls may indicate that they are better at complying with the explicit and implicit rules this new type of education involves. Far more than boys, girls are still socialized to conform and 'be good'. This leaves them better able to demonstrate the behavioural norms expected of them first by teachers, then by university lecturers. I clearly remember the day my then four-year-old daughter came home from school, her jumper adorned with a huge sticker. She told me the teacher had given it to her for 'sitting nicely'. My heart sank a little: I didn't want her to see 'sitting nicely' as the aim of her time in school.

The boys in her class who chose to run around rather than 'sit nicely' presumably got no such reward. Hoff Sommers notes that 'girls reap large academic benefits from good behaviour and accommodation to the school environment'.[40] By the time they reach higher education, students are no longer rewarded for sitting nicely; however, marks given out for group work, attendance and participation reward similar behavioural characteristics. Girls today might be getting more exam passes but in order to achieve this they are not expected, like students in the past, to immerse themselves in a particular subject or to know a great deal. Instead, educational success depends upon diligence, dedication and obedience.

This privileging of compliance spills over into the realm of emotion. Anti-bullying initiatives and sex and relationships classes, history and literature lessons all demand an empathetic and emotionally correct response from pupils. Understanding and demonstrating 'emotional literacy' can be more all-consuming of a pupil's sense of self than mastering a body of knowledge.

TEACHING VALUES

The teaching of knowledge has been replaced not just by a new set of skills but also by new values, at the heart of which is feminism. Feminism in schools is taught quite explicitly; not as part of the history syllabus or a topic in a citizenship or politics course but as a distinct set of practices children are expected to comply with. Lesson plans, written by and for teachers, show how feminism can be taught to even the youngest children. One suggests: 'You can introduce a global view of women's rights, as well as a musical touch, with this series of lessons on women's rights and music in West Africa. It uses case studies and musical clips to explore geography, rhythm and the way music raises the voices of women and girls in their struggle for equality.'[41]

Teaching feminism often means tackling traditional gender stereotypes through the promotion of positive role models and the choice of books, posters and displays in class. Teachers are advised that 'Building a positive self-image for girls needs to be woven into the fabric of education'.[42] In the

UK, the National Union of Teachers has published advice on
'challenging gender stereotypes through reading'. It notes,
'Many men and women feel constrained by the narrow roles
assigned to them by societal pressures, and girls and boys are
expected to conform to narrow ideals of masculinity and femininity from a very early age.'[43] As a result, it recommends
books with characters that 'challenge some of the conventional ideas of what girls and boys enjoy and aspire to – and
act as positive role models as children seek to establish their
own individual identities'.

Of course, providing children with a wide range of reading
material is to be welcomed. But politicizing children's reading
choices and denigrating traditional gender roles is unlikely
to instil a love of reading. Teachers are encouraged to use
books as a prompt for raising particular issues. For example,
one book aimed at very young children comes with the suggested discussion point: 'What does Dad mean when he says
that 'dogs don't do ballet'? Why does he think that?
For example, could it just be that he hasn't met a ballet
dancing dog before – or perhaps because he has some stereotypical ideas about what dogs do – and what they don't?'
Not only is this, frankly, bizarre – dogs don't do ballet! –
more significantly, in any class of young children there will
no doubt be some girls who love ballet and some boys
who don't. There may also be some dads who think ballet
is not for boys. Indeed, this lesson aims to challenge
exactly such views. But however politically well-intentioned
teachers may be, criticizing the views and values of home
and parents vastly alters the remit of the school away from
education and towards the promotion of a distinct political
outlook.

As girls get older they may be pointed in the direction of
books about feminism or to workshops promoting women's
careers in science and technology. Speakers such as Laura

Bates from *Everyday Sexism* are frequently invited to address school assemblies. One resource for teachers to use in Personal, Social and Health Education lessons involves a video featuring Bates who, we are told, 'began the *Everyday Sexism Project* to highlight how often sexist behaviour and even sexual assaults go unchallenged and unreported'. In the short film, 'women tell their distressing stories of everyday sexism, and invite us all to help make it stop by shouting back'.[44] At a time when, as this chapter has shown, girls are doing so much better at school than boys, using class time to reinforce a message of female victimhood and male chauvinism uses education to inculcate in children with a particular view of the world.

The desire to influence children's most private thoughts and their individual sense of themselves is evident in official guidance on tackling the use of sexist language and behaviour given to teachers. One guide states:

> We are aware that there is a spectrum of gender
> identity and that gender is wider than the binary of
> boys and girls and males and females. This is one of
> the reasons why gender stereotyping is unhelpful
> and damaging as sexism leads us to believe that boys
> and girls should present themselves in certain ways.
> Transphobia and homophobia can result from this.
> However, the focus of this guide is on identifying
> and challenging sexism, gender stereotyping and
> sexist and sexual language to prevent negative
> impacts on the wellbeing and aspirations of girls
> and young women.[45]

The role of the teacher becomes policing the values, thoughts and language of children to bring them in line with one particular ideological outlook. In America, elementary school teachers are advised to 'refrain from phrases such as 'that's just for girls' or 'boys will be boys', which, only serve to reinforce a false binary. Allow dedicated time for coeducation, as some age groups may self-select into exclusively single-sex interactions if left to their own devices.'[46] Not all adults believe that gender is 'on a spectrum' and not everyone believes that girls and young women require a special focus on their wellbeing and aspirations. Policing the interactions of the playground for children's political errors is a major incursion into a child's capacity to develop independent thought.

The explicit promotion of feminism in schools does not benefit girls who are taught from a young age that they are disadvantaged. For boys the denigration of masculinity can have an even more deleterious impact as they are left feeling guilty and ashamed for simply being boys.[47]

Women in Science

As girls generally perform better at school than boys, at least in terms of passing exams, feminists focus their efforts upon the few remaining subject areas where boys still appear to have the edge. The relative underperformance of girls in science and technology subjects garners a great deal of attention. Science is said to have a 'woman problem'.[48] Yet at age 16 British girls outperform boys in all science subjects. Aged 18, boys perform marginally better (under one per cent) at maths and chemistry, but girls do better in further maths, biology, computer science and physics.[49]

At university, particular attention is drawn to physics and electrical engineering, where women undergraduates in British universities comprise fewer than 20 per cent of students. However, across a broader sweep of subjects, the difference is less stark: roughly 55 per cent of students studying for a first degree in science are men compared to 45 per cent of women.[50] Even this statistic understates women's achievements in science: in subjects allied to medicine and veterinary science women comprise over 75 per cent of students.[51] Women's progress in these competitive vocational subjects is significant because it leads on to careers in science. The scarcity of men from medicine and veterinary science courses is rarely considered to be a problem.

The number of women already studying science at undergraduate level and embarking upon careers in science has not put an end to high profile campaigns such as Women Into Science and Engineering (WISE). In the UK, universities strive to achieve a gender equality charter mark for science, overseen by the Equality Challenge Unit's Athena Swan initiative.[52] Universities pour considerable resources into securing these awards that aim to recognize commitment to 'advancing women's careers in science, technology, engineering, maths and medicine' all the while ignoring the huge inroads women have made into the study, research and teaching of science over recent decades. Today, such schemes can appear to be solutions in search of a problem.

Solutions that Create Problems

I discussed with physics teacher Gareth Sturdy the initiatives he has observed that aim to get more girls studying science. He tells me about 'extra extracurricular physics clubs specifically designed to be 'girl friendly' that involve students making jewellery based on Feynman particle diagrams; taking selfies using pinhole cameras, and of course – lots of cake!' Sturdy is quick to point out that, 'These are often led by good, very well-intentioned teachers', and he tells me such clubs can be very successful, 'When these activities are advertised, many more girls turn up and as a result some schools have seen a huge increase in the number of girls continuing to study physics beyond the age of 16, especially if there is a strong female role-model.'[53]

Sturdy's concerns are to do with the message such clubs send about the nature of the subject: 'Of course, if you have cake or jewellery making, or you give chocolates out for right answers you will attract more students. But there is a danger that these are just gimmicks and the students don't always gain a great deal intellectually. It becomes a problem if the activities begin to make physics more gendered than it is already. At the end of the day, if girls will only do physics if jewellery and cake are involved, they're not necessarily suitable candidates for the subject.'

Whereas school campaigns to get girls into science can inadvertently reproduce gender stereotypes, the ongoing awareness raising about the problems women face in science, which becomes most acute in higher education, risks giving young women a false impression that pursuing careers in this area will involve them having to confront prejudice and hostility. In a further irony, it is mostly women who complete the paperwork and audits necessary to apply for gender equality awards such as Athena Swan, presumably in the time their male colleagues are writing research papers and applying for grants.

GIRLS UNDER PRESSURE

Girls are more likely than boys to leave school with a clutch of certificates but this success increasingly seems to come at a price. There is growing concern about the number of women and girls reporting mental health problems such as anxiety and depression or engaging in self-harm. Much of this is no doubt explained through a desire, by adults, to see children, perhaps especially girls, as vulnerable and to interpret every-day emotions through a prism of mental illness. However, it might also be the case that girls are under more pressure than in the past to meet the expectations of teachers and peers in relation to educational success. The issue of women and mental health will be explored more fully in Chapters Four and Five.

A further price to be paid for school success may come later in life. Although girls' diligence and obedience is rewarded with certificates that help them secure a university place and enter well-paid professional careers, it may be less beneficial in the longer term. Women are made into capable and diligent employees but progressing to the higher levels of some careers can require leadership, risk taking and an element of self-promotion. These tend to be the very qualities girls have been socialized out of through their education.

BACK TO SCHOOL

Beyond the workplace, women who become mothers can rapidly find themselves back in the classroom. As we will explore more fully in Chapter Four, today's parents are expected to play a far greater role in relation to their child's education. Many schools require parents to sign up to 'home

school partnership agreements' or 'contracts' which specify
the obligations of parents regarding everything from getting
their children to school on time and regular attendance at
parents' evenings to overseeing reading and times tables
practise.

While schools take over many of the duties traditionally
carried out by parents, such as teaching about sex, relationships and healthy eating, they expect parents to take greater
responsibility for teaching reading and supervising home-
work. Such expectations have currency because parents want
their children to succeed at school and they come to accept
that their input as parents determines educational success or
failure as much as schools and teachers. The primary responsibility for parenting tends to fall disproportionately upon
women who are often positioned as the 'main carer' by
schools. Schools, in turn, assume the duties of the mother
extend far beyond loving, nourishing and caring for her children and must also encompass a regular commitment to her
child's education.

CONCLUSIONS

The gender attainment gap appears to be both stark and
growing with girls having successfully overturned centuries of
limited educational opportunities and now, not just equalling
the achievements of boys, but outperforming them at every
level. Girls are doing better at school than ever before and
young women are notching up considerably more exam
passes and degree certificates than their male contemporaries.
This success leaves them better positioned to enter the world
of work. But exam results only go so far in liberating women.

Girls outperform boys in an education system that is seen
as a key site for the socialization of children into particular

values. Many teachers assume that if children were socialized differently then gender inequality could be eradicated and that this, more than teaching any particular body of subject knowledge, is their primary goal. When language use and behaviour is policed, then doing well at school can demand an exacting emotional toll and risk binding women to a lifetime of conformity.

Most recently, attention has been drawn to the underachievement of boys, and education is becoming a key battleground in the gender wars. It seems that girls and boys cannot just be 'pupils' or 'students' but, from their earliest days at school, must represent their gender. This may appear to benefit girls more than boys in the short term, but, in the longer term benefits no one. More than anything else, fighting a gender war through schools and universities is to the detriment of education.

CHAPTER TWO

WOMEN AT WORK

Glossy magazines, broadsheet newspapers, websites, books and television documentaries all seem to tell the same story when it comes to discussing women's experiences at work. We're told that life is 'still a struggle for working women'; that 'four in ten American women face workplace discrimination' and 'gender inequality in the workplace goes beyond the pay gap'. Listicles specify 'eight big problems for women in the workplace' or 'three key problems women in banking now face'. All working women, it seems, face an onslaught of obstacles, discrimination and microaggressions. They are paid less than the same men who speak over them in meetings ('manterruptions'), take credit for their ideas ('bropriation') and then ask them to make the coffee (maybe deMANding?).

Yet a look at the statistics tells us that women's achievements in education follow them into the workplace: not only are more women employed than ever before, they are entering the professions and taking more of the top jobs too. In this chapter we consider the experiences of women at work today and, in teasing out reality from in-between numerical successes and lamentable narratives, consider what, if anything, is really holding working women – and men – back.

MORE WOMEN ARE WORKING

Women's lives do not grind to an undignified halt the moment they leave school; the progress girls have made in education is paralleled by increased opportunities in the workplace. In Britain and many other developed countries, more women are in paid employment than ever before. In July 2016, close to 70 per cent of British women aged 16–64 worked outside the home, the highest figure since records began.[54] Among women graduates with no dependent children, this rises to almost 90 per cent.[55] In both Britain and America, women now comprise just under half of the total labour force, 46 per cent in the UK[56] and 47 per cent in the US.[57] In historical terms, this growth in the number of women workers represents not just a dramatic economic shift but a real social change too: it means that women of all ages, with children and without, are now likely to be in paid work, working at all levels and across all employment sectors.

In America, a smaller proportion of women are in work than in Britain; just 57 per cent of women are employed outside the home.[58] Black women are most likely to work and Asian women are least likely to have paid employment (60 per cent and 56 per cent respectively).[59] In part, these lower figures can be explained by the larger age range covered by the statistics: in the UK employment stops being recorded at state retirement age. If we look specifically at American women aged between 25 and 54, we see that 69 per cent are in employment – almost the same as in the UK overall.

In Britain, as in many other European countries where legislation to extend maternity leave and women's rights at work has been passed, the most significant change in recent decades is the rise of the working mother. British women with children are almost as likely to be in work (74 per cent) as those without (75 per cent).[60] In America, the only developed country that still does not guarantee women paid maternity leave, 70 per cent of women with children aged under 18 were either in work or actively looking for work in 2015. This figure was slightly lower for married mothers (68 per cent) and higher for unmarried mothers (75 per cent).[61] Elsewhere, the figures are higher still; 83 per cent of Swedish women with children work.

WOMEN IN THE PROFESSIONS

It's not just that more women are working nowadays: they are taking more of the top jobs too. The increasing number of female graduates has had an impact in the workplace. In America, women now make up 57 per cent of workers in professional and related occupations[62] while British women take exactly half of all professional jobs.[63] Many of these women are employed in traditionally 'female' occupations; education alone accounts for over one million British women workers.[64] However, whereas teaching was, not that long ago, one of the very few options available to women graduates, today the brightest women are more likely to reject teaching with its comparatively low wages and perceived low status.

More women are now entering professions that were once the preserve of men; in the UK there are now more women than men working as veterinary surgeons, doctors and lawyers. There are more women than men at junior levels in accountancy and academia while entrants to dentistry are almost equally split between men and women. The scale and pace of women's entry into once male-dominated professions can perhaps best be illustrated with veterinary science. In the US, the proportion of female graduates in this area leapt from 11 per cent in 1970 to 80 per cent in 2013.[65] This closely parallels the UK where, in 2014, 78 per cent of veterinary science undergraduates were female.[66] As a result of the shift in student demographics, women now account for 60 per cent of practising vets.

Women are not as well represented at the very top of the professions and we will explore why this might be the case later in this chapter and in the two subsequent chapters. Nonetheless, women's entry into the professions is significant: it suggests there are few practical or cultural barriers preventing highly educated, often middle-class women from choosing whatever career they are inclined towards.

Women's employment today represents, in historical terms, a significant social and cultural change. However, many working-class women always combined domestic responsibilities with paid work either carried out at home, in other people's homes as domestic servants, in family businesses, or in particular industries such as pottery and textiles. Upper- and middle-class women who needed to earn money had fewer employment options available to them: they were limited to 'suitable' occupations such as teaching or nursing. The most significant recent changes, then, are not in the total number of women working, but in the rise of the middle-class career woman, the increase in the number of working mothers and the challenge to previously gender segregated employment practices.

HISTORICAL CHANGES

In the twentieth century, women entered the workforce in large numbers during the two world wars. However, as soon as peace broke out, employers, trade unions and government campaigns endeavoured to get women back into the home. Women were legally barred from certain occupations, or from being promoted beyond a particular level. Women were prevented from working once married or pregnant. These formal restrictions were in addition to the myriad informal social barriers and practical obstacles that kept women from being employed. As we will explore in more detail in Chapter Eight, second-wave feminists of the 1960s and 1970s fought for women's right to work with considerable success. But even into the 1980s women's jobs were considered easily expendable. When employers needed more workers, women were recruited but when recession loomed they were first in line to lose their jobs, with home, marriage and children considered a ready-made alternative to employment.

Today, thanks in large part to a previous generation of feminist campaigners, the days when women were barred from certain professions or their progress legally restricted are long gone. Nowadays, not only do women face few formal restrictions on the type of work they can do, many employers also seek to overcome informal barriers to women's progress through mentorship schemes, recruitment drives and 'family friendly' working policies. This is not to suggest that women, especially when they have children, face no obstacles to career success; rather, as we will explore in Chapter Four, the problems women face combining motherhood and work today are very different to those they encountered in the past.

GENERATIONAL DIFFERENCES

Women's employment prospects have altered fundamentally in a very short space of time. As a result, it's easy to forget that older women today entered the workplace when all kinds of obstacles to their employment still existed. For example, it was only in 1977, when the Employment Protection Act came into effect in Britain, that women had a legal right to return to work after having had a baby. Before this time, pregnancy was a legitimate pretext for dismissal.[67] Women who began their working lives before 1995 entered the workplace at a time when female graduates were still in a minority. Today, these quite stark generational differences mask the full extent of recent changes.

The workplace is changing from the youngest members up. So, while a majority of accountants, doctors and lawyers over the age of 50 are male, the reverse is true for those under the age of 40. This generational lag needs to be kept in mind when discussing inequalities higher up in the professions. Although women comprise 62 per cent of lawyers, fewer than one-third are partners; but as the new female entrants progress through their careers, they will eventually swell the senior ranks too. Much is made of the apparent underrepresentation of women in senior positions today but to get to the top of any profession often requires many years of experience and several incremental promotions. People are unlikely to have amassed such a portfolio in their twenties or thirties. Feminism, with its focus on younger middle-class women, finds it difficult to account for the experiences of older women.

FEWER MEN WORKING

Women began to enter the workplace in ever greater numbers at the end of the 1980s. The nature of work itself began to change at this time with a shift away from manufacturing and heavy industry towards services and work that required 'soft skills' rather than physical strength. The employment sectors traditionally dominated by men were now in decline. Factories, steel works and coal mines were on the way out; in came call-centres, retail parks and care homes. Men have borne the brunt of this structural change: in Britain only 79 per cent of men aged between 16 and 64 are working today, a sharp decrease from 92 per cent in 1971.[68]

In America, proportionally fewer women are employed today than 20 years ago. After climbing for six decades, the percentage of working women aged between 25 and 54 peaked in 1999 at 74 per cent,[69] while latest statistics suggest just over 69 per cent of women in this age group are in work.[70] There are several possible explanations for this fall; what's immediately significant is that over the same period, male employment rates also fell, and to a far greater extent.

In both America and Britain, structural economic changes have disproportionately impacted upon working-class men.[71] As a result, there are fewer well-paid jobs for men without formal qualifications than there were in the latter half of the twentieth century. Employers in the service sector look to recruit women rather than working-class men. More jobs nowadays, from medicine and business to retail and restaurants, seem better suited to women.

NARRATIVE OF SEXISM

Despite women's resounding success at entering the workplace and dominating the professions, and the decline in male working-class employment, a narrative of sexism and female disadvantage persists. Instead of celebrating women's victories, we hear about sexist bosses, misogynistic air conditioning and men 'microaggressing' women through 'manspreading' in the office and 'mansplaining' in meetings. The message, coming at women and girls from every direction, is stark. As the authors of *The New Soft War on Women* put it: 'while women are doing spectacularly well in universities, in the workplace it's an opposite picture. Women are stalling out, and the higher they go, the harder it gets. A whole network of landmines is exploding women's progress as they try to move ahead.'[72]

The rise of the working woman has been met by constant reminders that the workplace is a battleground where women have to negotiate sexism at every turn. A plethora of books offer women 'battle tactics' to combat the 'sexist, subtly sexist, overtly sexist, and sometimes just oblivious behaviours that exist in even our most progressive offices'.[73] Self-help manuals urge women to 'Lean In' and exercise 'Feminine Authority'. 'Glass wall success strategies' compete with advice on how to shatter glass ceilings. Perhaps unsurprisingly, then, one survey tells us, '83% of women think gender discrimination exists in the workplace'.[74]

While metaphors of combat, war and battlegrounds may be over the top, the market for such books and the stories of workplace discrimination suggest something is not right for working women. There appears to be a growing chasm between women's statistical success and personal experiences.

ELITE CONCERNS

With few obstacles in the way of many women choosing professional careers, focus has shifted from the gender balance of entrants to the number of women at the top of any sector. The economist Vicky Pryce notes, 'Even today 93 per cent of executive directors are men', and 'among the FTSE 250, women's representation in the boardrooms is only just over 17 per cent'.[75] One often quoted fact is that there are more Chief Executive Officers named John leading the UK's top 100 companies than there are women.[76] This truism hinges upon the fact that John was the most popular UK and Irish male Christian name throughout most of the twentieth century before slowly falling out of fashion in the 1970s. It reveals as much about the age of CEOs as it does their gender.

As we have already noted, pointing to a lack of women at the top of any profession misses the historical legacy that persists when the workplace changes rapidly. What's more, a myopic focus on absent women from senior positions ignores both what has happened to men and the experiences of women who do not work at the very top of the career ladder.

Feminist self-help manuals for working women focus primarily on the concerns of women in elite occupations. In the case of Jessica Bennett's *Feminist Fight Club*, this is largely New York women with high profile media careers. Bennett outlines problems women face at work such as 'manterruption – a man interrupting a woman while she was trying to speak' which has the effect of 'causing us to clam up, lose our confidence, or cede credit for our work'. Or, 'The Bropriator' who:

> ... *appropriates credit for another's work: presenting the ideas of his team as his own, accepting credit for an idea that wasn't his, or sometimes even doing nothing at all and* still *ending up with credit – a convenient reality of being born male, where credit is assumed.*[77]

Challenging 'manterupptions' and 'bropriators' may make women in high-powered jobs feel better about themselves – although we can wonder at the need for a book to tell people how to have a simple conversation. But such advice is unlikely to be of much use to women with jobs rather than careers who are expected to carry out, rather than question, instructions.

Most women do not have corner offices to aspire towards. Neither do they receive bonus payments or have the flexibility to leave work early and then 'pick up on email after the children are in bed'. Although the current crop of self-help career guides for middle-class women make token mentions of the particular problems experienced by women of colour, there is, for the most part, little attempt at understanding the experiences of working-class women.

At best there seems to be a hope that concentrating on middle-class women and getting more women into the top jobs will have knock-on benefits for all women. However, there is little evidence that this is the case. In universities, for example, women academics meet to discuss why there are so few female professors and how more women can be helped to secure promotion. Often they do so in a room booked by a woman and cleaned by a woman while eating sandwiches prepared by a woman – yet these women are rarely invited to sit at the table and discuss *their* career prospects.

QUOTAS FOR WOMEN

For some campaigners, encouraging women to get promoted goes beyond 'fight club' tactics and circle time meetings. Pryce, writing in *Why Women Need Quotas*, suggests women are underrepresented on executive boards and that, 'There is no way the current situation can be transformed except through legislation to fundamentally change society's norms of what is and isn't acceptable.'[78] She argues companies need to have quotas in place to ensure women are represented on boards of directors.

However, as we have seen, even in the absence of legislation women are entering the workplace in greater numbers. In this regard, the demand for quotas to ensure a certain number of posts are filled by women appears to be a solution in search of a problem. Worse, quotas, like other forms of positive discrimination, undermine women with the implication that promotion has been granted on the basis of biology rather than merit. Women are quite capable of making it to the top without such special measures being put in place.

DIFFERENT WOMEN, DIFFERENT EXPERIENCES

Feminist journalists and commentators do acknowledge that not all women experience the workplace in the same way. Some women are at more of a disadvantage than others. Pregnant women are a particular target: surveys tell us a fifth of women have been harassed at work while pregnant and 'maternity discrimination is pushing people out of work'.[79] Meanwhile, older women 'are being forced out of the workforce' while another study shows that 'women face weight-based discrimination in the workplace'. Muslim women experience 'triple discrimination at work' and transgender women 'face challenges when looking for work'. For some women – just like some men – the journey from graduation to Chief Executive Officer may be seamless. Other women may not have such ambitions and, even if they do, may find they face setbacks and obstacles on their way.

One problem with differentiating women into ever more fragmented groups is that it ignores the experiences of the majority of women who are not fighting for a place on the board of directors. Alison Wolf, author of *The XX Factor*, reminds us that, 'Most people, including most women, work to live rather than live to work.' She explains this means that there are 'two quite different groups of women'. While a small and elite group of women compete with men as equals for the top jobs with high salaries and bonus payments, a majority of women still have traditionally 'female' jobs that first and foremost provide the necessary income to keep home and family together.[80]

The middle-class preoccupations of feminist campaigns and the tendency to see women's problems in the workplace as primarily caused by male behaviour preclude solutions that would help improve the lives of all men and women. Higher wages and a more flexible approach to working hours, for example, give people more freedom and control over their lives. Extra money can pay for the child care; cars and convenience food that help life run more smoothly.

Rather than fighting for higher wages for everyone, feminist campaigns represent the concerns of a small group of middle-class women. One of the more bizarre examples is the demand that companies have 'period policies' to allow women to take days off while menstruating.[81] Such 'progress' might be great for women who work in creative industries — although it rehabilitates the sexist assumptions of hormonal and irrational women in a radical feminist guise. Perhaps fortunately, then, such campaigns are unlikely to be extended to women who work as secretaries or receptionists. If women in less prestigious or flexible jobs take a day off because of their period they may lose a day's pay.

The dominant feminist narrative suggests all working women have interests in common: they all face sexism and discrimination at the hands of sexist bosses and colleagues. At the same time, we are also presented with an identity-driven division of women on the basis of weight, skin colour, age and sexuality. In this way, the problems faced by the most disadvantaged women appear to apply equally to the most privileged of the sisterhood. In reality, women in lower paid jobs have far more to gain by fighting for their interests alongside men in a similar position than they do hoping for crumbs from the feminist top table.

SEX SEGREGATION

It can seem as if feminism today has little to say to women who have jobs rather than careers. Wolf reminds us that, 'In 2010, fewer than 2000 people worldwide worked for Facebook. Walmart's workforce that year numbered over 2 million; a million more than at the century's turn and up from 21,000 in 1975.' She points out that for many men and women employment is still quite rigidly segregated along gender lines; 'Take the US. If you pick the twenty top female occupations – meaning the ones that employ the largest absolute numbers of women – you find that, in seven of them, the workforce is over 90 per cent female.'

A majority of women today still work in what have long been considered typically 'female' occupations. In the UK, women make up 82 per cent of the workforce in the caring and leisure industries, 77 per cent in administrative and secretarial work and 63 per cent in sales and customer service. Pryce notes that one-third of all the women who worked part time in 2013 were employed in sales and customer service jobs earning relatively low median earnings. Although Scandinavian countries are held aloft as models of best feminist employment practice, they are also the most segregated along gender lines because, as Wolf notes, 'they have gone the furthest in outsourcing traditional female activities and turning unpaid home-based "caring" into formal employment.'[82]

In Scandinavia, as in much of the developed world, the labour market is separated into an elite group of both men and women who work as equals in professional occupations and the vast majority of the population who work in lower paid and gender-segregated traditional jobs. Yet feminism, and its preoccupation with the concerns of a minority of elite women, focuses our attention on a tiny fraction of the workforce. There are more campaigns concerned with getting women into senior posts than there are into improving the pay and conditions of women who work for the minimum wage — perhaps cleaning, cooking and child minding for the Chief Executive Officers.

A FEMINIST ETIQUETTE

Feminism today, with its elite concerns, comes to be about enforcing a new etiquette through regulating people's interactions with each other. One example of how this plays out in practice is provided by the self-styled 'fearless feminist' and barrister Charlotte Proudman. Proudman made headlines in 2015 after she made public a private message sent to her via the professional networking site *LinkedIn*. An older male solicitor had got in touch with Proudman to tell her he thought her profile picture was 'stunning'. For the crime of sending this misplaced and unwanted compliment, Proudman exposed the man to ridicule, first on Twitter and then through the pages of the national press and television news studios.

The message to men in the workplace is to think twice before engaging with female colleagues. The message to women is, perhaps ironically, far worse: you are constantly at risk at work, if not from misogynistic insults then from sexist compliments. You can't be expected to laugh such comments off or joke with colleagues. Instead you must be traumatized and display your trauma to the world. Meanwhile, human resources departments have another example to use for their equality and diversity training workshops and there is an increase in the micromanagement of relationships in the workplace.

Challenging this perception of women as oppressed at work is a risky strategy. In 2016 Kevin Roberts was suspended from his post as chairman of the global advertising company Saatchi and Saatchi for suggesting gender bias was not an issue in the advertising industry.[83] Roberts argued that women are working in advertising in ever greater numbers, but they choose not to apply for promotion. For this he was taken to task by high profile women in the industry who poured scorn on the idea that women's absence from the top jobs was down to choice. They accused Roberts of offending women and argued he should simply not have been allowed to say what he did.

But Roberts has a point: women are doing well in advertising. They account for 46.4 per cent of all those employed in the sector and 30.5 per cent of senior executives. The proportion of women creative directors rose from just 3 per cent in 2010 to 11.5 per cent in 2014.[84] It is clearly worth investigating why more women do not choose to become creative directors – although the long and anti-social hours that make the role incompatible with family life probably provides us with a big clue. This is worth discussing.

PERSONAL CHOICE

If any debate about gender equality in the workplace that does not start by paying homage to women as perpetually disadvantaged is closed down immediately, then an honest appraisal of women's working lives today will be impossible. We need to be able to acknowledge the progress women have made – as well as what still needs to be achieved. Part of this discussion needs to be about individual choice. Women are not a homogenous group who either all want to be the next CEO or are all frustrated stay-at-home mums.

It shouldn't be outrageous to suggest that some women may want to concentrate on their careers in their twenties

and thirties but then take a step back for a while when they
have children. As Roberts argued, it's not just women but
young men too who are deciding that they have priorities
other than making it to the top of the business hierarchy.
No longer do young workers think lifelong loyalty to one
company is a worthwhile commitment or that sacrificing a
social life or family life for a promotion is aspirational.

Over time, people's priorities have changed and the world
of work has changed. It might be entirely positive that younger workers are rejecting long hours and loyalty or it might
suggest that work is uninspiring or that young people are
unable to commit to projects beyond their immediate self-
interest. What's certain is that for many people work is
simply not the source of emotional fulfilment and mental
stimulation that both bosses and campaigners may expect us
to believe. Ultimately, what matters is not so much the personal choices individuals make but that people have enough
money and support – including access to good quality and
affordable childcare – in order to be able to make these
choices as freely as possible.

There is more that can be done to allow people greater
freedom and control in juggling work with family responsibilities and personal interests. However, claiming that women
have no choices to make, or are limited by a patriarchal and
discriminatory working environment, is disingenuous and
does women themselves few favours. Women at work have
proved they are equal to men; it is now feminism that is telling them they are not and never will be.

CONCLUSIONS

Feminist campaigners present a view of the workplace as
hostile to women primarily because of the behaviour and

attitudes of individual men. But this does not stand up to scrutiny and may well contribute towards putting some women off applying for the top jobs. The determination to view the workplace solely through the prism of gender helps no one. Experiences of work vary far more according to the type of job someone does than their gender — people working in low-skilled and low-paid jobs in catering or in retail, for example, experience work differently to women working in advertising or accountancy, for instance, who are better paid but may be expected to be permanently available for clients. The interests of women are better secured in conjunction with their male colleagues rather than by opposing them.

A more nuanced discussion of the difficulties we all face in our working lives is not possible while feminist campaigners insist on scoring workplace victories according to gender. We need to move beyond a battle of the sexes in order to get more opportunities and freedom for everyone. In the next chapter we explore the position of women at work further through the particular issue of the gender pay gap.

CHAPTER THREE

THE GENDER PAY GAP

As the previous two chapters have shown, better educated girls have, as women, more opportunities in the workplace. As a result, young women today are earning more and have a far greater degree of financial independence than women of previous generations. Women's wages have not only increased in absolute terms, they have also increased in comparison to men's earnings. Yet despite this growing financial equality, the gender pay gap is rarely out of the news. Every day brings forward new statistics reporting to show the difference between men's and women's wages. But, as this chapter shows, when it comes to measuring pay, statistics can be weighed and measured to prove whatever point campaigners wish to make.

Discussion of the gender pay gap has become separated from reality. At a time when men and women are paid the same for the same work, and younger women earn, on average, more than men of the same age, belief in the pay gap is an expression of faith. Its existence has become a central tenet of feminism – calling it into question an act of blasphemy. The pay gap narrative suggests that gender is the key factor in determining a person's earnings and that women are at a disadvantage in the world of work, relegated to poorly paid jobs and, especially when children come along, to part-time work. Although this may be true for some women, particularly those without qualifications, it is certainly not true for all. This chapter separates fact from fiction and explores what purpose the pay gap obsession serves.

WOMEN ARE EARNING MORE

Over the past few decades, as women have entered the workplace in ever greater numbers, they have secured greater financial independence. Few women today are left entirely dependent upon 'housekeeping' money donated, perhaps reluctantly, from their husband's wages – a situation within living memory and once common for women of all social classes. The female breadwinner, once an oxymoron, is now a reality. Across Europe, one-third of working mothers are responsible for their family's main source of income,[85] whereas in the US, four out of every ten women are either the sole or primary family earner.[86] This figure has quadrupled since 1960 – a remarkably rapid social change that speaks not just to women's success but also to the changed nature of the labour market and the changing structure of the family.

Women today not only earn more in total than at any other point in history, they also earn more as a proportion of men's earnings. As a result, the gender pay gap, however it is measured, is the smallest it has ever been. On occasion, this fact is acknowledged. In announcing new plans to tackle inequalities in the workplace, then British Conservative Minister for Women and Equalities, Nicky Morgan, said: 'We are determined to tackle the barriers to women achieving their all. Business has made huge amounts of progress already in recent years — the gender pay gap is the lowest since records began.'[87] But the quiet demise of the gender pay gap continues to be ignored by many feminist campaigners who are reluctant to let go of what they perceive to be a powerful indicator of inequality between the sexes.

When the narrowing of the gender pay gap is acknowledged, it is presented as a success brought about by the efforts of feminist activists. Campaigns and strikes for equal pay have a long history, especially in America. In 1883, workers at Western Union Telegraph Company went on strike in part to ensure 'equal pay for equal work' for male and female employees. Although communications across the US ground to a halt, the strike was unsuccessful. In 1911, a long battle with the Board of Education led to male and female teachers in New York receiving equal pay.[88] In the UK, the most famous strike for equal pay took place at Ford Dagenham in 1968 when women sewing machinists demanded their work be paid at the rate for skilled labour. In 1976, Jayaben Desai led the Grunwick Film Processing Laboratory strike. Although this was not a dispute specifically focused on equal pay, the overwhelming majority of participants were female immigrants, dubbed 'strikers in saris'.[89]

These brave women do indeed deserve celebrating. However, their efforts are only partially responsible for the diminishing gender pay gap. Trade unions were reluctant to back strikes for equal pay and government equalities legislation, now much praised, was often viewed by employers as an obstacle to be overcome rather than an impetus for positive change. Today's levelling-off in pay differentials has come about because of a number of demographic and economic factors that have happened alongside, not simply as a result of, feminist campaigns.

DELAYING MOTHERHOOD

Over the past half century, as we saw in Chapter One, there has been a huge increase in the number of young adults going to university and growth in the number of women students has been particularly notable. One impact of this change is that men and women have been entering the workplace, marrying and having children, later in life. In the 1970s and into the 1980s a woman giving birth after the age of 35, especially for the first time, was considered unusual. In the UK today, women are more likely to give birth over the age of 40 than under the age of 20. The trend for later motherhood can be seen across all social classes and in all developed countries. The UK's teenage pregnancy rate is the lowest since records began.

Delayed motherhood is, as Alison Wolf notes, particularly a feature of graduates. She says that by 2006, American women graduates were most likely to have their first baby when they were aged between 30 and 35. For women who don't complete high school, a different picture emerges and they are likely to become mothers by the age of 25. In the UK, the proportion of women graduates having a baby before they reach 30 has halved over the past few decades, whereas a majority of women without qualifications become mothers by the time they are 22.[90] More than ever before, women are choosing not to have babies at all; since the mid-1970s, the proportion of American women who do not have children has doubled.[91] The fact that women are delaying motherhood, or not having children at all, has helped bring down the gender pay gap as more women are working full-time for more of their lives.

NATIONAL ECONOMIC CHANGES

Even more than delayed motherhood, the gender pay gap has narrowed because of changes in the nature of work. As national economies, especially in developed countries, have shifted focus from industry and manufacturing to services, men's wages have been growing at a far slower rate than women's wages. In 2016, British men and women both saw an increase in median earnings on the previous year. However, whereas men's earnings grew by 1.9 per cent, women's wages increased by a slightly more substantial 2.2 per cent. Between 1997 and 2016, women's pay grew by 81 per cent compared to 62 per cent for men.[92] The story from the US is similar: 'while middle income male salaries have grown little over the past few decades, women's have grown quite fast'.[93] This means that for many middle- and low-income families, the impact of men's stagnant wages has been offset by women working and earning more. Women's wages were once considered 'pin money' and a supplement to the main family income; today they are more likely to be seen as a necessity. Low-income families with only one wage earner struggle most.

PAY GAP OBSESSION

Despite the speed and scale of women's increased earning power, celebrations have been few and far between. Barely a week goes by without alarmist news stories reminding us, 'Women still far adrift on salary and promotion as gender pay gap remains a gulf' or that the 'Gender pay gap won't close until 2069'. Outrage often seems more important than accuracy. From America we have the 'potty mouthed princesses', young girls who 'drop F-bombs' in protest at the gender pay gap. They pose the question: 'Which is worse, swearing children or paying women less than men?'[94] In the UK, the more sober Fawcett Society petitions employers and the government as well as running high-profile media campaigns to raise awareness about gender pay inequalities.[95] On both sides of the Atlantic, there are bi-annual 'equal pay days' which mark the point in the year when women effectively start and stop earning relative to men.[96] Campaigners present an image of a large and persistent gender pay gap resulting from entrenched sexism in the workplace.

Bizarrely, the narrower the pay gap becomes, and the less likely anyone is to argue seriously that men and women should be paid differently for doing the same work, the more attention equal pay garners. Irrespective of facts, every public figure wants to be seen publicly condemning the gender pay gap. Theresa May, in her very first speech as British Prime Minister, standing outside the door of 10 Downing Street, took the opportunity to declare, it is wrong that 'if you're a woman, you will earn less than a man'.[97] Her predecessor, David Cameron, had promised to end the gender pay gap 'in a generation'.[98] In the run up to the American presidential election, Hillary Clinton criticized Donald Trump for saying 'women don't deserve equal pay unless they do as good a job as men'.[99] Clinton, and others, took this to imply that Trump thought women didn't deserve to be paid the same as men.

It's not just politicians. Oscar-winning actor Jennifer Lawrence expressed her anger at finding out 'how much less I was being paid than the lucky people with dicks'. She questioned not the film production company but herself, 'I'm over trying to find the "adorable" way to state my opinion and still be likable.'[100] Fellow Oscar-winner Patricia Arquette also spoke out against the gender pay gap: 'We see this pay discrepancy between women and men in 98 per cent of all industries,' she said. 'So it's impacting women across the board.' She continued, 'It costs the average woman almost half a million dollars over her lifetime, the gender pay gap. And for women with higher education, it costs them $2 million over their lifetime. So it's an enormous impact.'[101]

Wealthy celebrities together with politicians of all persuasions add to the voices of feminist campaigners. The YouTube star Laci Green argues she's a feminist, 'Because of the gender pay gap that still exists in America. Men are paid more for doing the same job. Over the course of her career, a woman will have lost out on an average of $450,000 due to the discriminatory pay gap. The number is even greater for Latina and Black women, according to statistics from the White House.'[102] In the UK, co-founder of the Women's Equality Party, Catherine Mayer, aims to 'draw attention to a persistent inequity, a gender pay gap that endures almost 46 years after the Equal Pay Act received royal assent'.[103]

Unfortunately for the pay gap campaigners, the frequent repetition of a claim does not make it true. The rhetoric surrounding the gender pay gap elides fact and fiction: men are not paid more than women for 'doing the same job'. This is simply false. The obsession with the gender pay gap gets in the way of a clear analysis of what's happening to earnings.

A MOVABLE FEAST

Despite all the attention given to the gender pay gap, there is surprisingly little agreement about either its size or the reason for its continued existence. In the US, some reports claim women are paid just 77 cents to every dollar a man is paid.[104] In the UK women are said to earn, on average, 76 pence for every £1 a man gets.[105] Such figures are indeed alarming. However, they depend upon a highly selective and ultimately misleading interpretation of pay data. As we'll explore in more detail below, this large gap is arrived at by comparing average wages; in other words it depends upon us ignoring such differences as employment type and total hours worked. The more we compare 'like for like' rather than average pay, the smaller the pay gap appears to be. Christina Hoff Sommers argues that 'when you control for relevant differences between men and women (occupations, college majors, length of time in workplace) the wage gap narrows to the point of vanishing'.[106]

The beauty of the gender pay gap is that it can be simultaneously large, small and non-existent. As Sheila Wild, former head of age and earnings inequality at the UK's Equality and Human Rights Commission, has argued, 'the statistics on the gender pay gap are so various and so nuanced that almost anyone can take anything out of it and say what they want'.[107] Campaigners and commentators make pragmatic decisions about what to measure and as a result the gender pay gap can be made to appear whatever size suits the objectives of the person doing the measuring.

THE PROBLEM WITH AVERAGES

Feminist campaigners, researchers and reporters are incentivized to present data so as to make the gender pay gap appear to be as large as possible. To achieve this, they most frequently cite figures that compare men's and women's average annual earnings. This measures the difference between the total annual pay of all men and all women irrespective of hours worked, occupation, qualifications, age or career stage. This measure produces the frequently cited claim that women earn roughly 24 per cent less than men. Some campaigners further inflate the 76 pence for every £1, or 77 cents for every dollar, claim by multiplying it 52 times to show a difference in lifetime earnings. Although this assumes people begin their working lives aged 18 and carry on working until they are 70, it nonetheless produces a conveniently memorable figure:

over the course of their working lives, we are told, women will earn $450,000 or £300,000 less than men.[108]

This might not be a complete fabrication, but it is certainly disingenuous. Measuring differences in total pay masks a multitude of variables: older workers who have built careers through numerous promotions often earn more than junior colleagues; people working part-time earn less in total each year than people working full-time, even though they may be paid more each hour; some jobs are handsomely rewarded, many others pay the minimum wage. An average – or mean – measurement includes the pay of everyone, even the tiny proportion of extremely high earners who make more money than almost everyone else combined. This further skews the statistics to make the gender pay gap seem even larger.

Ignoring all of these factors makes it seem as if women are paid less than men for doing the exact same work. Worse still, it presents all women as equally disadvantaged. In reality, the experiences of a woman working part-time in a shop are vastly different from those of a woman working full-time as a Chief Executive Officer of a large corporation. The grouping together of all women into one single group elides these differences and, as a result, further exploits the lowest paid women to justify pay increases for the already well-remunerated.

Arguments around an average pay gap do not stack up. If it really was the case that women could be paid 24 per cent less for doing the exact same job as a man, there would be far fewer men employed. Many countries have passed equal pay legislation, making it illegal to pay men and women differently for the same work. Unfortunately, it doesn't seem to matter if a passionate feminist argument bears only a passing relationship to reality.

LIKE FOR LIKE EARNINGS

Most campaigners agree, when pushed, that the gender pay gap is at a record low. Unfortunately, the desire to make headlines comes at the expense of nuance. Simply by using a median − rather than a mean − form of arriving at the average, and thereby minimizing the impact of the small proportion of extremely high earners, the gender pay gap shrinks considerably. When median hourly earnings are compared, rather than total wages, we arrive at a far more realistic, but less headline-grabbing, figure. According to the UK's Office for National Statistics, a comparison of median hourly earnings shows roughly a 9 per cent gender pay gap.[109]

This lower figure takes account of hours worked but not the jobs people do or the experience they have accrued. It also ignores the fact that total hours worked can have an impact on hourly pay. People who work more may be more likely to qualify for bonus payments that are dependent upon hours billed. Similarly, people who work more may gain experience at a faster rate, leaving them able to apply for promotion or a performance-related pay increase sooner than colleagues who work part-time.

When the wages of women and men working in the same jobs for the same number of hours, at the same level and for the same number of years, are compared, there is no pay gap at all. In fact, when we compare the pay of men and women in their twenties, no matter which way we measure the statistics, we find that women are the higher earners.[110]

PART-TIME JOBS AND PART-TIME WAGES

Campaigners wanting to raise awareness of the gender pay gap prefer the average statistic not just because it is large but also because, they argue, women are more likely to work part-time and this is itself a sign of the sexism endemic in society and in the workplace. As we saw in the previous chapter, despite the absence of legal barriers and huge shifts in social attitudes, work remains highly segregated along gender lines. This is far more the case for unskilled jobs; men are more likely to work as labourers on building sites while women are more likely to work as carers in nursing homes. It's also a fact that far more women than men work part-time, although recently this gap has been narrowing. The number of women working part-time in professional occupations has, over the past 20 years, been offset by a dramatic increase in the number of men employed part-time in poorly paid unskilled positions.[111]

Nonetheless, women remain far more likely to work part-time than men. In the US, 64 per cent of part-time workers are women.[112] In the UK, 41 per cent of women work part time compared to 11 per cent of men.[113] What these figures can't tell us is whether women freely choose to work part-time or have no alternative either because there are few other employment options, or, more usually, because child care and family commitments fall disproportionately upon women and make full-time work impossible. This is the topic of the next chapter.

Different women's experiences, and the choices available to them, vary enormously. For well-qualified women in professional jobs, particularly those who are married, working part-time allows them to supplement the family income and keep the status and stimulation of being employed outside the home while at the same time juggling the demands of intensive parenting. For these women, part-time work is a positive choice. For women without skills or qualifications, poorly paid part-time work may be the only option available. Furthermore, the high cost of childcare in comparison to earnings might make working more hours unviable for these women even if full-time employment was available.

As we've already noted, part-time jobs tend to pay less, not just in total but also per hour. When we compare solely female earnings we find that women who work part-time earn, on average, 32 per cent less each hour than women who work full-time.[114] However, when just part-time workers are compared, a very different gender pay gap is revealed: women are, on average, paid more than men. Looking at people aged 30 to 39; we find that 38 per cent of women work part-time compared with 8 per cent of men. But the gender pay gap for this group is actually −8 per cent; in other words, women working part-time earn substantially more than men working part-time.[115] This part-time gender pay gap in women's favour is increasing.[116]

The explanation for this negative gender pay gap lies in the different types of jobs men and women working part-time are likely to do. A significant proportion of women work part-time in highly paid, professional occupations. Even though their hourly rate of pay may eventually fall behind their full-time colleagues, they may still earn more in total than people who work full-time in unskilled jobs. The female doctor who chooses to work part-time while her children are at school will initially earn the same each hour as her male colleague working full-time. After 10 years she is likely to be earning less each hour as her incremental pay rises and promotion opportunities have not kept pace with his. However, she is still earning more, in total, than the male retail assistant who works full-time or the male lorry driver who works part-time. There are some signs that a very small number of men in elite occupations are beginning to opt for part-time work.[117] However, by far the majority of men who work part-time are in low-paid jobs and have taken part-time work, often supplemented by state benefits, in preference to no work at all.

Even though the number of men who work part-time is small, this is a growing proportion of the workforce. A report by the UK's Institute for Fiscal Studies shows that men today are four times more likely to be working part-time than they were in the 1990s and that 'men with low skills and in areas of the country with few jobs are among the worst hit by the loss of well-paid full-time employment'.[118] For many men it seems that part-time work is still less likely to be a positive choice and more likely to be a last resort. Campaigns around the gender pay gap overshadow news about the decline in wages for men in low-skilled occupations. Yet, as most people still live in couples, a drop in male earnings has an impact upon entire families.

GENDER DOES NOT DETERMINE EARNINGS

The continual evocation of gender in discussions around education, employment and earnings gives the impression that this is the key factor in determining a person's life chances. In reality, this is far from the case. Wages are determined by many factors other than a person's gender. Although rarely acknowledged, age is a big contributing factor in the gender pay gap. People over the age of 45 today began their working lives in an era dominated by very different attitudes. It was far less common for women to have careers; as we've seen, practical and social obstacles stood in their way. People currently in senior positions in any profession have built careers over a number of decades and promotions, and therefore more of the highest earners are, unsurprisingly, men. Older women entered the world of work without the educational advantages young women have today and when childcare was not so readily accessible; this historical legacy still has an impact upon their hourly earnings.

The ever-present focus on gender in discussions around pay prevents us from seeing that the real pay gap is not between males and females but between an elite group of both men and women in professional occupations and a growing number of people employed in low-paid, part-time, temporary jobs. What we have, today as much as ever, is a social class pay gap rather than a gender pay gap. A report by the UK's Social Mobility Commission published in January 2017 calculated that professionals from working-class backgrounds earn £6,800 less each year than colleagues who come from affluent family backgrounds.[119] This 17 per cent pay gap shows that Britain remains a 'deeply elitist' society according to the Commission's Chairman, Alan Milburn. Yet even this 17 per cent statistic is a comparison of the wages paid to people in 'professional' occupations. It is not a measure of difference between professionals and unskilled workers.

Professional jobs in medicine, law and business tend to pay better than low-skilled work in catering, cleaning or caring. In general, within employment sectors, doctors earn more than nurses, teachers more than classroom assistants and lawyers more than secretaries. The jobs people do, in turn, are determined by myriad factors including gender but also, perhaps even more significantly, their educational level and type of qualification, their family contacts, role models, aspirations and ambitions.

Significantly, the jobs people end up doing also depend upon the work that is available and accessible. I may dream of being an astronaut but sadly few such vacancies are advertised in my local paper. What this means is that, particularly when national economies are struggling to be productive and social mobility is low, working-class children tend to grow up to get working-class jobs while upper- and middle-class children go on to take better paying professional jobs. In other words, social class is a far bigger determinant than gender of the work people do and the wages they earn. The French sociologists Pierre Bourdieu and Jean-Claude Passeron, writing in *Reproduction, Education, Society and Culture*, demonstrate how social class positions are reproduced and legitimized through home and school.

Among cleaners, caterers, carers and shop workers the gender pay gap is very slight; minimum wage jobs tend to pay the minimum wage to both men and women alike. Among Chief Executive Officers, on the other hand, the gender pay gap is roughly 30 per cent: more men work as CEOs, many have been in post for longer and they tend to be in bigger, more established firms. Yet I imagine few female CEOs, even those who campaign loudly against the pay gap, would trade their position for a less well-remunerated job complete with smaller gender pay gap.

The small and shrinking remaining pay gap primarily affects women over the age of 45, particularly those who have taken time out from employment to raise children and have then returned to work part-time. As always, this historical legacy plays itself out most profoundly on those in unskilled jobs who live in areas of low economic growth. As a result, a sizable group of working-class women enter retirement with significantly lower pension provision than men of the same age. Yet among all the discussion of the representation of women on boards of directors, the pay of female professors and the starting salaries of female graduates, little is said about this group of women.

The narrative of the gender pay gap is worse than just a distraction from real-income inequalities. In overlooking social class differences and the enormous progress elite women have made in recent years, feminist campaigners claim all women suffer the injustice of being paid less than men. Rather than telling young women that they are doing better than ever before and have a world of opportunities available to them, feminists tell women nothing has changed and they are still badly treated in the labour market.

PROBLEMATIC SOLUTIONS DON'T DO WOMEN (OR MEN) ANY FAVOURS

Various solutions to the gender pay gap have been proposed. In 2015, the then British prime minister David Cameron introduced new legislation to make it mandatory for large companies to report wage differentials broken down according to gender. His proposal mandates every business with over 250 employees to 'publish the gap between average female earnings and average male earnings'. This would, he declared, 'cast sunlight on the discrepancies and create the pressure we need for change, driving women's wages up'. This 'naming and shaming' legislation is set to come into effect in 2018.[120]

All legislation runs the risk of instigating perverse incentives and this focus on publicly exposing companies that apparently underpay women is surely no exception. For example, one very straightforward way for a company to lower their overall gender pay gap would be to get more women into senior and better paying roles. For some women this might be a welcome opportunity to realize a long-held ambition: indeed many public sector employers, universities and multinational corporations already run mentorship schemes and other training programmes designed to help women advance their careers. But if such voluntary schemes do not have the desired effect then perhaps more pressure might be applied to women to push them into roles they are reluctant to take. At the same time, it is hard to imagine that women's requests to work part-time, flexibly or take a career break will be looked upon favourably.

Far worse than pushing women into top jobs is the potential for companies to tackle a pay gap by not recruiting women into less well-paying lower-level positions. Such junior posts can provide people, particularly those without formal qualifications or high-level connections, with a 'foot in the door' and an opportunity to work their way up in a business. Concern about increasing the gender pay gap might have the unintended consequence of denying some women this route to social mobility. Another solution to the pay gap already being trialled by some employers and perhaps likely to become more prevalent when naming and shaming legislation comes into effect is simply to pay women more. This is already happening in some British universities.

Paying Women Professors More

Data analysed by the *Times Higher Education* in 2016 shows that women working in UK universities on full-time academic contracts earn, on average, 11 per cent less than men in the same roles. For professors, this pay gap is smaller, with women earning 5.8 per cent less than their male counterparts: a difference of £4,570 a year.[121] There may be many reasons for this pay gap. Academics are often awarded an annual pay increment, so people who have been in work longer tend to earn more than new entrants to the profession. The pay gap data could be skewed by a preponderance of men at the end of their careers and women at the start of their careers. We can expect such a pay gap to decline over time − which is indeed what is already happening.

The gender pay gap in academia might also be down to the institutions academics work in: older research-focussed universities tend to offer higher salaries than newer teaching-focussed institutions. Similarly, the subject areas people work in also have an impact on their salary. Data from the Higher Education Statistics Agency show that women comprise 45 per cent of academic staff in UK higher education. However, there are quite considerable variations by discipline. Although women and men are almost equally represented in social studies and humanities, more men work in science, engineering and technology disciplines while more women are employed in education and subjects allied to medicine.

Although we may wish it were otherwise, people working at the cutting edge of scientific and technological research can command higher salaries because they have competitive employment alternatives in the private sector that are rarely available to those working in humanities disciplines. Furthermore, discipline impacts upon career structure — which, in turn, has an effect on salary. More women academics work in education or nursing departments and are likely to have spent the first part of their careers working as teachers or nurses. When they then embark on an academic career they compete against colleagues of the same age in other departments who are already in possession of a portfolio of publications.

Rather than taking account of real differences that might underpin the data, many universities prefer to demonstrate their feminist credentials and be proactive in tackling the pay gap. Mentoring schemes to support female academics in negotiating salaries and applying for promotion abound. Some British universities have gone further. At the University of Essex one-off pay increases, averaging about £4,000 a year, have been awarded to all female professors.[122] These special additional payments, awarded on the basis of biology, are presented as a logical solution to a gender pay gap assumed to result from deeply entrenched sexist attitudes rather than a combination of historical legacy and the choices women make. Making 'compensatory' payments to female professors creates the false perception that women are disadvantaged in academia and need special treatment to achieve equal status with their male colleagues. They suggest that women should be paid more just for being female, rather than for the quality of their research and teaching. Female academics have no need for such pity-payments.

As always, the focus on the gender pay gap in academia ignores other, far greater, pay inequalities. Many women employed by universities work in administration, catering or housekeeping – photocopying, cleaning offices and making coffee for academics. Likewise, many men are employed in maintaining buildings and ensuring campus security. These women and men are paid a fraction of a professorial salary but their jobs do not permit them the time to attend mentorship programmes and support networks. The women who keep the university infrastructure going on a daily basis are often too busy simply getting by to put effort into presenting themselves as victims of the patriarchy and in need of bonus payments for being female. Yet I suspect they may well be envious of the pay increase awarded to female professors.

CONCLUSIONS

The current obsession with the gender pay gap does women few favours. At a time when women and men earn the same pay for the same work and younger women earn more, on average, than men of the same age, campaigners rely on a disingenuous and highly selective interpretation of statistics to summon the pay gap into existence. As a result, the reality of there being many well-paid career opportunities available to women today is overshadowed by a view of women as poorly paid and taken for granted in the workplace. The politicization of the pay gap means it has taken on a symbolic importance for feminists and a continual round of high-profile initiatives raise this one issue above and beyond its real-world impact. The obsession with the gender pay gap means that women's lives are judged solely according to how much they are paid and a more nuanced discussion about both pay and the problems with combining work with being a mother is avoided. In the next chapter we explore why women are more likely than men to opt for part-time work.

CHAPTER FOUR

THE MOTHERHOOD PENALTY

Recently, attention has focused on the gender pay gap that emerges when people have children, what has come to be labelled 'the motherhood penalty'. A much-publicized 2016 report shows a gradual but continual rise in the average hourly pay gap, from virtually zero when men and women begin their working lives, to about 10 per cent when a woman first gives birth. By the time her first child turns 12, women are earning, on average, a third less each hour than men.[123] In this chapter we look at the pressures mothers face today and consider why women are still more likely than men to give up work altogether, or return only part-time, once they become parents. We ask whether the apparent freedom mothers have to choose staying at home, returning to work part-time or full-time, is just an illusion — designed to put a liberal gloss on the reality of women's lives.

PAYING MOTHERS LESS

Talk of a 'motherhood penalty' can make it seem as if sexist male bosses conspire to pay women with children less than

men. This narrative of sexism and female disadvantage stands
in opposition to reality: women who return to work immediately after maternity leave, even if that maternity leave lasts
for a year, find no loss of pay at all. On a 'like for like' basis,
they continue to earn the same as their male colleagues.
Likewise, women who return to work part-time suffer no
immediate penalty; indeed, women's weekly earnings fall by
proportionally less than the reduction in hours worked –
that is, their hourly wages actually tend to increase.[124] The
economist Heather Joshi points out that today's women graduates who postpone having children until the age of thirty
and then return to work 'will probably suffer no earnings
loss at all for a first child'.[125]

The alarming 'motherhood penalty' emerges from a comparison of average hourly wages that takes no account of the
jobs men and women do or the total number of hours they
work. Women returning to employment after maternity leave,
even if they come back part-time, initially earn the same each
hour as their male colleagues. However, over time, women's
wages drop. As we noted in the previous chapter, part-time
workers are slower to gain promotion and less likely to qualify for bonus payments. Women with young children are less
likely to make a major career move. They are also less likely
to work (or be seen to work) additional hours on top of the
working day if they are responsible for picking up a child
from school or nursery.

By the time her first child is 20, the average woman has
been in paid work four years less than the average man, and
has been in work of more than 20 hours per week for nine
years less than a typical man.[126] In other words, when people
have children, more women than men cut back on the hours
they spend in paid employment and this is reflected in their
earnings. Gradually, over the course of a decade, the cumula-
tive effect of women stopping work altogether or working

fewer total hours, is that their average earnings fall. The gender pay gap is not so much a motherhood penalty as a time away from paid work penalty.

Of course, we need to ask why more women than men decide to take time out or work part-time once they have children. Debates about working mothers are emotive and polarized. On the one hand, women are presented as eager to get back to advancing their careers but held back in a hostile and sexist labour market. On the other hand, women are considered to have a 'maternal instinct' that overrides personal ambition the moment a baby arrives. The truth, as always, is somewhere in between. Some women may be replying to emails from the maternity ward and back at their office a few days after giving birth. Other women may be only too happy to swap meetings and sitting at a desk for play groups and breastfeeding. Most women try to find a way of combining work and raising children that suits them and their family.

THE ILLUSION OF CHOICE

Decisions about whether or not to continue working after having a baby are personal and complex. Often, they are not taken by women alone but in conjunction with partners and perhaps other family members. Choices are influenced by attitudes towards work as well as towards motherhood. Good quality and affordable child care makes returning to work easier, as does having a high-status, well-paid and enjoyable job. Work that is poorly paid and tedious can make staying at home a more attractive option, especially for women who grew up expecting to play this role. Often, compromises are involved. Part-time work, if only for a few years, is popular because it allows women to earn money, maintain a career and still be a 'hands-on' parent.

Feminists are often quick to point out that the rhetoric of 'choice' is misleading and what may appear to be an individual woman's chosen life course is in fact the only option available to her. For example, a woman may choose to give up work after having a baby, but if her partner works exceptionally long hours and refuses to give up his job, and there is no suitable childcare or other help available, then she doesn't really have much of a choice to make. Continuing to work would be nearly impossible. Similarly, a woman whose job involves considerable amounts of travel, or frequently working late into the evening, but whose child attends a nursery that shuts at five o'clock may say she has chosen to work part-time although her only other option was to leave work entirely.

Time and again it seems that women are more likely than men to prioritize children over work. Anne Marie Slaughter, the first woman Director of Policy Planning at the US State Department, became one of the most high-profile women to leave her job in order to spend more time with her teenage children. Slaughter chronicled her decision in a widely read article entitled: *Why Women Still Can't Have It All.*[127] Like many feminist commentators, Slaughter pointed to the practical obstacles and social pressures that combine to ensure women put motherhood first.

TRADITIONAL ROLES

To explore what shapes the decisions women make, we need to dig deeper than current debates about whether women can 'have it all'. As always, the legacy of history continues to have important repercussions. The movement of economic production out of the home with the industrial revolution meant that men took on the role of breadwinner while women were pushed into taking sole responsibility for domestic life. As a consequence, women became primarily defined as wives and mothers. Their relegation to the home, where their labour carried no financial value, made them economically dependent upon men. Although a proportion of working-class women needed to earn money too, the default position of housewife meant their labour was poorly paid and insecure.

Frederick Engels, writing in *The Origin of the Family, Private Property and the State* in 1884, located women's oppression in the institution of the family. He argued that the role women were forced to play in the home prevented them from fully participating in public life. In the 1960s and into the early 1970s, feminists such as Betty Friedan and Germaine Greer argued that a combination of formal legislation and informal practices meant women were still oppressed because they were unable to participate in all aspects of society in the same way as men. Lack of access to contraception, abortion and childcare placed real limitations on women's capacity to engage fully in the workplace or public life more broadly.

In her 1974 book *Housewife*, Ann Oakley describes 'gender differentiation between the roles of female and male' as 'the axis of the modern family's structure'.[128] This division does not occur because of natural instinct or simply because of children's socialization. Social and cultural practices that stem from outside the family have an impact too. As we have already noted, in the years following both the First and Second World War there were concerted efforts led by government and backed by trade unions to get women out of work and into the home. One consequence was that support for children's day nurseries was withdrawn.

Women who wanted to work faced poor job prospects and low pay. This meant that male employment was most important for a family's financial security and, if women worked outside of the home, it was their work not the man's that had to fit around the needs of children. In the 1970s, at the time of the UK's Equal Pay Act, nurseries that would take babies and stay open long enough to allow women to work were rare. Nurseries at this time were described as, 'little more than an appendage of the social security system, an inadequate net to catch those women the state considers to be incompetent at one of their prime tasks under capitalism: child rearing'.[129] Mothers wanting to work were forced to depend on informal arrangements with family and friends. In this context, equal pay legislation was destined to be of limited success and the political demand for childcare became a radical challenge to women's continued oppression.

Many things have changed for women over the past half century but the pace of change has not been even in all areas of life. Writing in 1978, the Irish journalist Mary Kenny confidently declared, 'By the age of twenty-three, most women are married and have children. Ninety-five per cent of all women in the world eventually marry and have children.'[130] This is far from the case today. However, the title of Kenny's book is revealing: 'How to run a home and bring up a family without giving up your job – essential reading for every working mother.' Women were marrying and primarily responsible for the children – but they were increasingly working too. In Britain in 1978, 750,000 women with children under 5 worked, but perhaps because of the difficulties in combining work and family life, more than two-thirds of women who worked were employed part-time.[131] In 1980, the proportion of women returning to some form of work when their baby was 8 months old reached 24 per cent of all working mothers.[132]

In a lecture delivered in 1982, the then British prime minister Margaret Thatcher claimed, 'The battle for women's rights has largely been won.'[133] However, the subsequent economic downturn meant her words were premature and the number of women in employment fell in the mid-1980s with Thatcher herself calling on women to return to the home. In reality, many women with children had never left the home and those that had still bore the brunt of housework and childcare. The sociologist Arlie Hochschild coined the term 'the second shift' to describe the hours women spent looking after home and children in addition to their paid employment.

Today there are far more 'working mothers' but many, it seems, are still 'running a home and bringing up a family' too. Whether through tradition, convenience or choice, it's mum rather than dad who is far more likely to be phoned up, first by nursery and later by school, when their child is sick. It is still the mother's job that is often considered more flexible when the child needs to stay at home. Whether or not the burden of this second shift pushes women to 'choose' to work part-time or give up entirely depends upon the willingness of her partner to share responsibility for housework and childcare or being able to pay for childminders and babysitters to ease the load – as well as her own personal preferences.

CHANGING FAMILIES

Much has changed for working mothers in recent years. Trade unions are more likely to be campaigning against the gender pay gap than reminding women their place is in the home. Nurseries and after-school clubs, although often expensive, have proliferated. However, even though our lives are very different today, history still leaves its imprint. Slaughter notes, 'Men are still socialized to believe that their primary family obligation is to be the breadwinner; women, to believe that their primary family obligation is to be the caregiver.'[134] Right from early childhood, we are told, role models, books and toys all help prepare girls for a life of domesticity where careers come second to the more important role of being a mother.

Such stereotypes were more rigidly policed in the past, but they undoubtedly still hold sway today. However, the tendency for increasing numbers of women to delay motherhood, or not have children at all, suggests the influence of such childhood conditioning is diminishing. Similarly, men's attitudes towards housework and childcare are also beginning to change. The authors of *The New Soft War on Women* note, 'Married fathers in two-earner couples have dramatically increased the amount of time they spend in both child care and house work over the past twenty-five years.'[135] A study from the University of Warwick likewise claims that men no longer have such a strong perception that housework is the role of a woman. While women still do most around the home, researchers found, men are now doing more. Interestingly, they point to an emerging class divide with working-class men carrying out more household chores than high earners.[136]

As some of Hochschild's *Second Shift* couples illustrate, money can, to a limited extent, substitute for time through the purchase of take-out food and domestic help. Today, women have more employment opportunities, men are beginning to take on a greater share of housework and childcare is more readily available. It should be more possible than ever before for women to combine work and motherhood. But the fact remains that some women who have money for childcare and partners willing to share the load do still choose to be more involved at home, perhaps seeing a domestic role as more central to their sense of identity than men.

Slaughter moves on from discussing the socialization of children and pinpoints 'a maternal imperative felt so deeply that the "choice" is reflexive'.[137] The notion that women are biologically programmed with a maternal instinct and hormonal drivers ready to kick in and circumvent our brains returns us to the realm of workplace 'period policies' discussed in Chapter Two. Whereas an older generation of feminists challenged the belief that women existed at the whims of their hormones and biology, today's feminists breathe life back into this old idea.

The danger with propagating notions of a nebulous but overwhelming maternal instinct is that it becomes a pedestal women who want to be good mothers are compelled to climb aboard. Hanna Rosin, author of *The End of Men and the Rise of Women*, writes, 'I've seen so many friends nearly quit their jobs because they did not want to stop breast-feeding or deal with the stress of pumping breast milk at work. In that myopic, desperate moment of early motherhood, women demote their own ambition to the near moral equivalent of starving your baby.'[138] The notion of a 'maternal instinct' suggests motherhood is the natural state for a woman and women who happily return to work full-time are denying their true nature. It also suggests that fathers who are not in possession of such an instinct can never come up to scratch.

For young women yet to confront the reality of juggling family and work, belief in a maternal instinct encourages them to begin preparing for their biological destiny. Sheryl Sandberg, the Chief Operating Officer of Facebook and the author of *Lean In* notes, 'Women are making room for kids they don't have, years before they try and get pregnant ... the men, meanwhile, are super aggressive and focused. They are in your office every day. "Can I do that? Can I lead this?" They don't have to be talked into things.'[139] In practice, this means that some women end up deprioritizing their careers before they have even begun to have children.

NEW PRESSURES ON MOTHERS

Just when there are few barriers to mothers working outside the home, it seems that new pressures come to the fore. When people married and had children at a younger age, becoming a mother was simply a routine part of life. Indeed, for many young women it marked the transition to adulthood. Today, thanks in part to improved access to contraception and abortion as well as to better education and employment opportunities, becoming a parent rarely 'just happens'. For many people nowadays the decision to have a baby is taken consciously; children become part of an overall life plan (even if this plan is little more than an aspiration).

Women are having fewer children than in the past but the trend towards smaller families does not mean that home life necessarily takes up any less time. Betty Friedan, writing in *The Feminine Mystique*, commented on the tendency for housework to fill the time made available to it. Today, it is not housework but looking after children that expands to fill ever more time. Kenny noted in 1978 that, 'As families get smaller they also get more intense.' She continues, 'The fact that women are having fewer children doesn't necessarily mean – as I had once believed – that they expend less energy on motherhood; indeed, they probably expend more, since everyone takes child-bearing and child-raising so seriously now.'[140]

When having a baby 'just happened', children were simply part and parcel of an adult's life. Children were expected to fit into the adult world, not the other way round. The job of socializing and disciplining children was undertaken not just by parents but by teachers, religious and community leaders, extended family members and neighbours. Ellie Lee, Director of the University of Kent's *Centre for Parenting Cultural Studies*, notes that 'the task that should properly be shared by *all* adults – that of shaping and developing the next generation – has come to be thought of and fetishized as "parenting"'.[141] Today, the job of child rearing has become far more privatized; it is seen as solely the responsibility of the nuclear family. Yet at the same time as raising children has become the sole responsibility of parents, there is an increasing expectation that it will be carried out in a particular way.

The fact that having children is considered a deliberate choice means that parents are under pressure to raise their children in the 'correct' way; that is, in a manner determined by an army of professionals offering advice and guidance on what is best for the child. Lee explains: 'bringing up children is seen as far too difficult and important to be left to parents'.[142] As a result, parents spend more time and effort raising their children despite being considered the least qualified person in their child's life.

RELINQUISHING AUTONOMY

The word 'parent' is today used less as a noun and more as a verb; rather than simply being a parent, people do 'parenting'. Despite there being a long history to publications and organizations offering parental advice, Lee argues that '"parenting" has acquired specific connotations more recently' with 'an explicit focus on the parent and their behaviour that emerges as the general, distinctive attribute of the contemporary term "parenting" and the determinism it brings with it'.[143] Today, clear expectations as to how parenting should be done properly come from psychologists, parenting experts, health professionals, teachers, parenting charities and campaign groups, neuroscientists and government ministers.

Parents are encouraged to worry about the mental and physical health of their babies not just from before birth but even from before conception. In the UK, the NHS advises prospective parents: 'Preconception care is an opportunity for you and your partner to improve your health before you start trying for a baby. A healthcare professional can help you to assess your health, fitness and lifestyle, to identify areas that you may want to improve.'[144] Although the NHS guidance is careful to include 'you and your partner', the pressure to seek out and follow advice falls disproportionately upon women who get pregnant, give birth and are expected to breastfeed their babies exclusively for at least six months.

At their very first appointment with a midwife, British women are presented with an extensive list of foods to avoid or consume in moderation. The list is as specific as it is long with advice on exactly how much caffeine is acceptable, how many cups of herbal tea to drink each day and what types of cheese to avoid.[145] The message to pregnant women is clear: you are no longer a rational adult able to exercise common sense. Instead, for the sake of your future baby, submission to the rules is required. As pregnant women want what's best for their babies, they relinquish autonomy over their own lives.

Rules are strictest around smoking and drinking alcohol. There are proposals to submit pregnant women who are persistent smokers to carbon monoxide testing with shopping vouchers as a reward for abstinence.[146] Although this is not yet a routine feature of antenatal care, the fact it can be proposed at all shows the extent to which medical professionals hold the individual rights and personal freedoms of the living adult woman in lower regard than the life of the foetus. Likewise, there is no evidence to suggest that moderate alcohol consumption, having a couple of glasses of wine a couple of times a week, is detrimental to the developing foetus. Yet because health professionals operate a precautionary principle and don't trust women to apply common sense and follow nuanced guidance, women are advised to abstain from alcohol altogether for the duration of their pregnancy. This made-up 'rule' then gets policed by people, such as bar-tenders, who have no relationship to the pregnant woman yet still feel entitled to tell her what to do on behalf of the unborn child.

Practically, the impact of following such rules to the letter is that women cannot relax and socialize with friends and colleagues as equals without having attention drawn to their 'special' status as a mother-to-be. It is not sexist bosses, outdated laws or religious conventions that prevent pregnant women playing a full part in society but a view of women as nothing other than the carrier of a future baby. Rather than this being seen as an imposition, many women consider the sacrifices they are expected to make when pregnant as important and worthwhile; they accept the idea that putting the needs of the child first, even before it is born, is of paramount importance. As Katie Roiphe puts it, 'Doing something unhealthy, or creating an unhealthy environment for a child, is currently so taboo that we are tyrannized by the fear of it: we are almost unable to think in other terms.'[147]

Women, and to an increasing extent men, find their lives change when they have children. Of course, having children demands sacrifices are made – this has always been the case. Impromptu nights out, holidays and taking jobs in another country might not be curtailed but certainly require more planning. This comes as little surprise to most parents. What's new today is that adults who have been quite capable of conducting their own lives find, upon becoming parents that they are subject to guidance on what to eat, drink and wear, how to exercise, socialize and run their lives. It is assumed that the child, even before birth, has interests distinct from those of the parents and professionals are needed to ensure the child's needs are met. For some women, perhaps distant from their own mothers and anxious to do everything 'correctly', this instruction might be welcomed. For others, it is a fact of life, to be taken on board or smiled at in public and ignored at home.

For those who want to run their lives and raise their families in a way that goes against the norm, the weight of interference, leading to children being removed or threatened with removal from the family home, is truly appalling. Rebecca Schiller, author of *Why Human Rights in Childbirth Matter*, details the experiences of women who, through choice or circumstance, through a missed antenatal appointment or the decision to have a home birth, have not followed the approved route for childbirth. She explains, 'It is perhaps unsurprising that a society increasingly dictatorial about pregnant women's behaviour, that fetishizes parenting and points the finger of blame all-too-frequently at the mother, is punishing women in this way.'[148]

DOING PARENTING

The pressure — often self-inflicted — to be a textbook parent does not disappear when a baby is born: it intensifies. The importance placed on 'bonding' and the mantra that 'breast is best' lead women to interpret failure as potentially disastrous for their child's future life chances. Jess Phillips explains: 'For some reason, we all sign up to the idea that women are doing something sacred in a baby's first year that no one else could manage.' She takes the breastfeeding obsessives to task: 'I know all the statistics about how natural birth is safer and how breast is best, but up and down the country new moms are weeping over the heads of their newborns because they can't get the hang of breastfeeding and have for some reason been led to believe by some crappy meme on Facebook that if they give them baby formula they will basically be feeding them crack.'[149]

As children grow up, demands on mothers don't lessen but change in response to new anxieties. Parents today are expected – and in turn take it upon themselves – to be ever-vigilant about where their children are and what they are doing. As a consequence, the days when children stayed home alone, played out in the street and walked to and from school unaccompanied have largely vanished and many parents instead end up shepherding their children from school to a series of clubs and structured activities. Sharon Hays, author of *The Cultural Contradictions of Motherhood*, notes that 'modern American mothers do much more than simply feed, change and shelter the child until age six'. This 'more', notes Charlotte Faircloth, 'involves devoting large amounts of time, energy, and material resources to the child'.[150]

Mothers are not just held responsible for their children's physical safety and educational development but for their mental health too. Parenting expert Steve Biddulph claims, 'Affluent, time-poor British parents are responsible for a youth mental-health epidemic.' He advises mothers not to be hung up about their looks, to limit their child's 'screen time' (both perhaps easier said than done) and not to go clothes shopping with their daughters. Such advice conflicts with many mothers' instincts yet, as no parent wants to risk the mental health of their child, it is often welcomed – even when not always acted upon. Frank Furedi, writing in *Paranoid Parenting*, explores how the belief that everything a parent does has an impact on their child's life makes raising children an almost impossibly fraught task.

I asked Dr Jan Macvarish, author of *Neuroparenting,
The Expert Invasion of Family Life*, why parenting has
become such an all-consuming endeavour. Macvarish says
that 'Raising children used to be something people just got
on with but now, almost everyone thinks about parenting as
a conscious act that has particular outcomes and needs to be
carried out to a certain standard. The idea that parenting is
something you can get wrong has become widely accepted
and because of this, raising children has become something of
an ordeal.'[151]

Macvarish argues that one reason for this shift lies in our
collective concerns about the future: 'At a time when we
don't seem to be in control of the future, the very fact of
having another biological generation come into being
through the child becomes a site of considerable anxiety.
Children carry the weight of our insecurities; they have
become a repository for every social problem.' She suggests,
'Parents have become charged with making this transition to
the future happen in a positive way that solves the problems
we face now. So much is loaded onto the shoulders of parents
today that wasn't attributable to them in the past.'
Macvarish explains, 'When social problems are talked about
today all discussion coalesces around the idea that the early
years are formative. There is no longer any sense of people
being part of broader society or of the possibility of bringing
about structural social change. Instead, social problems are
located in individuals and parents are supposed to solve these
problems. Parenting has become both the cause and the solution to all problems.'

A focus on parenting rather than political solutions to
social problems allows campaigners to distance themselves
from politics and defer instead to seemingly neutral experts.
The latest science of parenting involves a focus on babies'
brains; something Macvarish has labelled 'neuroparenting'.

She writes that brain claims suggest the correct scientific approach to raising children has now been determined and is beyond doubt: 'The basis for this final achievement of certainty regarding child rearing is said to be discoveries made through neuroscience about the development of the human brain, in particular, during infancy.'[152] Most mothers will be familiar with claims about the significance of what they do in pregnancy and the first few years of their child's life such as the importance of breast milk or playing babies classical music. Macvarish argues, 'The rhetoric of babies' brains is deployed to challenge the fundamental rights and responsibilities which have shaped British family life for the past 100 years or more, in particular, the general presumption that parents know best when it comes to caring for babies and getting toddlers to school age.'[153] The pressure is on parents to create the perfect environment for their child by seeking out and following expert parenting advice. The 'good' mother is the one who is most dedicated to this cause.

The working mother, on the other hand, seems to be selfishly putting her own needs above those of her child. Steve Biddulph makes this point clearly when he blames the mental health crisis in teenage girls on mothers who are too busy working to spend time with their daughters, urging 'career success comes at great cost'.[154] It seems as if whatever mothers do today they are in the wrong. If they work full-time, they risk damaging their child emotionally. If they dedicate themselves to full-time parenting, they are criticized for being a 'helicopter mother' and denying their children independence. Simply loving and looking after your children is no longer enough.

This intensification of parenthood, and in particular the focus on the role of the mother, makes the decision to combine having children with working full-time more difficult. Jennie Bristow explains that it has become 'morally unacceptable' for 'women to devote themselves to their work more than, or as much as, to their children – by going back to work less than six months after their baby's birth, working longish hours or a five-day week, attending international conferences rather than Nativity plays'.[155] No matter how good or cheap nurseries might be, no matter how much time dads spend with children or doing housework, the intense pressure and effort required to be the perfect mother makes the idea of leaving work altogether, or working only part-time, appear not just attractive but actually necessary – irrespective of whatever a woman's ambitions might once have been.

DISAPPEARING WOMEN

In a previous era, feminists fought for women to be recognized as independent and autonomous beings distinct from first their fathers, then their husbands. Later, they recognized the danger of swapping obedience to men for sublimation to the child. In 1970, Germaine Greer wrote in *The Female Eunuch*, 'Childbearing was never intended by biology as a compensation for neglecting all other forms of fulfilment and achievement. It was never intended to be as time consuming and self-conscious a process as it is.'[156] Yet almost 50 years later many women find their identity has indeed become subsumed within that of their child.

Katie Roiphe describes the trend for women with interesting adult lives to represent themselves on Facebook with a photo of their child. 'These photos signal a larger and more ominous self-effacement, a narrowing of worlds,' she argues, 'yet this style of self-effacement, this voluntary loss of self, comes naturally.' Judith Warner, writing in *Perfect Madness, Motherhood in the Age of Anxiety*, labels the new 'problem with no name' as the 'Mummy Mystique'. She explains,

'We have taken it upon ourselves as supermothers to be everything to our children that society refuses to be: not just loving nurturers but educators, entertainers, guardians of environmental purity, protectors of a stable and prosperous future.'[157] As a result, she argues, 'Too many of us allow ourselves to be defined by motherhood.' Women who readily define themselves by motherhood are more likely to feel guilty about working full-time and prioritizing their own needs; they are more likely to leave work altogether for a few years or return part-time.

FLEXIBLE WORKING

One solution to combining intensive motherhood with employment is 'flexible working' – allowing people to work at different times of the day, from different locations or only during school term times. Flexible working sounds great but rarely seems to live up to the hype. Particularly for women in low-skilled, low-paid jobs, flexibility can be a way of selling insecurity. 'Zero-hours contracts', where employees do not know from one week to the next when or even if they will be working have, rightly, been criticized. Dressing such contracts up as a way for people to combine work and children is little help to people who need a regular source of income. Likewise, the entitlement British women now have to take a full year's maternity leave may not be best for their careers. As Vicky Pryce notes, 'Generous maternity pay and leave arrangements seem to widen the experience gap between men and women because it means women take longer out of the labour market.'[158]

Flexibility can also mean an expectation for employees to be permanently 'on-call' and replying to work phone calls and emails. Rosin points out that women who work flexibly, 'work all the time', she explains, 'work and play and kids and sleep are all jumbled up in the same twenty-four-hour period'.[159] Unfortunately, as work is currently organized, particularly the higher up the career ladder individuals go, it neither coincides neatly with the school day nor lends itself to flexibility. Being a partner in a law firm, the editor of a newspaper or the creative director of an advertising agency requires a level of dedication, commitment and availability that flexibility rarely permits.

Flexible working might allow some women to juggle the competing demands of work and family life. But it can only ever be a partial solution to the problems today's feminists return to again and again: the gender pay gap and the underrepresentation of women in the most senior positions. At the moment, women are under pressure to be hands-on mothers whose first priority is always their children. At the same time, they are expected to dedicate themselves to their careers and seek out promotion opportunities at every turn. Doing both requires superhuman levels of organization and stamina. Yet while success is judged in terms of wages and job titles on the one hand, or having perfect children on the other, then there is no room for a broader discussion about what would make life better for everyone today.

CHOOSING MOTHERHOOD

Feminism tends to promote work as the key to women's happiness and search for meaning in their lives. Writing in a preface to *The Feminine Mystique*, author Lionel Shriver notes that 'Friedan may have placed excessive faith in the world of work to engender the creative fulfilment she envisions for her sisters'. This view of work reveals much about the type of people who become feminist campaigners. Shriver continues:

> *The jobs that involve innovation, imagination and*
> *exhilaration are available only to so many people.*
> *Not everyone can be an architect, a research physi-*
> *cist, or a filmmaker. Working the checkout till at*
> *Wal-Mart can be every bit as monotonous and*
> *soul-destroying as scrubbing the kitchen floor —*
> *maybe more so. Work is not always a privilege.*
> *For many women in the workforce today, a job is*
> *a fiscal necessity but hardly a source of joy.*[160]

For many women, being a mother seems more meaningful and fulfilling than paid employment. Motherhood carries an identity and a status that yesteryear's 'housewife' does not.

Although we can certainly question the extent to which women freely choose to leave work or cut their hours, to deny that women have any choices to make presents them as mere automatons acting out a pre-determined role over which they have little control. Indeed, the freedom women have to make such choices and to determine their own life course is surely feminism's biggest victory. What's needed is more freedom and choice to enable women and men to combine parenting and work more easily.

CONCLUSIONS

Combining a full-time job with intensive motherhood is exhausting. It can mean spending time at work expressing breast milk, evenings spent cramming in quality time with young children, and disturbed nights broken by a co-sleeping toddler. Ultimately, even for the most ruthless and best organized women, combining motherhood and work involves compromises. No one can be in two places at once, or, for that matter, expect to be paid for a job they don't do. That some women then choose to work part-time or not apply for a promotion is entirely understandable. For some women this is a positive choice – they want to spend time with their children and welcome the opportunity to step off the career ladder.

Today's feminism, fixated on the experiences of young professional women, cannot account for what has changed within families. There is awareness that life is different for women when they have children and this in part explains the obsession with the pay gap and the 'motherhood penalty'. Yet many feminists struggle to explain what's problematic with parents losing autonomy over their own lives when they have children because they are all too ready to see a celebration of breastfeeding, baby-carrying and an idealized version of motherhood as an aspiration to be juggled alongside the role of career-woman. The cry is often for men to do their fair share of parenting, or for employers to be more accommodating, rather than a broader discussion of the demands and expectations placed upon parents.

Feminism needs to let women off the hook and recognize that everyone makes different choices. Some women might want – or need – to get back to work days after giving birth. When the French Justice Minister Rachida Dati did just this in 2009, she became the subject of international consternation. Likewise, some women might want – or need – to leave work and become full-time mothers and they should be allowed to do so without feeling as if they are letting the side down by not 'leaning in'.

Women's freedom to make choices about their lives is to be celebrated. Rather than pushing mothers to get back to work or to stay at home, we should look at how best to support women in whatever decisions they choose to make. Part of this discussion needs to be recognition that neither work nor motherhood may be a source of a woman's true fulfilment. By presenting work and home as binary choices, feminism removes the potential for public life and private relationships that go beyond motherhood and the workplace.

PART TWO

PRIVATE RELATIONSHIPS, PUBLIC CONCERNS

CHAPTER FIVE

VICTORS OR VICTIMS?

The first part of this book has presented a contradiction. As we have seen, girls in most Western countries are doing better at school than boys. They are entering higher education in greater numbers than men; they are taking degrees across a broader range of subjects than ever before and are leaving with higher qualifications. As a result, women have better employment prospects and the gender pay gap, narrowing for everyone, has been all but eradicated for younger women today. Over a period of some four decades, the life chances and opportunities available to many young women have been transformed. Feminism has been a remarkable success story.

But what's striking is the absence of celebration. Instead, as we have seen, previous victories are reappraised and new sites of disadvantage are uncovered. Statistical successes stand in stark contrast to lamentable narratives. Women are, all too often, presented in the media and by campaigners as victims at home, in the workplace and in the street. This chapter explores the gap that exists between women's progress at school and at work and the perception of women's lives today. We look at why a view of women as victims has

gained such currency and the impact this has upon the lives
of women and men today.

DESPERATELY SEEKING DISADVANTAGE

It can appear as if every day new abuses or injustices against
women are brought to our attention.

In 2016 Nicola Thorp was sent home from her temporary
office job without pay for breaching her employer's 'appearance guidelines'.[161] As a receptionist, Thorp had been
expected to wear high-heeled shoes. Her refusal to do so led
to a petition and a subsequent inquiry followed by a report
from Members of Parliament recommending that such discriminatory practices be outlawed. It is easy to see the imposition of such a dress code as a huge infringement on women's
rights. However, many people, men and women, are expected
to wear uniforms to work that are far more restrictive than a
footwear stipulation.

Elsewhere, an investigation conducted by *The Times*
exposed the hidden cost of being female. The newspaper
showed that women were being overcharged for everyday
necessities such as razor blades and clothes.[162] Again, this
hunt for examples to prove women are disadvantaged
by sexist and exploitative business owners takes us into
highly selective terrain: the cost of replica football strips and
video games could be used to show the expense of being
male. It also ignores the fact that men and women make
choices: no one is forced to buy anything, whether in pink
or blue.

In the same week that Theresa May was inaugurated as
British Prime Minister, many women Members of Parliament
were busy launching a campaign to *Reclaim the Internet*.
Labour MP Yvette Cooper argued, 'for some people online

harassment, bullying, misogyny, racism or homophobia can end up poisoning the internet and stopping them from speaking out'. The campaign, named to echo the *Reclaim the Night* marches first organized by feminists campaigning against rape and sexual violence in the 1970s, drew upon research claiming to expose, 'the huge scale of social media misogyny'.[163]

Anyone who uses social media knows that there are those who, often hiding behind a cloak of anonymity, fall far wide of the line between criticism and personal insults. Indeed, there is no doubt that some of those who take pleasure in meting out such online abuse deliberately choose women as their target. There is arguably more of a need for social media users to regulate their community. But to suggest that the internet is a scary place for women who somehow need to 'reclaim' it is disingenuous. One study suggests more men than women have experienced online abuse[164] and, as Cooper acknowledges, 'some kinds of sexism (such as aggressively accusing women of being a "slut" or a "whore") were as likely to come from young women as young men'.[165] Her argument that this reflects 'a wider and ingrained culture of abuse' shows a determination to stick to a narrative of female victimhood even if this means ignoring inconvenient facts.

Such campaigns and news stories construct a narrative of women as victims. Writing in her part-autobiography, part-feminist manifesto, *Everywoman*, Labour MP Jess Phillips tells us, 'Women have a rough deal.' 'We get beaten, abused and raped more often,' she informs us, 'it's crap that caring responsibilities still mostly fall to us, and our razors and deodorant cost more because they are pink.'[166] This seamless shift from rape to the price of deodorant allows all women to be included in a common experience of victimhood.

OVERLOOKING DIFFERENCES

A view of women as victims is exacerbated by eliding the experiences of women and girls. Campaigners raise awareness of 'violence against women and girls'. On the presidential campaign trail, Hillary Clinton made numerous references to 'all the little girls watching' and frequently addressed her message to 'women and girls'. This lumping together of women and girls assumes women should be addressed along with female children rather than men. But the problems women and girls encounter, and far more importantly the different capacity adults and children have to solve problems, makes the comparison invalid. It elicits sympathy for women but ultimately takes away their adult autonomy – something a previous generation of feminists fought to have recognized.

A further sleight of hand used to confer victim status on privileged women in Western societies is to draw comparisons between women's lives in very different global circumstances. Women all around the world form a 'class' with interests in common, we are told. The logic of this hollow statement is that because women in Rwanda have limited access to sanitary products; because women caught up in South Sudan's civil war have been raped; because some women in rural India face forced marriage then *all* women are, by association, victims of abuse. What's more, when all women and girls are grouped together then the cause of their problems is shown to emanate from men rather than the society they live in.

Female Genital Mutilation

When feminism becomes separated from a broader political analysis of power relations, campaigners can draw equivalence between the experiences of girls in developing countries and wealthy women in the developed world.

Female genital mutilation (FGM), or cutting, is one example of an issue affecting some girls in certain African countries as well as in parts of Indonesia, Malaysia and India,
but is used to show that women everywhere are oppressed.
This benefits neither girls in the developing world nor
women in developed countries. FGM is a traumatic procedure and a backward cultural practice that serves no medical purpose but feminists have never completely agreed on
how to deal with it. At times it has been ignored or even
quietly condoned out of a fear of appearing to criticize the
practices of other cultures, particularly when those cultures are foreign, black and Muslim. More recently, some
feminists have become far more vocal in criticizing FGM.

The latest incarnation of anti-FGM campaigns raise a
number of problems. Most obviously, raising awareness
about FGM in the developed world has become more
vociferous just as the prevalence of FGM in practice is
decreasing. In Africa today, the chance that a girl will be
cut is about one-third lower than it was 30 years ago.[167]
Significantly, it is in decline primarily because of the economic development and broader cultural shifts taking
place in previously impoverished societies. These social
changes have been driven largely by the efforts of African
people themselves. The campaigning of Western feminists
has had a minimal impact. Where FGM is still practiced it
is often in a far less severe form than was common in the
past. Clitoral hood removal or clitoral pricking procedures
are increasingly carried out by medics and are arguably
less severe than male circumcision.

Much current campaigning around the issue of FGM
focuses on girls of African heritage who are living in the
West. Bríd Hehir, a retired nurse who blogs about FGM[168]

told me, 'There's no evidence to suggest that FGM is being carried out in Britain, no children are presenting with it. The few cases being recorded in under-eighteens are for genital piercings, something completely different.' I asked Hehir why, if FGM is in decline, the campaign against it has such momentum: 'A number of issues come together,' she says, 'there's a coincidence of interests.' 'There's a belief in the extreme vulnerability of children and a perception that child abuse is prevalent which makes people less likely to interrogate the issue but simply to accept, at face value, what they are told. At the same time, there's a real desire among some politicians to show that they connect with women and care about girls. Together, this means that there is a lot of funding available for anti-FGM campaigners, and activists are incentivised to exaggerate the prevalence and extent of the practice.'

Sending Signals

This suggests that the current campaign against FGM in the West has more to do with sending signals at home than it does with challenging what happens abroad. This is not without consequence. Western feminist awareness-raising about FGM results in an intrusion into the lives of many girls of African heritage in the UK. Hehir tells me, 'Health professionals are now checking more girls for signs of FGM and there is a mandatory reporting duty which requires health and social care professionals and teachers to report "known" cases of FGM in under 18s which they identify in their professional work to the police.'

In the eyes of campaigners, a lack of evidence of FGM having been carried out is not considered proof of its absence but rather that it is being better hidden. Monitoring and reporting from health professionals does little to help girls and mothers of African heritage. On the contrary, it singles them out in a way that would be labelled 'racial profiling' if it was concerned with any other issue. Hehir tells me, 'Targeted communities feel stigmatized and are angry. They do not get credit for the work they've done to stop the practice here and instead they've been criminalized. They are viewed suspiciously, for example, through screening at airports during the so-called but non-existent "cutting season."' The purpose of the anti-FGM crusade in the UK seems to be to send a reminder that some women and girls are victims; therefore, all women are victims.

In response to the accusation of racial profiling, the campaign against FGM has been expanded to encompass Western women who opt for cosmetic surgery such as labiaplasty or vaginoplasty. Such procedures are discussed by critics in the same terms as FGM and the adult women patients are considered to be just as much victims of ingrained patriarchal attitudes as the mothers who prepare their daughters for FGM. This false comparison suggests women, as adults, are not able to make decisions about their own lives and bodies. They are not presented as making rational and conscious choices but as having 'internalized the male gaze' and been misled into believing their bodies should look a certain way.

The implications of this were spelled out by a British doctor who faced prosecution for FGM after carrying out cosmetic genital surgery on a woman who requested it. Upon being cleared, the surgeon, Professor David Veale, commented 'FGM is an abhorrent practice conducted on girls against their consent and motivated by a desire to control female sexuality, but [cosmetic genital surgery] is provided for adult women with capacity to consent and motivated by a desire to improve their appearance and sexuality. It's no different to any other cosmetic surgery.' He continued, 'I don't like the procedure. But the bottom line for me is freedom of choice. You have a freedom of choice if you have capacity for consent to do what you wish with your own body.'[169] The feminist-led crusade against FGM, conducted in the name of vulnerable girls, ends up reducing adult women to the status of children with no autonomy to make free choices about their own bodies. The principle of women having control over their own bodies — so vital in securing provision of medical services such as abortion — is undermined by the extension of anti-FGM activism to adult women.

INFLATED CLAIMS

The better women do in education and employment, the more effort is needed to sustain the notion that women are disadvantaged. Claims to victimhood are often backed up by advocacy research; that is questionnaires, observations and interviews that provide data to support the researcher's pre-determined conclusions. As we will explore in more detail in the following chapter, surveys purporting to show that women are victims of everything from rape culture to online harassment and sexualized bullying at school, all tend to follow a similar pattern. They extrapolate results from a small and self-selecting group of interviewees whose experiences are interpreted and categorized by researchers rather than the respondents themselves. We've seen how even statistics on pay are subject to selective interpretation to suit the argument being promoted. In this way, feminist research promotes an already established narrative rather than the pursuit of truth.

Indeed, the very suggestion that an 'objective' or 'neutral' stance is possible when discussing topics such as sexual harassment would be derided by many feminist researchers as a myth emanating from a masculine world view.

Promoting this bigger truth is more important than technical accuracy. In February 2017, it emerged that a viral video of a woman cyclist taking revenge upon a van driver who verbally harassed her had been staged. The truth emerged just 24 hours after the video was published online. However, in just this time, the short clip had been viewed over 10 million times on social media. People believed it was real because it confirmed their existing biases of uncouth men (especially working-class van drivers) hassling middle-class women. Even when the truth about the film was known, commentators were quick to point out that the bigger truth, that women are victims of harassment, was not in any doubt.[170]

PERSONAL STORIES

Many feminist researchers argue that an individual's account of their own experiences is more truthful than statistics. The subjective voice of the individual stands in opposition to monolithic and masculine data sets. According to this way of thinking, the more disadvantaged a person is, the more oppressed and 'subaltern' they are, the more powerful and closer to truth are the experiences they have to share. Ironically then, many of the personal narratives promoting victim feminism come from high-profile women in powerful positions. In the UK, women members of Parliament such as Diane Abbott, Harriet Harman and Jess Phillips have spoken out about the misogyny experienced by women in the public sphere.[171] Actors such as Jennifer Lawrence, Patricia Arquette and Mila Kunis have been vocal about Hollywood sexism.[172]

Harry Potter actor turned feminist campaigner Emma Watson makes headline news with her claims that women and girls are vulnerable. She has been rewarded with a UN Goodwill Ambassadorship for her efforts. Actor and activist Lena Dunham runs a high-profile blog, *Lenny*, in which she details the sexism she encounters.[173]

But personal narratives don't just come from people in the public eye. The British *Everyday Sexism Project* aims to 'catalogue instances of sexism experienced on a day to day basis. They might be serious or minor, outrageously offensive or so niggling and normalised that you don't even feel able to protest.'[174] The site encourages women to share stories on the basis that by doing so, 'you're showing the world that sexism does exist, it is faced by women every day and it is a valid problem to discuss.' The argument that 'you're showing the world that sexism does exist' suggests that sexism only becomes 'real' and women only become 'victims' once they have received public affirmation of their experiences. Laura Bates, the project's founder, has become a high-profile proponent of the view that women are victims everywhere from public transport to school, from the street to the workplace.

Of course, women have every right to tell their stories and this can be a useful way of shedding light on areas of life glossed over by statistics or not researched at all. At the moment, however, the narrative of women as victims seems to be the only story that gets heard. The personal stories of women who are quite happy with their lives and not struggling to confront sexism and misogyny are not told — perhaps because such women have little need for the affirmation that comes with placing personal revelations in the public domain. Victim feminism presents a selective view of the world that sends a message to young women that life will be difficult and the world is against them. The more this message stands in contradiction to the reality of women's lives today, the more feminists seek out increasingly obscure examples of prejudice.

This search for new sites of inequality takes feminism a long way from hard-fought battles for the right to vote, divorce and work in the same jobs as men for equal pay, and have access to childcare, contraception and abortion. The determination to present sexism as an 'everyday' occurrence necessitates a focus on smaller and more trivial concerns such as men spreading their legs on train seats or interrupting women speaking. On one random day, women took the time and trouble to record on the *Everyday Sexism* website their issues with men standing too close to them, paying unwanted compliments, asking unwanted questions, giving up seats on public transport and not cleaning up after parties.[175]

All these examples point the finger at behaviour that is subjectively experienced as 'bad' by some women. While one woman feels moved to write that she is offended by men offering her a seat on a train because, she assumes, they 'get public "virtue points" from doing something so visible to everyone seated in the carriage', another woman might be offended by *not* being offered a seat. It no longer matters how trivial the incidences of sexism might appear when the role of each is to support a pre-determined narrative. For this reason petty annoyances make front-page news.

Victim Feminism on Campus

Expanding the definition of 'victim' continues apace within academia. Universities are said to be in the grip of an 'epidemic' of sexual harassment. According to one UK newspaper, 'a combination of rampant abuse, inaccessible processes and a culture stacked against victims doesn't just result in inaction but in the bolstering of a structure where predatory staff are protected by power while the access of women to employment and learning within higher education is seriously threatened'.[176]

Accepting this view of women students as fragile and at risk of physical, sexual or psychological harm poses frequent challenges to free speech on campus. When it is assumed that words can harm vulnerable women, and that all women are vulnerable, it seems only logical to vet campus speakers and 'disinvite' those likely to cause offence, including feminists who challenge the logic of victim feminism. There are numerous examples of this on both sides of the Atlantic. In 2016, students tried to stop the feminist writer Christina Hoff Sommers from speaking at Oberlin College because her denial of the existence of rape culture would apparently traumatize students. Protesters explained: 'By bringing her to a college campus laden with trauma and sexualized violence and full of victims/survivors, OCRL is choosing to reinforce this climate of denial/blame/shame that ultimately has real life consequences on the wellbeing of people who have experienced sexualized violence.' The protesters added for good measure, 'We could spend all of our time and energy explaining all of the ways she's harmful. But why should we?'[177]

We see from their statement that, even though Hoff Sommers would inflict no physical harm on the students, the mere presence of a rape culture 'denier' comes to be perceived as detrimental to their mental health. In the act of protest, these students find affirmation of their suffering. At Occidental College students protested commencement speaker Harvard Law School Professor Randall L. Kennedy because of his criticisms of the rape culture documentary, *The Hunting Ground*.[178] Alt-right controversialist Milo Yiannopoulos's habit of proclaiming 'feminism is cancer' has seen him disinvited from universities across the US and the UK.[179] When he speaks it is often in conjunction with a 'safe space' for 'triggered' students, usually women, to reside.

Abortion

Discussion of abortion has become a particular flashpoint on campus with pro-choice speakers disinvited from Catholic colleges[180] and pro-life speakers from non-religious institutions. Even President Obama came under fire. His invitation to speak at Notre Dame was protested by those who felt his pro-choice views were out of line with a Catholic University.[181] Elsewhere pro-life students have been asked to remove posters and displays used for over three decades. 'We've reviewed your pictures with our advisors and have determined that your display contains triggering and disturbing images and content,' announced the student committee of Johns Hopkins University.[182] In the UK, a debate on abortion at the University of Oxford was cancelled after feminist students promised to 'take along some non-destructive but oh so disruptive instruments to help demonstrate to the anti-choicers just what we think of their "debate"'.[183]

Particular ire was raised because the debate was to take place between two men. Niamh McIntyre, one of the students involved in the protests proudly declared: 'I helped shut down an abortion debate between two men because my uterus isn't up for their discussion.'[184] Although McIntyre argued abortion is an issue for those with a uterus she was happy to contend, in the same article, that 'access to abortion impacts the lives of women, trans and nonbinary people every day, and the threat pro-life groups pose to our bodily autonomy is real, not rhetorical'.

Transwomen

At the same time as it is argued that men can't discuss abortion, there are also campaigns to disinvite those who challenge the idea that gender is nothing more than a feeling and anyone can become a man or a woman. Again, the argument is made that discussion poses an existential threat to transgender people. This has seen campaigns against celebrated feminists of a previous era, such as Germaine Greer who has, in the past, written, 'The insistence that manmade women be accepted as women is the institutional expression of the mistaken conviction that women are defective males.'[185] Rachael Melhuish, the women's officer at Cardiff University wanted Greer's invitation rescinded because she has 'demonstrated misogynistic views towards transwomen, including continually misgendering transwomen and denying the existence of transphobia altogether'. As Greer retorted, 'What they are saying is that because I don't think surgery will turn a man into a woman I should not be allowed to speak anywhere.'[186]

Trigger Warnings

The desire to protect supposedly vulnerable women students from offence reaches beyond banning speakers from campus and has led to the demand for trigger warnings to be issued by lecturers particularly for law or English literature classes in which discussion of rape or sexual assault may feature. The idea behind the trigger warning is that students will be given advance notice of a topic they may potentially find distressing. Feminist writer Laurie Penny argues they are the opposite of censorship and a means of opening up debate through 'asking that classes and discussion spaces take the possible experiences of their members into account'.[187] However, trigger warnings do more than just allow students to prepare themselves mentally beforehand so they are not taken by surprise in class. They allow students to avoid classes altogether and serve as a means of encouraging academics to self-censor.

Jeannie Suk, a Professor of Law at Harvard University, claims that the increased anxiety among both academics and students about discussing sexual assault and rape cases is impeding criminal law professors' ability to teach the law properly. Ultimately, she argues, this will be at the expense of students and the rape victims whom some of them will eventually represent. 'Student organizations representing women's interests now routinely advise students that they should not feel pressured to attend or participate in class sessions that focus on the law of sexual violence, and which might therefore be traumatic,' Suk says, 'One teacher I know was recently asked by a student not to use the word "violate" in class – as in "Does this conduct violate the law?" – because the word was triggering. Some students have even suggested that rape law should not be taught because of its potential to cause distress.'[188]

Suk is right – allowing students to opt out of studying whole areas of the law is in the best interests of neither them nor their future clients. Trigger warnings are not about enabling access to education for those who have suffered a traumatic experience. Even in their own terms they make little sense. People are more likely to have flashbacks to a particular event prompted by a smell or a colour than by explicit discussion of certain topics. Trigger warnings are far more about making a generalized statement of the sensitivity of women, the fragility of their

identity and their need to be protected. The result, however, is an erosion of academic freedom and an enshrining
of the view that women should be held to a lower standard than men. Campus censorship carried out in the
name of feminism assumes that women are less able to
stand debate and less able to engage in rational discussion
than men. This sets the clock back on equality and infanti-
lizes women. Whereas women in the nineteenth century
fought for entry to higher education and for access to the
same knowledge as men, today's feminists are fighting to
be protected from knowledge they consider distasteful.

INTERNALIZED MISOGYNY

Feminism's impetus to see women as victims extends from
blaming men to blaming women for their own oppression.
The aftermath of the 2016 US Presidential election led to
much discussion of the '53% of white women' who voted for
Trump. Amid the disbelief that women might have decided
not to vote with their vaginas and back Clinton, and shock
that a significant number of women apparently made a positive decision to back Trump, an explanation emerged. As one
commentator put it, 'misogyny is not a male-only attribute'.
In this view, Trump's victory comes about because of female
weakness: 'One way to be desirable to men may be to align
oneself with their interests in the hope they might protect
you.'[189] This argument takes the logic of victim feminism —
that women are held back by men through physical, sexual
and verbal violence — and manages to turn it against women
still further: in order to protect themselves women become
complicit in the abuse directed against them, they defend the

men who demean them and beat them to it by degrading themselves.

The idea of internalized misogyny takes us back to the very beginning of second-wave feminism. In her landmark 1969 work, *Sexual Politics*, Kate Millett explains, 'having internalized the disesteem in which they are held, women despise both themselves and each other'.[190] If women who despise themselves are to be pitied, then women who refuse to do this and stand proudly by their decisions to vote for Trump, wear high-heeled shoes, have cosmetic surgery or earn money through pole dancing, are vilified. Yet a feminism that dictates only some of the choices women make are valid, or that women who make the 'wrong' choices deserve pity or contempt, is no champion of women. It seems that a view of women as irrational, misguided and lacking in autonomy is today more likely to come from feminists than many men. This feminist policing of women allows campaigners to sustain the fabrication that women are victims of an outdated and patriarchal culture. Yet few women challenge the view of themselves as victims and those that do are quickly brought into line.

Women who take responsibility for their actions are chastised by feminists for promoting dangerous attitudes. In her 2016 autobiography, *Reckless*, Chrissie Hynde describes one particular incident when, on drugs, she went with a gang of bikers and was subsequently raped. Feminism dictates that Hynde should describe the trauma she suffered at the hands of her male abusers. She should elaborate upon the lifelong repercussions being a blameless victim of this crime has had upon her. The lesson learnt — and now taught to others — should be that all women, however tough they may appear, are victims. Only Hynde refused to get on board with this script. 'Now, let me assure you that, technically speaking, however you want to look at it, this was all my doing and I take full responsibility,' she wrote, 'You can't fuck around with people, especially people who wear "I Heart Rape" and "On Your Knees" badges.'[191] Her refusal to 'blame others for my transgressions', led to her being condemned by feminists. It also exposed the limitations of the 'sisterhood'.

We can contrast Hynde's treatment by feminists to the heralding of Labour MP Jess Phillips. In *Everywoman*, Phillips informs readers, 'The things I bragged about while smoking fags around the back of the gym should have been shared with the police instead.' Instead of taking responsibility for her misspent youth, Phillips offers herself up as a victim and tours schools to talk to young people 'about rape and sexual exploitation'. J K Rowling has declared Phillips to be 'a heroine'. A key goal of feminism today is, it seems, to teach women and girls to see themselves as victims and in Phillips's case this is done, quite literally, in the classroom.

THE ATTRACTION OF VICTIMHOOD

In exaggerating women's disadvantages and pinpointing male behaviour as the cause, victim feminism imbues young women with a false and degraded sense of their own position in society. Women are encouraged to see themselves as passive objects, unable to stand up for themselves or to exercise control over their own lives. What's curious, then, is why victim feminism has gained such traction in public debate.

Phillips illustrates some of the attractions with victimhood for feminists today. It not only provides access to platforms, resources and power but it also, more importantly, leads to a moral beatification. Contemporary political culture reveres the victim and continually reinforces the moral authority of those who suffer. The victim is placed on a pedestal, a heroine, blameless. The only demand the victim makes of us is to believe her. Phillips expresses this clearly in her feminist advice to readers 'just believe her'. The popularity of the Twitter hashtag #IBelieveHer further illustrates the blamelessness of the 'victim'.

The obligation placed upon others to 'just believe' becomes a moral imperative. To believe is to affirm the woman's identity as a victim. The assumption of blamelessness, however, is at best a hollow victory. To be blameless is to have lacked all ability to control your own destiny. It is a victory that ultimately leads to a demand for protection not equality. Through expressions of victimhood, women gain recognition and affirmation but at the expense of having to present themselves as vulnerable. Through this process women come to internalize vulnerability as a part of their identity.

The 'victim' first became an object of academic and social interest in the mid-1960s. At this point, the word 'victim' began to appear far more frequently in books and academic papers. This notion of the vulnerable self was identified by Christopher Lasch in his 1979 book *The Culture of Narcissism*. In the intervening decades, the idea of the individual as fragile has become widely accepted and references to 'victims' have grown steadily with particular escalation throughout the 1970s and 1980s.[192]

These two decades in particular saw the uncovering of all kinds of harassment and abuse at home, school, work and in all areas of life. News reports discussed sexual abuse, child abuse, ritual abuse, satanic abuse, domestic violence and sexual harassment. New medical conditions and syndromes were being discovered and recognized. For example, post-traumatic stress disorder was first added to the American Psychiatric Association's Diagnostic and Statistical Manual of Mental Disorders in 1980. Experiences that had previously been thought of as personal or social problems became reconsidered as medical or psychological conditions. Dyslexia, for instance, became recognized as a condition requiring specific interventions in the 1980s.

One objective of feminism today seems to be securing recognition that all women, however successful, are victimized. This victim status sits easily alongside an assumption of equality: women are equal, indeed superior, to men because of the suffering they endure and the disadvantage they have overcome. Likewise, claims of victimhood can be made loudly and confidently: women are made strong by their collective pain, they are survivors. Victim feminism is an assertive demand for affirmation of this status. Journalist Julie Burchill wasn't writing specifically about women when she coined the term 'cry bully' but this is an apt description of today's feminists. Christina Hoff Sommers calls this 'grievance feminism' or 'fainting couch feminism' and she argues it is based on 'twisted theories of patriarchal society'.[193]

WOMEN'S MENTAL HEALTH PROBLEMS

The notion of the vulnerable self has a particular resonance with girls who receive messages about female fragility from teachers, overprotective parents and trendy feminist campaigners. Recent years have witnessed a growth in campaigns and awareness raising initiatives around the issue of mental health that are often aimed specifically at young people. From their earliest years in school many children, especially girls, adopt a vocabulary of 'stress', 'depression' and 'anxiety.'[194] Lessons in mindfulness and meditation urge them to focus inwards and consider their personal emotional state rather than running around outside or exploring topics that will take them beyond their own internal monologue.

At university, poster campaigns advertise support services and urge students to look after themselves and each other. Soap operas, advertising campaigns and the Tweeted struggles of YouTube stars reinforce the message that young people are mentally vulnerable. As a result, young women have become increasingly open about discussing their mental health. One journalist reports: 'My female friends and I have discussed, without shame, everything from depression to panic attacks to suicide attempts to miscarriages to cocaine-induced paranoia (drugs and alcohol use are so obviously a factor in mental illness) to eating disorders and OCD.'[195]

In 1981, sociologist Ann Oakley observed in relation to Sylvia Plath that 'the function of mental illness' is to serve 'as an acceptably feminine escape route'.[196] Once, this 'escape route' was stigmatized or barely mentioned by more conservative members of society, or criticized by feminists such as Oakley as a means of avoiding discussion of the real conditions of women's oppression. Today, in contrast, it has become legitimized and the subject of public display. When there is no longer any shame attached to discussing feelings of anxiety or depression, not joining in marks one out as different. Just as women rarely admit to feeling completely happy about the way they look, so too will few admit to being totally mentally robust and resilient. Young women who openly display their suffering are lauded for bravery and honesty. Stigma has been replaced with kudos.

In an age of identity politics, mental health problems come to define people. They mark some individuals out as more fragile and special than everyone else. This vulnerability can be publicly displayed through self-inflicted scars; the practice of self-harming makes a young woman's suffering visible to the world. Writing in *The Second Sex*, Simone De Beauvoir recognized the trend for girls to self-harm, remarking that such actions were, 'more spectacular than effective'. She

describes the girl as remaining 'anchored in the childish universe whence she cannot or will not really escape; she is
struggling in her cage rather than trying to get out of it'.[197]
Girls today, labelled 'cotton wool kids' and 'generation snow-
flake', have been kept securely in their cages by parents, as
we've already seen, determined to protect their daughters
from harm. Cosseted girls who never venture outside their
own homes unaccompanied are likely, once they gain such
freedom, to find the world a genuinely scarier place. When a
view of women as vulnerable is internalized, it becomes a
self-fulfilling prophecy and, in turn, a state to be revered.

Self-care

'Self-care' has recently become a key feminist activity. It
arises from the assumption that women are vulnerable
and that sexism is such a pervasive part of life that fighting
against it can be exhausting. In this context, self-care
becomes a political act, defined by Dr Christine Meinecke
at *Psychology Today*, as not self-indulgence or self-
pampering, but 'choosing behaviours that balance the
effects of emotional and physical stressors'.[198] This idea of
feminist self-care has its origins in the writing of Audre
Lorde who wrote, 'Caring for myself is not self-
indulgence, it is self-preservation, and that is an act of
political warfare.'[199] Today's feminists have taken this
one sentence to heart. But Lorde wrote this in *A Burst of
Light*, compiled as she fought against liver cancer. As self-
declared 'feminist killjoy', Sara Ahmed, tells us, 'the
expression "a burst of light" is used for when [Lorde]
came to feel the fragility of her body's situation: "that
inescapable knowledge, in the bone, of my own physical
limitation"'.[200] For Lorde, self-care really was a matter of
self-preservation. Thankfully, however, not all women

have to face a terminal illness. Yet the notion of self-care has been taken up with alacrity by a younger generation of feminists.

The feminist website *Bustle* argues self-care is 'very important to help people with depression, anxiety, and other difficulties, get through everyday life. But in a wider context, self-care ... is both an important general practice, and a fundamentally feminist idea.'[201] A different website, *Everyday Feminism*, suggests, 'life can be too much for folks who are politically conscious or radicalized'.[202] It offers self-care tips because it's 'not fair to expect you to go out and yell for other women in protests, write editorials, or even get into arguments with that sexist uncle at Christmas when you're not taking care of yourself in the process'. The writers argue that self-care is at 'the very core' of feminism.

The message to budding activists is that you must 'value yourself, take time out ... listen to your body, and do what you want without resistance. Resisting patriarchy is hard enough; doing it while resisting your own needs makes it even harder.'[203] We can only imagine what a previous generation of feminists who campaigned tirelessly, risked their lives, were imprisoned and went on hunger strike might make of this demand on women today to put their own needs first. Like the popularity for Danish hygge with woolly socks and scented candles, self-care is feminism with bubble baths, chocolate and prosecco. Even while battling cancer, Lorde pointed out that self-care risked leading women away from engaging in political struggle.[204] The focus on self-care among young women campaigners today is revealing of a feminism that is situated not as a challenge to, but firmly within the context of broader social and cultural trends.

CONCLUSIONS

Feminism has always been driven by a need to highlight areas where women are disadvantaged in comparison to men; this was necessary to win the right for women to participate in society as equals. Exposing areas of disadvantage doesn't automatically turn women into victims. However, over the past few decades, legal changes have combined with a shift in cultural assumptions about what women can achieve, yet feminism clings to the assumption that women are oppressed despite the fact that this claim carries little meaning today. Victim feminism is not simply a continuation with the past then; rather, it emerges at a distinct moment when feminism stopped demanding sexual equality and began instead to focus on the differences between women and men and to position men as the cause of women's oppression.

As we will explore in the next chapter, victim feminism emerged first in the 1970s with the erosion of the boundaries between public and private life and the construction of problems such as child abuse, domestic violence and sexual harassment at work, not as issues between individual men and women but as social problems inflicted by men as a class upon women as a class. In embracing victimhood, feminism has moved from a perception of women as autonomous beings, desiring freedom and able to cope with the world in the same way as men, to presenting women as being in need of special protections, trigger warnings and safe spaces. The following chapters explore the process through which this has come about and the consequences it has for women's lives today.

CHAPTER SIX

SEX AND RELATIONSHIPS

Forget laid-back hook-up culture and jokes about friends with benefits. For many young people today, sex is problematic. It's not sexually transmitted diseases or pregnancy they worry about so much as each other. During a campus debate, I asked a group of students why they thought attendance at sexual consent classes should be made mandatory. Surely, I argued, people didn't need to be taught the difference between rape and consensual sex; and statistically, their campus was one of the safest places in the country. 'But,' one young woman was clearly horrified by my question, 'We could be raped. I don't leave my room on campus after dark even to walk to the library.' Others in the group were quick to correct the 'not going out after dark' narrative, not from a position of bravado but from a more sober understanding that a rapist was more likely to be someone known to them, perhaps a boyfriend or someone they had invited back to their room, rather than a random stranger.

This chapter looks at men's and women's private relationships and explores how feminism moved from celebrating sexual liberation to seeking to regulate sex and relationships.

This changed dynamic in feminism took off in earnest at a time when old certainties about people's behaviour, garnered from their membership of community organizations, trade unions, churches and political parties, could no longer be assumed. The old morality and values that once regulated people's lives was being jettisoned. An ascendant feminism that transcends both the public and private realms of people's lives provides schools, universities and other state institutions with a clear set of seemingly radical values to embrace. In this way, feminism comes to the fore in establishing a new means of regulating both social life and intimate relationships. In this chapter we explore how feminism works to regulate private relationships through a focus on three key issues: sexual harassment, pornography and rape culture.

WHATEVER HAPPENED TO THE SEXUAL REVOLUTION?

The era of sexual liberation proved to be short-lived. Almost 50 years on from the dawn of second-wave feminism and it seems that chaperones, curfews and prudish sermons preaching a morally-approved way to have sex are all back. Only this time they do not stem from religious conservatives or old-fashioned relatives but from feminists with 'I heart consent' badges. The message to young women is clear: sex without explicit, verbal and ongoing consent is rape and all men are potential rapists. But this lesson is only ever partially imbibed. Young people are not opting *en masse* for self-imprisonment; most are still going out, getting drunk, hooking up, and later forming relationships and having children. It's not that young people have been scared out of having sex altogether, it's more that for many, relationships coexist with angst: intimacy has come to be associated with anxiety.

Talk of 'rape culture' and 'sexual harassment' dominates feminism today. But these words only rarely describe specific incidents; rather, their repetition fulfils a need to present women as victims of violence and abuse perpetrated by men. Old ideas of sexually chaste and vulnerable women having to ward off predatory men are being rehabilitated at a time when women, especially those in wealthy, Western countries, have greater financial and legal independence than ever before. Yet this independence brings with it not just new power but also, it seems, new fear. The young women consigning themselves to their rooms after dark have been put there not by tyrannical fathers but by their own anxieties.

Sexual liberation now seems as dated as flower-power. It has been cynically written off as a con – fun for men but disastrous for women. But this is to forget how much women's lives have changed for the better. Not that long ago, cohabiting couples were 'living in sin' and babies born 'out of wedlock' were stigmatized. When marriage was one of the few routes for women to secure their future, sex before marriage could be ruinous. Young people, especially young women, were policed by an older generation intent on upholding religious and moral standards. The consequences of digression were serious. As Alison Wolf reminds us: 'Pregnancy was more likely to be a prelude to a shotgun marriage than to an illegitimate child; but if the man couldn't be persuaded or forced to do the "right thing," then women faced social ruin, and their babies, for the most part, a miserable fate.'[205]

The 'Pill', safe and reliable contraception that allowed women to control their own fertility, emerged just as the women's liberation movement was beginning to take off. Young women, already questioning the regulations and restrictions placed upon them, challenged the double standard that dictated only men could enjoy sex. Women wanted a sexual revolution so they could enjoy this freedom too. Chrissie Hynde, lead singer of rock band *The Pretenders*, sums up the mood of the times: 'Never mind LSD – a passing fad – the pill was king, and like Cher it needed no second name.'

For Hynde this was something to celebrate: 'In the name of women's lib, women were becoming like men, and that was good news for me because I wanted what the boys had. In thinking we were in charge of our own sexuality, now we could say "yes" instead of "no".'[206] Wolf agrees, 'Those of us who came to adulthood post-Pill stand on another shore, an ocean apart from all generations before us. Sex can be safe. You can relax about it. Women can avoid an undesired pregnancy, completely, securely, and on their own.'[207] But today, erstwhile proponents of the sexual revolution express retrospective qualms. Even Hynde sounds a note of caution: 'Now we could fuck and run like they did, even if it didn't really suit our nature.'[208]

Contraception and abortion freed women from the constraints of their biology. Campaigners fought to secure access to them even when this meant taking on the church as well as national governments. As Mary Kenny recalls, feminists in Ireland famously boarded trains from Belfast in the north laden with condoms to distribute in the Catholic south where it had been illegal to sell 'birth control artefacts' since 1935. Kenny explains, in 1971 'a group of us in the Irish Women's Liberation Movement decided to go to Belfast – then, as now, within the United Kingdom – purchase condoms and spermicides, and bring them back across the Border and declare them at Connolly Station (to the mortifying embarrassment of the customs officers).'[209] In France, a Suppression of Contraception Act was passed in 1920 and was not repealed until 1967 while several American states also had legislation to prevent the sale or distribution of birth control products.

More than any other form of contraception, the pill allowed women to separate sex from pregnancy. Hynde again taps into the mood of the time, 'Sex was becoming a recreational lifestyle choice. If you were to mention the word 'procreation' you'd probably get thrown out of any protest, commune or crash pad for being a bummer. Only a straight person would think like that.' This drove other social changes: men and women began to delay getting married and when they did they had fewer children.

PROBLEMATIZING SEX

No sooner had the sexual revolution begun than feminists started to argue that sex was problematic. Writing in 1969, Kate Millett describes intercourse as 'an assertion of mastery, one that announces his own higher caste and proves it upon a victim who is expected to surrender, serve and be satisfied'.[210] Later, Andrea Dworkin describes bluntly 'the role of the fuck in controlling women'.[211] At the very moment sex stopped being about procreation, it began to be seen, by some, as a form of oppression and a means of patriarchal domination. Dworkin's 1987 book, *Intercourse*, elaborates her theory that heterosexual sex is used by men to control, possess and dominate women.

These new ideas developed in climate that was already reappraising the sexual revolution because of the emergence of the AIDS virus. Panic-fuelled campaigns drew a link between casual sex and the transmission of AIDS. As Katie Roiphe points out in her exploration of attitudes to sex on campus in the early 1990s, 'Now instead of liberation and libido, the emphasis is on trauma and disease.'[212] For young women at this time, she explains, 'the shift from free love to safe sex is itself part of our experience. Our sexual climate, then, incorporates the movement from one set of sexual mores to another.'[213] Not for the first time we see a coincidence between the aims of radical feminism and more socially conservative moralists.

Those revising the history of the sexual revolution in the 1980s were consolidating around one half of a divisive split within feminism. As we will explore in more detail in Chapter Nine, second-wave feminism in the 1970s became increasingly fractured according to race, social class and sexuality; there was a growing divide between socialist, radical and liberal feminism. For a while, it looked as if the answer to this splintering could be found in the promotion of a common enemy: the patriarchy. All women, feminists at this time told us, shared an experience of being objectified and sexualized by men in a way that reinforced patriarchal power relations and kept women in a subordinate social position.

BATTERED WIFE SYNDROME

During the 1970s and the 1980s, feminists played a significant role in shedding light on previously private issues such as domestic violence. This was an important and much needed step. However, domestic violence began to be understood less in relation to the financial and practical power imbalances that existed in many relationships and more in the context of female psychological vulnerability and innate male aggression. In this way, domestic violence went beyond the immediacy of any individual woman's situation and social issues were reconsidered as diagnosable syndromes. The American psychologist Martin Seligman developed a theory of 'learned helplessness' in the 1960s and this was taken up by fellow psychologist and feminist Lenore Walker. Walker had a longstanding interest in the issue of domestic violence and founded the Domestic Violence Institute to conduct further research. Walker's theory of 'learned help-lessness' led her to develop the 'cycle of abuse' model to explain abusive relationships. The cycle of abuse suggests that victims of domestic violence remain trapped within a situation, destined to play itself out repeatedly, until the rela-tionship is abandoned altogether or some external interven-tion takes place. It focuses primarily on the psychological characteristics of the 'co-dependent' individuals within an intimate relationship.

Walker published her findings in 1979 in *The Battered Woman*. Here, she considers issues such as marital rape and child abuse as well as domestic violence. She explores the impact of exposure to violence on children, the personal-ity characteristics of different types of batterers and new psychotherapy models for batterers and their victims. From this perspective, domestic violence stops being a feature of individual relationships within a specific set of circumstances. Instead it becomes a psychological condition associated with a particular personality type. Stopping domestic violence becomes a question of employing the correct psychological interventions as well as offering practical support. This focus on psychological harm enshrines women and children as victims of domestic violence – and men as perpetrators – even after the abusive relationship has ended. The woman is now said to be suffering from 'battered wife syndrome', later to become a legally recognized defence for spouse murder. It assumes that women, having been traumatized at the hands of their husbands, are so psychologically damaged they can no longer act rationally or exercise control over their actions.

SEXUAL HARASSMENT

At the same time as the identification of battered wife
syndrome came the 'discovery' of sexual harassment. Second-
wave feminists tried to explain why gender inequality continued despite equal pay and anti-discrimination legislation.
This led to the articulation of sexual harassment – an issue
which, up until this point, had no specific name. There was a
particular focus upon sexual harassment within the workplace where gender inequality seemed to be entrenched. The
legal scholar Catharine MacKinnon successfully argued that
sexual harassment was a feature of sexual discrimination and
needed to be outlawed if women were to have equal opportunities in education and work. Linking sexual harassment to
formal processes of discrimination meant drawing equivalence between an individual woman's experiences of being
mistreated, perhaps groped or propositioned in the office,
with policies such as a marriage bar.

This expanded the definition of discrimination and moved
sexual harassment away from a problem experienced and
dealt with by individuals within a specific context to it being
seen as a broader explanation for women's disadvantage. The
cause of women's lack of opportunities and continued underperformance in education and work became located within
their experiences of sexual harassment rather than in practical obstacles such as lack of access to childcare or in social
pressures on women to remain at home once they had
children. Instead, the explanation for continued inequality
between the sexes was laid firmly with the collective bad
behaviour of men. Mackinnon explained that sexual harassment was not tangential to women's inequality but 'a crucial
expression of it'.[214] Nonetheless, it turned out to be far more
difficult a problem to solve than some other obstacles working women faced.

Following a 1976 court case, sexual harassment in America became legally recognized as a form of discrimination under the 1964 Civil Rights Act. Heightened awareness of the issue meant that suddenly sexual harassment was uncovered everywhere; writing in 1979, MacKinnon reports that seven out of ten women had experienced sexual harassment 'in some form at some point in their work lives'.[215] For a previously unidentified problem to encompass so many people in such a short space of time is quite remarkable. Daphne Patai, author of *Heterophobia*, is cynical about the processes that led women to attach this label to their experiences. She suggests the efforts, particularly virulent on university campuses, to uncover and name this newly discovered problem are best described as a 'Sexual Harassment Industry'. Patai argues this industry offers women a 'training in victimhood', through which they 'learn how to identify the injuries they suffer' and come to see themselves first as 'victims' then as 'survivors'.[216]

According to Patai, the sudden explosion in the number of sexual harassment victims suggests the offence is too broadly defined and the problem overstated. However, this is not to deny that sexual harassment takes place: Lin Farley, Catharine MacKinnon and other feminists who first drew attention to sexual harassment did indeed identify a particular problem. In the 1970s, women had a much lower status in the workforce than they do today. They often held poorly paid and insecure jobs and had few employment rights. As Mackinnon correctly points out, because women are 'economically vulnerable they are sexually exposed'.[217] Women's low status could be exploited by unscrupulous bosses safe in the knowledge that those wanting to keep their jobs had little option other than to put up with unwanted advances. Mackinnon makes clear, 'following the woman's refusal, the man retaliated through use of his power over her job or career'.[218] The Sexual Harassment Industry was less quick to point out that not all male bosses harassed their female employees – and neither did all women see all sexual advances as unwelcome.

The problem for women was not just that feminist campaigns defined sexual harassment far too broadly; more importantly, they did not focus on improving women's pay and conditions or raising their status in the workplace. Instead, sexual harassment came to be viewed as a problem solely of men's bad behaviour. Mackinnon spells this out: 'The common denominator is that the perpetrators tend to be men, the victims women.'[219] This suggests that the power imbalance that enabled sexual harassment to occur was not driven by women's precarious employment conditions but by the innate characteristics of men and women. Again, MacKinnon makes this point clearly: 'The relationship between a woman's anatomy and her social fate is the pivot on which turn all attempts, and opposition to attempts, to define or change her situation.'[220]

TEACHING VICTIMHOOD

Campaigns against sexual harassment focus on exposing and correcting men's offensive behaviour. This means women have to recognize themselves as victims so that men can be held to account for their indiscretions. As a result, workplace relationships, perhaps between friends or family members, become problematized and situations that were previously viewed as trivial, or something women could easily deal with themselves, are re-interpreted as abusive. Any solution to women's problems that requires women see themselves as victims can only ever be a hollow victory.

Teaching women to see themselves as victims increases the perception of sexual harassment as a significant problem. It's no surprise then that, despite the fundamental transformation in women's working lives since the 1970s, the problem of sexual harassment has not gone away. Instead, over the course of four decades, definitions of sexual harassment have become ever more expansive and are now incorporated into the law. The UK's Equality Act (2010) describes behaviour as sexual harassment 'if it is either meant to, or has the effect of violating your dignity, or creating an intimidating, hostile, degrading, humiliating or offensive environment'.[221]

Legally, sexual harassment encompasses, 'sexual comments or jokes, physical behaviour, including unwelcome sexual advances, touching and various forms of sexual assault, displaying pictures, photos or drawings of a sexual nature, sending emails with a sexual content'.[222] By this definition, sexual harassment is entirely subjective – what one woman experiences as unwelcome another might see as a compliment. Whether or not a picture, email or joke violates someone's dignity or creates an offensive environment can only be determined by the recipient. The need, identified by Patai, for a Sexual Harassment Industry not only to train women to see themselves as victims but also to step in and reprimand the male perpetrators becomes clear.

A 2016 survey conducted by the UK's Trade Union Congress (TUC) reported that over half of all women have experienced sexual harassment at work.[223] The problem with subjective definitions of harassment is apparent in the methods the TUC researchers used to gather their headline-generating data. The claim that 'over half' of women have experienced sexual harassment refers to 52 per cent of roughly 800 women surveyed. A third of those questioned had been subjected to unwelcome jokes and a quarter had experienced unwanted touching. The largest category of

positive responses came from women who had heard a comment of a sexual nature being made about another woman or
women in general. In other words, a woman who overheard
colleagues share a lewd joke a decade ago, who had never
interpreted this as sexual harassment, comes to be counted as
a victim.

REGULATING PUBLIC LIFE

The TUC researchers express concern that: 'Women seemed
reluctant to extend the meaning of sexual harassment to their
own experience; this was not because they failed to understand what constituted sexual harassment. Rather, it was
because women had defined certain acts in terms of serious-
ness and therefore, did not define their own experience as
serious enough.' In other words, women who understood the
meaning of sexual harassment had decided that their experiences were not serious: yet they were still recorded as victims.
The results of surveys like this are reported in good faith
because people have come to accept uncritically a narrative
of women as victims. Feminism comes to be concerned not
just with correcting male behaviour but with regulating how
women see themselves.

The issue of sexual harassment quickly spread beyond the
workplace. Today, it is presented as a problem for women in
all aspects of their lives. Towards the end of 2014, a video of
an actress walking through New York became a viral hit. A
hidden camera filmed the woman as she was 'cat-called' over
100 times. This footage was then edited down to a two-
minute clip and viewers watched as the woman, 'endured a
barrage of comments like: "What's up, Beautiful?" "Smile!"
and "God bless you, Mami"'.[224] This was said to illustrate
the hostile environment women face every day. However,

women generally do not walk for ten hours at a stretch, alone, and looking for examples of cat-calling to film. As with all such projects, the makers of this video found exactly what they set out to discover.

The perception that women are bombarded by harassment from the moment they leave their homes leads, inevitably, to calls for greater regulation of public life. In the British city of Nottingham, men's 'uninvited verbal engagement' of women is now recorded by police as a hate crime equivalent to racial abuse. This has major consequences for civil liberties. The right to risk an uninvited comment is integral to our freedom as citizens – one that many people welcome rather than perceive to be a risk. A feminism that tells us women need police protection from such exchanges is no champion women's liberation. Yet challenging incursions into our civil liberties conducted in the name of feminism is complicated by the promotion of such new legislation as pro-woman.

PORNOGRAPHY

Campaigns against sexual harassment took off when feminists in the 1970s looked to the cultural sphere – and the attitudes and values it promoted – as the cause of sexual inequality. Pornography in particular was singled out for objectifying and degrading women. Writing in a 1974 essay, feminist activist Robin Morgan made the now famous claim that 'pornography is the theory and rape is the practice'.[225] This heralded a strange alliance between radical feminists and conservatives. Catharine MacKinnon's characterization of pornography as the active subordination of women found echoes in the work of the conservative campaigner against sex education, abortion and the Equal Rights Amendment, Phyllis Schlafly who likewise argued that 'pornography really should be defined as the degradation of women'. Schlafly claimed pornography subordinates women 'for the sexual, exploitative, and even sadistic and violent pleasures of men',[226] further sharing with MacKinnon a presumption that pornography might have a particular impact upon a man 'who is already prone to violence against women'.[227]

The focus on pornography represented a broader feminist critique of heterosexuality as the means through which men, in the form of the patriarchy, collectively exercised power over all women. Dworkin argued that 'as long as men desire women for intercourse, and women are used as sexual objects, regardless of laws and other public reforms, women's status will be low, degraded'.[228] In the 1960s, Betty Friedan argued that the 'lavender menace' of lesbianism was a threat to the women's movement; just two decades later 'the destruction of heterosexuality as a system' had become an aim for some feminists.[229] Feminism was beginning to assert its influence in the realm of private relationships. Although MacKinnon's claim that heterosexual sex is rape, and Dworkin's cynical retort that romance is merely 'rape embellished with meaningful looks' never gained popular traction among women, such views did have an impact upon the direction of feminism at this time.[230]

Dworkin and Mackinnon argued that pornography was not simply speech or free expression but an act of discrimination and therefore it did not warrant protection under the First Amendment. This argument was partially successful in a legal attempt to get pornography recognized as a violation of women's civil rights. In 1984, an anti-pornography civil rights ordinance was enacted in the city of Indianapolis allowing women harmed by pornography – even indirectly – to claim damages. However, this legislation was soon overturned by the Supreme Court that sought to uphold freedom of speech.

Not all members of the women's movement agreed with what was seen as a censorious and explicitly anti-male turn in feminism. Those, like Dworkin and MacKinnon, who supported legal restrictions against pornography and sexual harassment, and saw heterosexual intercourse as the primary source of women's oppression, were characterized as 'sex-negative'. Nadine Strossen, author of *Defending Pornography* and former chair of the American Civil Liberties Union, refers to feminists wanting to restrict pornography as 'pro-censorship'. She says their claim that women are 'being manipulated as tools of "pimps" or "pornographers"' contains 'at least as subordinating or degrading a view of women as does the pornography they decry'.[231] She sums up the feminist anti-pornography argument as being based on nothing more than speculation that it may lead to discrimination or violence against women. 'If we should restrict pornography on this basis, then why shouldn't we suppress any expression that might ultimately have a negative effect?' asks Strossen.[232]

Feminists such as Strossen, Kathy Acker, Camille Paglia and Wendy Kaminer who campaigned against censorship and suggested that sexual freedom was an important part of women's liberation were labelled 'sex-positive'. Sex-positive feminists claimed that women could consent to take part in pornography and, far from being damaged by it, could get just as much pleasure from it as men. They argued that linking pornography directly to rape assumes a degraded view of men while, at the same time, absolving individual rapists of responsibility for their actions. Battles around pornography and sexual harassment sharply divided feminists in the 1970s and 1980s and, in the short term at least, led to a further splintering within the women's movement.

CHILD ABUSE

In the UK, a significant event in the positioning of women and children as victims of abuse by men within their own homes was the 1987 Cleveland child abuse crisis. A new method of detecting abuse, examining anal dilation, was used on children in a hospital in Middlesbrough, a town in the north east of England. Over 120 children were removed from their families and taken into the care of social services before the technique was finally discredited. Health professionals and social workers were all too ready to believe that the sexual abuse of children was widespread. The feminist writer Bea Campbell, reflecting in the aftermath of the scandal, chose to criticize not the doctors who instigated the test for sexual abuse with little evidence, or the social workers who removed children from their families on the word of a single doctor, but the police who 'quickly took the side of the fathers'.[233] She explains, 'For the police there is a particular problem: as a praetorian guard of masculinity, sexual abuse faces them with an accusation against their own gender.'[234] The upshot of the Cleveland scandal was not a retreat away from public intervention into the private sphere but calls for more recognition of men as perpetrators of abuse within the home.

Women were to see themselves as victims, or at very least potential victims, irrespective of anything they might or might not have experienced personally. Throughout the 1970s and 1980s, not only does the word victim proliferate in use, its definition also expands. It is no longer used solely to describe a specific event in the past tense, for example, 'to have been a victim of a crime'. Instead, it comes to describe a permanent state in the present. This broader meaning has remained and today we talk of victims of sexual harassment, child abuse and domestic violence not as people who have been through, and emerged from, a terrible ordeal, but as people who carry with them a permanent psychological mark of their experiences. Being a victim becomes an intrinsic part of who they are, it is incorporated into a woman's sense of identity.

Feminism has internalized the view of women as victims to such an extent it is no longer relevant whether an individual woman has had personal experience of violence, abuse or rape. Women who have personally suffered are merely typical of the suffering endured by all women. From the late 1970s onwards, to be a feminist was to recognize women as victims and men as perpetrators of abuse. To perform feminism at events such as *Reclaim the Night* marches involved raising awareness and gaining public recognition for the myriad ways women are abused. Once invested in victim status, women are pushed to defend this position. Any attempt to challenge the perception of women as victims strikes at the heart of what it means to be a feminist and also at what it means to be a woman. It is perceived as an existential threat rather than just a presentation of a counterargument.

RAPE CULTURE

Over recent years, the issue of sexual harassment has morphed into a more generalized discussion of 'rape culture'; a term which was first used in the 1970s. The discourse of rape culture presents the most extreme forms of sexual violence as everyday occurrences by focusing on a broader set of attitudes and beliefs rather than on specific crimes. One author, writing in 1993, described rape culture as 'a society where violence is seen as sexy'.[235] Rape culture is said to be manifest in song lyrics, advertisements and pornographic images that sexually objectify women, as well as in male-dominated sports and fraternities where discussion of rape is trivialized in jokes and comments. Rebecca Solnit, author of

Men Explain Things to Me, argues the term rape culture is useful precisely because it 'insists that a wider culture generates individual crimes'.[236]

The narrative of rape culture shifts attention away from a particular act carried out by a deviant individual to present rape as being socially legitimized behaviour on a continuum with other actions such as suggestive comments. Discussion of rape culture began to take off in earnest in 2011 after a Toronto policeman told women students to protect themselves from rape by not dressing like 'sluts'. This comment was roundly interpreted as a demand on women to change their behaviour rather than on men to stop committing rape. Periodically, a British judge hits the headlines for similar reasons, perhaps for commenting that women, who get so drunk they cannot remember what happened, make less credible witnesses in rape trials. Such attitudes are said to be symptomatic of rape culture in blaming victims for being raped. 'Slut walk' protesters claim men and women should be equally free to drink as much as they want and dress how they choose without fearing being raped.

The separation of a rape culture from actual incidence of rape helps propagate a view that all women are potential victims. It creates a climate of fear by eliding words with actions, song lyrics with sexual assault and fraternity chants with rape. As such it trivializes rape and distances the behaviour of the rapist from responsibility for their actions. Critics such as Wendy McElroy argue rape culture redefines rape not as a crime committed by one man against one woman but as a more generalized 'political act committed collectively by men against women'. She explains that rape culture 'is a social construct that derives from the concept of "the patriarchy", a system of oppression by which women as a class are said to be victimized by men as a class through the omnipresent threat of sexual violence'.[237]

The concept of rape culture is underpinned by an assumption that rape is common, under-reported and surrounded by myths. But accurately assessing the prevalence of rape is notoriously difficult. The Crime Survey estimates that 85,000 women in England and Wales are raped each year but, as Luke Gittos, author of *Why Rape Culture is a Dangerous Myth* points out, this is not a measure of recorded crimes. Instead, it is based on a calculation that 0.5 per cent of women have been victims of rape or sexual assault by penetration in the previous 12 months. This figure is then multiplied up to represent the population as a whole.

Respondents to the crime survey were not asked if they had been raped but if they had been penetrated without consent, which, as Gittos suggests, does not necessarily make someone a 'victim' of rape or serious sexual assault, even in law. The crucial point, missed by the rape culture crusaders, is that 'rape requires that the perpetrator lacked an honest belief in consent'. The figure of 85,000 'fails to capture those circumstances where a complainant may have been incapable of consenting, but the perpetrator did not know they lacked such capacity and honestly and reasonably believed they were consenting'.[238] Interestingly, 19 per cent of those who reported penetration without consent did not report the incident to the police because they said it was a 'private/family matter and not police business' while a further 11 per cent said the matter was 'too trivial and not worth reporting'.[239] In other words, women who do not consider they have been raped are being recorded in crime statistics.

RAPE MYTHS

Of the assumed 85,000 rapes each year, 15 per cent are reported to the police and only 1,000 result in a conviction.

Campaigners argue a huge number of rape cases go unreported but, by its very nature, unreported crime is difficult to
quantify. Further, it is assumed that only a tiny proportion of
rapists are ever punished and the gap between the number of
reported rapes and the number of convictions is put down to
the attitudes of all involved in the judicial process. As Helen
Reece, then Associate Professor of Family Law, notes, this
suggests that 'reform has proved relatively ineffective because
a range of agents hold "rape myths"'. In contrast, Reece
argues, 'the claim that rape myths are widespread may be
challenged on three grounds: first, some of the attitudes are
not myths; secondly, not all myths are about rape; thirdly,
there is little evidence that the rape myths are widespread. To
a troubling extent, we are in the process of creating myths
about myths.'[240] Campaigners are unperturbed by the accuracy of statistics because they are less concerned about actual
incidences of rape than they are about attitudes and behaviour that are said to create 'an environment in which rape
and sexual violence is seen as more acceptable'.[241]

Proponents of rape culture argue rape has become normalized. In America, discussion around rape culture was ignited
by a case in Steubenville, Ohio, involving the sexual assault
of a teenage girl. Feminists criticized the media's focus on the
loss to the boys rather than the harm to the victim as an
example of 'the normalization of rape'. A similar charge was
levelled at coverage of student Brock Turner, found guilty of
three counts of sexual assault, which made frequent references to his doomed swimming career.[242] In the UK, professional footballer Ched Evans was imprisoned for rape but
later had his conviction overturned. This did not stop campaigners from arguing he should be prevented from resuming
his playing career. This focus on a few high-profile individuals takes us far away from a rational investigation into the
likelihood of a woman being raped.

Alarmingly for women, what is becoming normalized in the rape culture narrative is the assumption that men and women should be treated differently before the law. Campaigners argue women cannot give full consent to sex, especially if they have consumed alcohol: if both parties are drunk at the point at which they have sex, the man should be held responsible for rape. Even when a woman says yes to sex, the man needs to prove that the woman knew what she was consenting to. This recalls Catharine MacKinnon's claim that 'in the context of a patriarchal society, women cannot give informed consent'.[243] As Patai argues, this represents an astonishing recapitulation of 'traditional, pre-feminist stereotypes about men and women, according to which women have been socialized into passivity and weakness'. The upshot, lost on many of today's feminists, is that 'men have freedom and responsibility but women have none'.[244] The assumption that women are passive and have no sexual agency sets feminism back decades.

CAMPUS SEX PANICS

The panic about rape culture is particularly virulent in higher education. The 1990s campus is described by Katie Roiphe in *The Morning After*: 'We arrive at college amid a flurry of warnings: "Since you cannot tell who has the potential for rape by simply looking, be on your guard with every man."'[245] Today these warnings come with the pseudo-scientific backing of statistics. In the US, it's often uncritically reported that one in five women are raped at college.[246] Meanwhile, in the UK, we're told that a third of female students have been groped and one in four has experienced 'unwanted sexual advances'.[247] The more such claims are repeated the more veracity they appear to accrue but dig beneath the surface and the evidence crumbles away.

The 'one in five' statistic comes from a 2007 Campus Sexual Assault Study conducted by the American National Institute of Justice, a division of the Justice Department.[248] The research was conducted at just two universities, but politicians, journalists and campaigners have since applied this small sample across all US college campuses.[249] It is rarely acknowledged that this frequently cited figure has even been criticized by those who conducted the research that led to it.[250] In the UK, most often quoted is a 2010 report which claims that 68 per cent of women students have been victims of sexual harassment.[251] This data is based on a tiny sample size of just 2000 self-selecting participants who completed an online survey that grouped together behaviour ranging from sexist jokes and inappropriate touching to serious sexual molestation. Again, we see that these figures are extrapolated to the student population as a whole. Christina Hoff Sommers, a critic of rape culture hysteria, argues we are in the throes of 'one of those panics where paranoia, censorship, and false accusations flourish – and otherwise sensible people abandon their critical facilities'.[252]

Such is the strength of the rape culture narrative that fact and fiction become blurred. In November 2014, *Rolling Stone* magazine published the story of 'Jackie', a young woman who alleged she had been gang raped at a fraternity party.[253] The absence of evidence to substantiate her account was not to stand in the way of a story that appeared to confirm all feminists' worst fears of women's safety on campus. Yet Jackie's claims unravelled and the story was later retracted. This would no doubt have happened more quickly if there wasn't an exceptionalism surrounding rape victims that moves us away from 'innocent until proven guilty' towards an uncritical 'I believe her'. Any attempt at questioning an alleged victim's narrative is said to re-inflict trauma and normal legal procedures, it is argued, should be jettisoned.[254] Campaigners seeking to raise awareness of rape culture appear unconcerned about evidence – their efforts are spent promoting what they assume to be a greater truth. That, as a consequence of this distorted narrative, some women students are afraid to walk across campus unaccompanied after dark is never the fault of the awareness raisers. On the contrary, it is considered further justification for self-perpetuating fear-mongering.

In the eyes of feminist campus crusaders, rape is everywhere. As MacKinnon and Dworkin's offspring, they might not go quite as far as to claim that all heterosexual intercourse is rape but certainly they see all unpleasant or regretted-after-the-event sex is rape. As Roiphe puts it, 'the word "rape" itself expands to include any kind of sex a woman experiences as negative'. She continues, 'You can change your mind afterward. Regret can signify rape. A night that was a blur, a night you wish hadn't happened, can be rape.'[255] As a result of this linguistic overreach, sex has become so problematized that some young women genuinely do not know whether or not they have been raped.[256] In the past, the severity of the crime of rape and the physical nature of the attack would leave little room for doubt. Today, these certainties no longer hold. Although no young woman would ever say she wanted to be raped, the accounts of college rape survivors seem to suggest a perverse determination to interpret past relationships so as to reach this conclusion.

Writing in 2000, Nadine Strossen declared, 'We are in the midst of a fully-fledged "sex panic," in which seemingly all descriptions and depictions of human sexuality are becoming embattled.'[257] The panic has not gone away. In this context, all the rituals of growing up and forming relationships – flirtation, drinking, showing off, hooking-up, regret and doing it all again — become interpreted as a prelude to the act of rape. Raising awareness of rape culture is unlikely to prevent one rape from taking place. In fact, the opposite is the case and it can only lead to an exponential growth in the number of rapes reported. This is disastrous for young people. It leads to a generation of frightened young women and falsely accused young men expelled from college, ostracized and possibly facing legal charges. It paves the way for consent classes, chaperones and the regulation of young people's private relationships.

AN EXPANDING PROBLEM

Dworkin and MacKinnon never did succeed in getting pornography outlawed and today it is more accessible than ever before. Soft pornography has become part of daily life with sexualized images used in advertisements, music videos and even in children's clothing. But this is hardly a victory for sex-positive feminism. Sexual harassment was afforded legal status as discrimination, chiming as it did with an era more willing to recognize women as victims. In the 1980s, the AIDS panic ushered in a new fear of sex being played out not in arguments about religion and morality but through the prism of health. There was to be no return to an era of sexual liberation. Today, the prevalence of pornography, and especially self-pornography, all too often represents a retreat from the necessity of involving another person in a sexual relationship. Nude selfies are less indicative of a more liberal attitude towards sex than a reluctance to leave the privacy of one's bedroom.

Dworkin and MacKinnon may not have won the sex wars in the short term but their arguments against objectifying images of women, the blurred lines between heterosexual sex and rape and the need to regulate expressions of sexuality found most resonance with a later generation of feminists. Today, the subjective and socially constructed concept of sexual harassment is still presented as a persistent problem. Rhetoric is inflationary: we move at a stroke from harassment to violence to abuse; from woman to girl, from victim to survivor. Definitions of sexual violence have become ever broader:

> Sexual violence against women is often perpetrated by intimate partners, as well as by strangers, and takes many forms, including rape, sexual assault, unwanted sexual advances or comments, trafficking, and sexually coercive behaviour. Globally, one in three women has experienced either physical or sexual violence.[258]

Violence against women, feminist campaigners tell us repeatedly, has become 'pandemic' and, as Rebecca Solnit, author of the viral essay *Men Explain Things To Me*, points out, 'it gets explained by anything but gender, anything but what would seem to be the broadest explanatory pattern of them all'.[259] While feminists may wish men in general, rather than specific groups of men, were more frequently labelled as the perpetrators of sexual violence, there is no escaping gender as an attribute of victims. Time and again we are reminded that it is women who are the victims of sexual violence. Loose definitions lead to the charge that 'violence against women and girls is at epidemic levels'.[260] Words like 'epidemic' create a highly charged vision of an escalating threat to women. This violence is rarely explained by war, poverty or inequality between men and women. Instead, it is put down to inherent traits within men. Masculinity is the problem women face.

According to Solnit, masculinity is primarily associated with violence, 'Violence is one way to silence people, to deny their voice and their credibility, to assert your right to control over their right to exist.'[261] To broaden the definition of violence to such an extent trivializes the experiences of women who have been raped or sexually assaulted. But broad definitions are preferred by campaigners because they enable all women to attach to themselves the label of victim. Obviously, this is not to say that no women in the West are victims of sexual violence or that all lead prosperous and stable lives. However, women who do experience violence are not best helped by relativizing their experiences to the point of meaninglessness.

Sexual violence and rape are undoubtedly serious problems, but when definitions are this broad then the surprise is that only one in three women is a victim. When all actions perceived by women as unwanted are on a continuum with rape and violence, and all women are incorporated into the category of victim, identifying and helping women who have suffered actual physical or sexual harm becomes increasingly difficult. Crimes such as domestic violence, sexual assault and rape all deserve to be taken seriously rather than expanded and inflated to such an extent that they lose all meaning.

EXPANDING DEFINITIONS

In the 1990s, the definition of violence expanded — and the corresponding group of victims increased — with the idea that language can inflict actual psychic harm on people. The opening lines of a 1993 book, *Words That Wound*, describe how words are used 'as weapons, to ambush, terrorize, wound and degrade'.[262] We are told that 'victims of vicious hate propaganda experience physiological symptoms and emotional distress ranging from fear in the gut to rapid pulse rate and difficulty in breathing, nightmares, post-traumatic stress disorder, hypertension, psychosis, and suicide'.[263] One contributor calls the use of racist language, 'spirit murder'.

This equation of words with violence makes sense only when harm is experienced subjectively: if I am offended then a statement is, by definition, offensive. It also assumes a fragile sense of self; not a robust individual but an 'identity' that is constructed through language and can, therefore, be dismantled through language. The crime of 'spirit murder' is the invalidation of identity and language is the source of oppression. When being a woman becomes an identity like any other, one that is fragile and vulnerable to invalidation, threats are everywhere. To be a woman is to be a victim; to be a feminist is to fight against spirit murder and for recognition of women as victims.

Today, the definition of violence envelops ever more women in the category of victim. In March 2017, organizers of a women's strike against President Trump explained that women experience:

> the violence of the market, of debt, of capitalist
> property relations, and of the state; the violence of
> discriminatory policies against lesbian, trans and
> queer women; the violence of state criminalization
> of migratory movements; the violence of mass
> incarceration; and the institutional violence
> against women's bodies through abortion bans
> and lack of access to free healthcare and free
> abortion.[264]

What's notable here, alongside a definition of violence far removed from any actual physical threat, is the checklist of special interest groups; lesbian, trans and queer women, who have victim status, not because of specifically violent situations they find themselves in, but as a result of who they are.

CONCLUSIONS

Even though young women today are largely freed from the moral and religious pressures of a previous era, they are far from sexually liberated. The desire to present women as victims of sexual harassment and rape and discriminated against through pornography removes sexual agency from women. If young people are to enjoy sex and forge intimate relationships with one another, they need to be freed from a narrative of risk. For older generations, this means backing off and leaving millennials to work things out for themselves, even if they make some mistakes along the way. After all, this is what people have done since the beginning of time.

The rape culture narrative benefits only feminist campaigners who get an opportunity to socialize young men and women into forming relationships in a way that meets with their approval. The next chapter explores the consequences of this in relation to the collapse of intimacy and the demonizing of masculinity.

CHAPTER SEVEN

THE TROUBLE WITH BOYS

A clear set of preoccupations come together around the demand that women be recognized as vulnerable. This plays out most clearly in the discussion around rape culture and the assumption that heterosexuality is the site of women's oppression. Feminism takes on its own regulatory dynamic and, even when women are not presented as vulnerable, the impetus to enforce a moral framework and assert specifically feminist values holds sway. In this regard, feminism plays into a broader dynamic to regulate not just public life but intimate relationships that are deemed to be a site for potential abuse. This chapter explores the repercussions of problematizing and policing heterosexuality and masculinity.

TITLE IX

Universities, having lost faith in the teaching and pursuit of knowledge, have developed a new role in relation to the socialization of young people. In *What's Happened to the University?* Frank Furedi describes socialization as 'the process through which children are prepared for the world ahead of them'. He argues that 'During the past century responsibility for socialization has gradually shifted from the parent to the school.' However, Furedi notes, 'The institutionalisation of the process of socialisation has in recent decades seamlessly extended into the sphere of higher education.'[265] Today, one of the most explicit ways in which universities socialize young men and women is through the teaching and enforcement of particular ways to conduct sexual relationships.

In the US, colleges are regulated by Title IX, a law prohibiting sex discrimination in federally funded education programs. Title IX states:

> No person in the United States shall, on the basis of
> sex, be excluded from participation in, be denied the
> benefits of, or be subjected to discrimination under
> any education program or activity receiving Federal
> financial assistance.[266]

As Robert Shibley, author of *Twisting Title IX* points out, this brief statement is followed by myriad exceptions. Title IX was not initially intended to have the expansive reach it has today. It began to take on far greater significance following a 1977 case developed by Catherine Mackinnon in which a federal court found that colleges could be liable under Title IX not just for explicit acts of discrimination but also for not responding to allegations of sexual harassment by professors. As Shibley notes, this meant that 'sexual harassment could now be considered discrimination and was thus within the province of Title IX'.[267]

As we have already seen, definitions of sexual harassment began to expand in the 1970s; in education the term came to encompass a 'hostile environment' in which women felt uncomfortable or unwanted because of their sex. By this measure, sexual harassment could be both entirely unintentional and without a specific target. A hostile environment could be created by fellow students irrespective of the actions of an institution's staff and managers. Shibley draws out the consequences of this move: 'Schools were now officially on the hook for policing sexual behavior taking place solely among students.'[268] Over recent years the US Department of Education has issued increasingly explicit directives urging colleges to 'take immediate and effective steps to end sexual harassment and sexual violence'. Despite the efforts of colleges to comply, each year many are investigated for violating Title IX policies.

TEACHING CONSENT

On both sides of the Atlantic, consent classes are used to educate students about the difference between rape and consensual sex. Such classes are rapidly becoming a standard part of university induction procedures; indeed, proponents argue, if students are being taught about fire regulations and health and safety requirements, then why shouldn't they be taught about rape too? By this logic, teaching consent is as straightforward as showing students how to locate the fire escape and no more complex than asking someone if they'd like a cup of tea or a slice of cake. Students are taught that sex should only proceed following an unambiguous 'yes' from both parties. If one person is reluctant then they must not be put under any pressure to change their minds. Unfortunately for the consent instructors, in real life sex and relationships do not follow such a pre-determined course. Consent is not as straightforward as students are led to believe.

The idea that people should engage in a process of explicitly requesting and granting permission prior to having sex is a recent development. When I was in my first year at university in the early 1990s, I joined in with members of the women's group who were making a 'No Means No' banner for a *Take Back The Night* march. At the time I remember thinking the slogan seemed a bit patronizing: surely everyone knew the meaning of the word 'no'. Today, this message seems positively enlightened; it suggests that women know their own minds and are capable of saying no to unwanted sex. It also implies a clear distinction between rape and sex – at the heart of which is the word 'no': when one partner says 'no' and the other proceeds to have sex regardless then this is rape.

Affirmative consent policies, or 'yes means yes' as it is sometimes called, teach students not to rely on one partner saying 'no'. Students are taught not to assume that people are always able to say 'no' and that the absence of 'no' should not imply consent. Sex could be rape even if the word 'no' is never uttered. Instead of waiting for a 'no', students must have an explicit and enthusiastic 'yes'. What's more, they cannot assume that a 'yes' given at one stage in proceedings is enough; consent must be ongoing and sought anew every step of the way. Likewise, a 'yes' from someone who is drunk doesn't count, people must be sober in order to consent. The assumption throughout is that a woman might not know her own mind; she might do one thing but actually mean another, only to change her mind altogether a few moments later. Men, on the other hand, are assumed to be predatory, determined to have sex whether the woman wants it or not. The emphasis on affirmative consent leads students to believe that spontaneity and passion are dangerous because sex not preceded by citing rehearsed scripts and formal negotiations is rape.

Students are presented with a simplistic notion of consent that sets an unattainably high standard for the conduct of private relationships. Often, people's lives and emotions are far from straightforward. Consent is not always black and white; there are blurred lines and misunderstandings in all human interactions. People drink alcohol before having sex precisely because it's fun and relaxing. Likewise, seduction, an elaborate form of persuasion, makes relationships thrilling. Without alcohol or persuasion, few students would ever have sex. People drink, enjoy rituals of teasing and seduction, have sex, and then, in the cold light of day, sober up and sometimes change their minds about the seducer. Sometimes they regret having had sex. But working through these misunderstandings, making mistakes and learning from them, until the next time, is how young people grow up.

What underpins consent classes and Title IX policies is an assumption that students cannot be trusted to grow up or negotiate having sex with each other without a team of experts to advise them. In the fevered imagination of rape culture campaigners, unregulated relationships are dangerous and abusive. Passion, emotion, desire and instinct – especially when fuelled by alcohol – are to be reined in at all times. Sexual consent classes do not preach abstinence; on the contrary, tutors employ a self-consciously pro-sex rhetoric. Likewise, few universities issue strict rules prohibiting sex between students; instead, consent classes work through internal regulation and play on students' fears of either being raped or being a rapist. To avoid the horror of this occurring, even inadvertently, students must exercise self-vigilance.

TEACHING MISTRUST

Not that long ago, students' sex lives were far more formally regulated than they are today. Social, religious and cultural norms, driven in part by a very real fear of unwanted pregnancy and the stigma surrounding it, were enforced by

authoritative adults in the guise of net-curtain-twitching
neighbours at home and tutors acting in *loco parentis* on
campus. Universities had single-sex accommodation and
enforced curfews. Later on, the increased availability of contraception and the relaxing of such stifling social conventions
were experienced as progressive and liberating. In 1970, the
legal lowering of the age of majority in the UK from 21 to 18
reflected a view that students, as adults, were free to make
their own mistakes in sex and relationships, as in every other
part of their lives.

In the years that followed, sex was separated from pregnancy and largely liberated from outdated formal restrictions
but a connection to intimacy and emotion, even if not always
in the context of a relationship, largely remained. Consent
classes, just like school sex education lessons, teach young
people to separate sex from intimacy. Citing phrases practiced in the classroom will not prevent pregnancy or sexually
transmitted diseases, but it ensures an emotional distance
between people exists even within the privacy of the bedroom. When rules are followed and rehearsed scripts are
cited, then sex is permitted. But private, intimate relationships
that are driven by passion and instinct rather than obedience
to a set of rules are to be feared. Intimacy becomes
problematized.

Just as school children are taught to be suspicious of stran-
gers, that other children may be bullies, that it is best to avoid
'exclusive' friendships and that sexual relationships can be
violent and abusive, consent classes teach young adults to
avoid making themselves vulnerable by emotionally investing
in other people. Consent classes and policy documents fill a
gap left open by the end of moral and religious instruction.
But whereas previous generations of students went to great
lengths to rebel against what were perceived as stuffy regulations, today it is more likely to be young and trendy feminists

teaching consent classes. And whereas breaking the rules to have illicit sex created a bond between people, consent classes teach students never to trust anyone else – even when they say yes they may really mean no.

GENERATION VIRGIN

Over the past 20 years, the number of young people who cite school lessons as their main source of information about sex has increased. The *British Medical Journal* reports that between 1990 and 2012 the proportion that learnt about sex in class from a teacher rather than from parents or friends grew from 28.2 per cent to 40.3 per cent. School sex lessons are about a lot more than simply biology; in the UK they must have 'due regard' to government guidance and encompass wider personal and social aspects of sex and relationships.

It seems that sex education might be having an impact. The American General Social Survey has been gathering data on people's sex lives since 1989. Over that time, the proportion of young adults aged between 20 and 24 who reported having had no sexual partner after the age of 18 increased from 6 per cent among those born in the 1960s, to 15 per cent of those born in the 1990s. They are less likely to have had a sexual partner since turning 18 than Generation X'ers were at the same age.[269]

In Britain, the most recent National Survey of Sexual Attitudes and Lifestyles similarly shows that 23 per cent of British 16–24 year-olds have not had sex in the past year. This means that today's young adults have less sex than any group under the age of 55. It seems that the guilty secret behind today's swipe-right hook-up culture is not promiscuity but abstinence. Even when students do hook up it doesn't automatically mean they have sex. One report claims that although 81 per cent of students reported engaging in sexual behaviour during a hook-up only 34 per cent said that this was sexual intercourse.[270] Another study found that for women in their first semester at college, only 27 per cent of their most recent hook-ups involved vaginal sex.[271]

Bemused Boomers and Generation X'ers struggle to explain exactly why millennials are so reluctant to have sex. Commentators on both sides of the Atlantic are quick to point to compulsive smartphone use with social media and video games providing a series of permanently accessible virtual distractions.[272] The ubiquity of online pornography may act to suppress rather than enhance the desire for a far more complicated real-life relationship. Others have pointed to the shift towards abstinence-only sex education in America and the growing popularity of virginity pledges.[273] Today's young adults are less likely to be married, less likely to have secure employment and more likely to live in the parental home than in the past, suggesting to some that millennials are, apparently, just too poor and stressed-out to have time or energy left for sex.[274]

For the most part, however, these are excuses rather than explanations. For previous generations, challenging religious taboos and rebelling against the strictures of parents and teachers lent sex an illicit excitement. In the UK, sex education does not preach abstinence, and virginity pledges are practically unheard of, yet still we see the same rejection of sex. If today's young adults wanted to have sex badly enough, they would turn their phones and laptops off. Indeed, they'd be in more of a rush to start an independent life of their own rather than putting up with the scrutiny of the parental home. It's not that young people are too busy online to have sex; rather they are seeking out virtual distractions in order to avoid real-life interactions.

Their reluctance to leave the safety and security of home gives us the biggest clue as to why young adults are abandoning sex: they've grown up too scared to risk all on another person, too nervous to overcome vulnerability with desire. Perhaps saddest of all the recent statistics is the *National Survey of Sexual Attitudes and Lifestyle* finding that 33.8 per cent of men and 44.4 per cent of sexually active young women report not enjoying sex because they experience pain and anxiety. Furthermore, almost 10 per cent of women said they experienced no excitement or arousal during sex. It seems it's not that young people find work and housing so stressful they've no energy left for sex, it's sex itself they find stressful. For a generation brought up on sex and relationships education, consent classes, crusades against rape culture, talk of objectification and warnings about body-shaming, sex has become so over-complicated they're too scared to try it and too fearful to enjoy it when they do.

HETEROPHOBIA

Consent has become a focus for concern in a climate where not rape but Daphne Patai's notion of 'heterophobia' has become normalized. Mackinnon's view that sex is an exercise in power, a symbolic act of male domination that women have been conditioned to submit to as a result of having internalized society's sexist and patriarchal norms has moved from being unorthodox to mainstream feminist thought. Germaine Greer, writing in 1999, explains, 'A woman's pleasure is not dependent upon the presence of a penis in the vagina; neither is a man's.' She continues, 'We must ask therefore why intromission is still, perhaps more than ever, described as normal or full intercourse. The explanation seems to lie in the symbolic nature of intercourse as an act of domination.'[275] This narrative of oppression playing out through sex between domineering men and passive women implies women can never truly consent to or enjoy heterosexual sex. Today, this is reflected in the views of feminist journalists who decry the 'cold sexual contempt' they see driving too many men. Donald Trump, with his throwaway remarks about 'grabbing women by the pussy' is portrayed as the embodiment of men's sense of entitlement to women's bodies.

The assumption that all men are potential rapists is premised on contempt for women as much as men. Women are presented entirely passively; sex happens to them, it's something they are forced to endure and cannot enjoy. The idea of women desiring, even actively pursuing, sexual encounters with men on their own terms is anathema to the heterophobes. The popularity of erotica such as *Fifty Shades of Grey* suggests that, to the disdain of feminists, for a significant number of women being sexually dominated is a fantasy not an opportunity for political protest. That men and women not only have sex but enjoy it is a threat to feminists who see sex as confirming and reinforcing outdated gender roles. It challenges their disregard for biology and their belief that both gender and sexuality are merely social constructs.

When feminist thinking on sexual harassment, rape culture and consent is challenged, especially by women, the response can be dramatic. Laura Kipnis, a feminist cultural critic and professor challenged her university's interpretation of Title IX legislation which banned relationships between members of academic staff and adult students in a 2015 essay in the *Chronicles of Higher Education*. Kipnis argued that the new codes infantilized students while vastly increasing the power of university administrators. She was shocked at the reaction her article prompted: 'One student said she'd had a "very visceral reaction" to the essay; another called it "terrifying."'

Two students proceeded to file a complaint against Kipnis under Title IX and the university embarked upon a lengthy and bureaucratic investigation. As Kipnis says, 'With the extension of Title IX from gender discrimination into sexual misconduct has come a broadening of not just its mandate but even what constitutes sexual assault and rape.'[276] It is worth remembering that Kipnis did not actually sexually assault anyone: her crime was entirely intellectual; she had an incorrect thought and dared to utter it in the public domain. When it comes to sex, it's not actions that count so much as intentions. Thought-crimes against feminism are, it seems, all too easy to commit.

TOXIC MASCULINITY

Kipnis's 'Title IX Inquisition' shows the extent to which young women have absorbed feminist messages about their vulnerability and need for protection. This same narrative also demonizes young men who stand accused of threatening women and promoting rape culture. It can appear today as if the very existence of men, or, more specifically, masculinity, poses a threat to women. Such ideas began to take root in the feminism of the late 1970s. Mary Daly, writing in her 1978 book *Gyn/Ecology*, argues the 'evil of men' is at 'the root of rapism, racism, gynocide, genocide and ultimately biocide'.[277] Feminism at this time, as Lynn Segal put it, sought to contrast 'the problem of "male" psychology and behaviour' with 'a more nurturant, maternal, co-operative and peaceful "female" psychology and behaviour'.[278]

Such views persist, and today, attributes that have traditionally (and stereotypically) been characterized as masculine, such as competitiveness, aggression, strength, ambition and risk-taking, are seen as problematic. Such macho qualities are

held responsible for everything bad in the world, from the
2008 financial crisis to climate change. More 'feminine' characteristics such as collaboration, co-operation, sensitivity
and empathy are prized instead. Hoff Sommers argues that
'gender scholars have spent the past twenty years trying
to resocialize boys away from such "toxic" masculine
proclivities'.[279]

Today's panic is not directed at all men but rather at stereotypical masculine behaviour or 'toxic masculinity'. The
word 'toxic' reveals the sense in which masculinity is seen as
poisonous, not just detrimental to women but dangerous to
men too. On both sides of the Atlantic, university managers
and academics take issue with a certain type of male student,
especially those into sport, alcohol and 'banter', in other
words, stereotypical 'laddishness'. Particular concern is
expressed about men in groups; in the UK there is panic over
'lad culture' and in the US, debate ensues about the possibility, rather than the desirability, of banning fraternities.[280]
While the legalities are debated, some institutions have introduced mixed-sex and alcohol-free regimes, effectively ending
the tradition of all-male college associations.

Those behind the new schemes work on the assumption
that the presence of women will civilize the fraternities, which
stand accused of promoting sexism and alcohol-fuelled
risk-taking. Meanwhile, in the UK, misbehaving rugby club
members at the University of Oxford are being sent for re-
education at sexual consent and 'good lad' workshops.[281]
The rugby club at the London School of Economics was
banned for sexism, misogyny and homophobia. To make
amends, the young men were expected to stand in public
wearing poster boards displaying their errors. Meanwhile,
at Duke University, 'male-identified students' are offered the
opportunity to 'discuss masculinity, feminism and intersectionality in a new program by the Women's Center'.[282] All

too often, men at university are seen as a problem and young men in groups even more so.

Such concerns go beyond the antics of all-male sports' teams on an alcohol-fuelled night out and carry over into the classroom. Male students are indicted for messing about, not taking their studies seriously and generally being disruptive. One group of British academics has received funding to investigate the behaviour of men at university. Their advocacy research poses loaded questions such as: 'How may lecturers and universities begin to challenge and change problematic "laddish" attitudes and behaviours?'[283] Perhaps unsurprisingly, these surveys have found that men 'just don't seem to really care, they just think it's cool to sit there and talk'.[284] Even relatively mild-mannered male students are considered to dominate seminars in a way that silences female voices.[285] For some lecturers, it seems, the presence of men in their classroom is a particular challenge to be managed, rather than simply being part and parcel of the everyday experience of teaching.

PROMOTING FEMININE VALUES

In a changed industrial landscape where neither brute strength nor risk-taking is valued, schools and broader society now reflect this shift towards the promotion of feminine values. Men are expected to get on board with the new, more emotive and therapeutic, ethos. Those who are reluctant to do so struggle at school and receive 'reverse mentorship' in the work place. The idea of reverse mentoring is that older workers are paired with younger ones in order to educate them on how 'new ways of thinking can improve them'.[286] Feminist reverse mentoring allows young women to educate older men about the 'correct' way to act in the workplace;

one scheme is designed 'to help managers understand how behaviour actions and words impact on others'.[287]

This means that those relics from a bygone era, such as the Nobel prize–winning scientist Sir Tim Hunt with his joke about the 'problem' of women in labs, or Saatchi and Saatchi boss Kevin Roberts with his suggestion that gender bias wasn't an issue in the advertising industry, are derided as pale, male and stale and are held up for public ridicule. Here we see how feminism can be used as a means of regulating not just the behaviour of men but their words, attitudes and values too.

With feminism, and more specifically the feminine, on the ascendancy, it can sometimes seem as if the only acceptable man is a man who wants to be a woman. Although undoubtedly most problematic for men, when there is no place in society for masculinity everyone loses out on a powerful force for good. Women, as much as men, can be aggressive, determined, ambitious and ruthless. Problematizing masculinity has the perverse effect of entrenching gender stereotypes and denying individual preferences. Women may be just as likely as men to prize individualism and ambition over the collaborative and the domestic. Even if women do not esteem such values themselves, they may admire men who do. Passion obeys no rules; certainly not all women share in the desire for an emoting and sensitive partner.

COMPETING CLAIMS FOR VICTIMHOOD

The assault on masculinity combined with the contemporary feminist tendency to pitch men against women has led to the emergence of a burgeoning men's rights movement. Campaigners for men's rights point to issues such as the underperformance of boys in education and the negative media portrayal of men as, for example, 'deadbeat dads' to argue that men's interests need defending in a far more coherent way. They suggest that their particular concerns, such as a higher suicide rate and unequal treatment in family courts when a marriage breaks down, are overlooked or trivialized. Men's rights activists claim men are more likely than women to be victims of violent crime and that domestic violence can be perpetrated by women as well as men. This raises some important issues and provides a useful counterbalance to the dominance of feminism. However, this is not a defence of masculinity but a demand that men have recognition for their particular problems.

While there is indeed a crisis of masculinity in societies that no longer have a useful role for men to play, the men's rights movement does little to tackle this issue. Rather than making the positive case for masculine values, all too often men's rights activists argue that men are victims too. They want greater awareness of the difficulties faced specifically by men. They argue men experience pressure to 'man up', maintain a stiff upper lip at all times and not reveal any vulnerability. Men's rights activists want men to be free to emote in public and to demonstrate sensitivity: they want recognition that they, too, suffer. The result is that both men and women fight to claim the mantle of victimhood. As Christopher Lasch prophetically noted in 1997, '*The Chronicle of Higher Education* lists 28 recent and forthcoming books on men and masculinity and leaves us with the sinking feeling that this is only the beginning. The market for self-pity, it appears, is inexhaustible.'[288]

Campaigners for men's rights argue that men are as much victims of gender stereotyping as women, but unlike women men are not just battling against tradition, they are also under attack from feminists, a group they see as a conspiratorial club that aims specifically at degrading men and denying them their rightful place in the world. What the men's rights activists miss is that modern feminism is as detrimental and limiting to the majority of women as it is to men. If sexual equality is to be a meaningful goal, it has to be about more than an equality of victimhood. Arguments over who is the most oppressed serve only to pitch men and women into battle against each other in a competition of grievances. There is no room for considering what people have in common and how society can be made to work in the best interests of everyone.

CONCLUSIONS

Today's feminism awards status based on competing claims to victimhood. Women especially are taught to see themselves as victims and as at risk from predatory men. One result of this is a proliferation of consent classes and campus rules designed to regulate personal relationships. This has the effect of eroding intimacy and trust between men and women. As a result, heterosexuality is presented as problematic and masculinity, especially, as toxic. In response, a men's rights movement has emerged that competes with feminism over who is most deserving of the victimhood mantle. There can be no winners from this race to the bottom.

PART THREE

—

FEMINISM THEN AND NOW

CHAPTER EIGHT

NOT YOUR GRANDMOTHER'S FEMINISM

The victim feminism portrayed in the previous chapters is premised upon the notion that women are oppressed. Popular articles and blogs tell us, 'Yes, women are still oppressed,' and point out, 'Five ways women are oppressed today.' Elsewhere, we are told that women are oppressed by the media, by advertising, by conservative politics and – of course – by men. It seems as if any specific meaning of oppression is lost in such inflated claims and instead oppression has become convenient shorthand for anything feminists find unpleasant.

Challenging women's oppression has been a goal of political and social reformers for over two centuries. From Wollstonecraft's *Vindication of the Rights of Women* to Mill's *The Subjection of Women*, via Cady Stanton and the Pankhursts, through to de Beauvoir, Friedan and Greer, central to this battle has been an attempt to understand and explain the specific nature and cause of women's oppression. Continuing this project today is important if we are to evaluate whether women are oppressed in a way that men are not.

This chapter explores the changing nature of campaigns for women's rights from their origin in the nineteenth century through to second-wave feminism in the 1970s. Over this time the position of women in society has changed beyond all recognition and the role of feminism in helping bring about sexual equality has been significant. At the same time, as we shall see, many feminist arguments for equality have, from the outset been premised on a problematic assumption that men and women are fundamentally different.

NATURALLY DIFFERENT

In his 1762 book, *Emile*, or *On Education*, the French philosopher Rousseau argued a view common among thinkers of his day: that men and women's natural differences, evident even in a pre-social state of nature, explained the contemporary inequality between the sexes. It was for this reason, he argued, that boys and girls should be educated differently: 'Give, without scruples, a woman's education to women, see to it that they love the cares of their sex, that they possess modesty, that they know how to grow old in their menage and keep busy in their house.'[289] A belief that the inferior position of women in society was down to the historical impact of biological differences between the sexes continued into the twentieth century and is evident in the work of anthropologists such as Levi Strauss.

Mary Wollstonecraft, writing 30 years after Rousseau, proposed that it wasn't biology but the ways that men and women were treated that explained the differences between them. In her powerful polemic, *A Vindication of the Rights of Women*, published in 1792, Wollstonecraft is critical of the way women conduct themselves. However, she argues their behaviour does not result from their innate disposition but from their lack of education. She suggests that education, far from responding to pre-existing biological differences actually helps create differences between the sexes. Women are not born as such inferior beings, Wollstonecraft claims, but are brought up to become 'more artificial, weak characters than they would otherwise have been'.[290] Their education and upbringing prevent women from having 'sufficient strength of mind to acquire what really deserves the name virtue'. Wollstonecraft is clear that endeavouring to keep women 'always in a state of childhood' degrades both men and women. She proposes we 'strengthen the female mind by enlarging it'.[291]

WOMEN AS SLAVES

Wollstonecraft drew a parallel between the position of women and slaves: 'They may be convenient slaves but slavery will have its constant effect, degrading the master and the abject dependent.'[292] The analogy of women with slaves was to become a recurrent theme of women's rights campaigners throughout the nineteenth century and into the early decades of the twentieth century, an analogy that highlighted the fact that at this time women were considered to be the property of men with no legal rights of their own. In most American states, the law considered married women to be extensions of their husbands, with men having full rights over their wife's body, property, earnings and children. In both Britain and America, women were considered legally indistinct from their husbands.[293]

Karl Marx described women's status within the family structure as akin to slavery: 'The modern family contains in germ not only slavery (servitus) but also serfdom, since from the beginning it is related to agricultural services. It contains, in miniature, all the contradictions which later extend throughout society and its state.'[294] The idea that women were enslaved merged into later arguments that women formed a distinct social class. Engels makes this point most clearly and links the formation of women as a distinct class to the emergence of monogamous marriage. 'Monogamous marriage comes on the scene as the subjugation of the one sex by the other'; he writes, 'The first class oppression coincides with that of the female sex by the male.'[295]

John Stuart Mill, writing in *The Subjection of Women*, makes an important amendment to the slavery analogy. He suggests, 'All men, except the most brutish, desire to have, in the woman most nearly connected with them, not a forced slave but a willing one, not a slave merely, but a favourite.'[296] Mill argues that because men wanted willing slaves, women couldn't be ruled by force or fear. For this reason, men 'turned the whole force of education' into enslaving women's minds. The enlightenment idea of equality, as encapsulated in Thomas Paine's *Rights of Man*, was not extended in practice to all people at the time of its formulation. But in its philosophy lay the intellectual basis for equality and the possibility, for the first time, of questioning assumptions that underpinned the way society was structured. The possibility of equality between the sexes, and the possibility that society could be different, allowed Wollstonecraft, Marx, Mill and Engels to question the position of women.

In America, women such as Elizabeth Cady Stanton, Lucy Stone and Lucretia Mott, all leading advocates of women's rights, first found their voices within the abolition movement. The campaign against slavery provided some women with a limited platform and with a means of confronting arguments about inequality which proved formative for women's rights campaigners. It allowed them to organize and plan conventions and publications. The first women's convention was held in America in 1848. Here, Cady Stanton presented her 'Declaration of Sentiments', a list of resolutions outlining the rights of women modelled on the Declaration of Independence.

The declaration summarized women's position thus: 'The history of mankind is a history of repeated injuries and usurpations on the part of man toward woman, having in direct object the establishment of an absolute tyranny over her.'[297] The blame for women's position was laid firmly with man: 'He has endeavoured, in every way that he could, to destroy her confidence in her own powers, to lessen her self-respect, and to make her willing to lead a dependent and abject life.'[298] All resolutions were passed unanimously except one: Cady Stanton's late addition of a resolution for women's suffrage.

For these first campaigners for women's rights, questioning the basis of racial inequality brought sexual inequality into stark relief. Christopher Lasch notes that the struggle against slavery provided the basis for the first critique of patriarchal authority.[299] But in doing so it also made clear the tension for early feminists between the promotion of black civil rights and women's rights. The abolitionist and women's rights advocate Sojourner Truth, declared in a speech given in 1851: 'I think that 'twixt the negroes of the South and the women of the North, all talking about rights, the white men will be in a fix pretty soon.'[300]

Truth's speech contained the now famous refrain, 'Ain't I a woman?' She demanded to know where there was room, in the emergence of campaigns for black civil rights on the one hand and women's rights on the other, for the problems experienced by black women. Despite Truth's efforts to bring the two groups together, the campaign for women's rights became primarily identified with wealthy white women. By

1896, a separate organization had formed, the National Association for Colored Women, led by Mary Church Terrell and including Harriet Tubman and Ida B. Wells-Barnett.[301]

Educating Girls

Much early campaigning for women's rights was not focused on the demand for suffrage but on other aspects of women's lives. Following Wollstonecraft's lead, there was an emphasis on the need to secure a decent education for girls. Cady Stanton was influenced by her own formal schooling in the 1820s having been curtailed prematurely. While her male classmates continued on to college, none at that time would permit women. Wollstonecraft's argument that girls' inferior education stunted women's intellectual and emotional growth proved controversial at the time but later found favour. Campaigners for educating girls to a similar level as boys argued this would pave the way for a greater equality between the sexes. By 1869 Mill notes, 'The claim of women to be educated as solidly, and in the same branches of knowledge as men, is urged with growing intensity.'[302]

While some women in the nineteenth century were content to be treated differently, others fought for access to 'the same branches of knowledge as men' and ideas that could take them beyond the limited horizons of the lives they were expected to lead. At a time when movements for social reform were becoming increasingly popular in both America and Britain, societies and political associations designed to advance the interests of women sprang up. The drive for girls' schools became part of this push for social reform. In England, the first schools offering an academic education to girls began to be established at this time with Cheltenham Ladies College opening in 1854 and the Girls' Public Day School Trust established in 1872. By 1880, basic schooling became compulsory for all English children aged between 5 and 10. For the majority of those able to continue their education beyond this elementary level, there remained segregated schools and different curricular for boys and girls.

The quest for access to the same knowledge of the world as men led young women to demand entry to the universities. However, as Lucy Stone, Cady Stanton's contemporary in the American campaign for women's rights, was to discover, entry alone didn't equate to an education. Stone managed to secure a place at Oberlin, the first US college to accept women. But, as Betty Friedan tells us, Stone, 'had to practise public speaking secretly in the woods. Even at Oberlin, the girls were forbidden to speak in public.' In the eyes of the college, the purpose of her education remained 'intelligent motherhood and a properly subservient wifehood'.[303]

By the 1860s, British women were permitted to sit in on lectures in Liverpool and Manchester and in 1869 Emily Davies co-founded Girton College in Cambridge, the first residential university college for women. Having fought against social convention, legal limits to their independence, inadequate schooling and sometimes poverty to get to university, once there, women had to overcome institutional rules and social prejudice as well as prove themselves to be academically capable, morally virtuous and physically healthy in a way that was not expected of men. In the US, the establishment of women's colleges, including Georgia Female College, Mount Holyoke Seminary and Elmira Female College, and more specifically their affiliations with universities such as Harvard, Columbia and Brown, allowed women to participate, in a limited fashion, in the educational opportunities afforded to men.[304] As students, women had to put up with male academics refusing to teach them as well as a plethora of petty regulations that 'stated exactly whom one could meet, in what circumstances, when, where, wearing what, and for how long'.[305]

The reluctance of American universities to allow women to enrol led to the emergence of single sex colleges such as Smith, Mount Holyoke, Wellesley, Barnard, Radcliffe, Vassar and Bryn Mawr, which were designed to meet the specific educational needs of women. By the beginning of the twentieth century, most public secondary schools and colleges in the US had become predominantly co-educational but, as in the UK, this alone did not guarantee equal opportunities. In 1918 the Commission on the Reorganization of Secondary Education made a case for the creation of a two track system: one track steered students, primarily males, towards college preparatory coursework, and the other track provided vocational training. Girls, even those with a strong academic record, were encouraged down the vocational track and required to take classes in domestic science or home economics.

Right up until the 1920s women at some universities were expected to be accompanied by chaperones wherever they went. Even though women took the same courses and exams as men and were judged by the same standards, many women students worked without any chance of graduating with a final degree qualification. Men were determined to 'keep women away from the places that endorse exclusive forms of power'.[306] It was not until 1948 that women were permitted to graduate from the University of Cambridge and 1959 before women's halls at Oxford became fully incorporated into the university.

VOTES FOR SOME WOMEN

The campaign for girls to have access to education was, for many pioneers of women's rights, a more important priority than securing the vote. Indeed, it was only when the importance of educating girls had become more widely accepted that the demand for suffrage began to take off. Campaigns for suffrage, on both side of the Atlantic, did not bring about a more liberal climate so much as emerge out of it. The British suffragist and union leader Millicent Fawcett was correct when she noted that:

> Women's suffrage will not come, when it does come, as an isolated phenomenon, it will come as a necessary corollary of other changes which have been gradually and steadily modifying during this century the social history of our country. It will be a political change, not of a very great or extensive character in itself, based upon social, educational and economic changes which have already taken place.[307]

Other significant women's rights campaigns in the late nineteenth century focused upon the rights of women to divorce and to maintain access to their children following separation, to inherit, to hold property and to practice in professions such as law and medicine. The movement for women's right to vote was considered at least at first to be of more symbolic rather than practical significance to improving the position of women; it highlighted the fact that women were denied citizenship rights and that their political interests were subsumed under those of men.

The demand for suffrage brought political differences between campaigners for women's rights to the fore. Today it is often assumed that the suffragists, represented by Millicent Fawcett, and the suffragettes with the Pankhursts as

figureheads, shared a common goal but disagreed over tactics, with the suffragists being in favour of peaceful protest in
comparison to the more militant suffragettes. But this ignores
a number of significant political differences between the two
groups. One such disagreement arose over which women
were to be included in suffrage campaigns.

Helen Taylor, the daughter of philosopher and women's
rights campaigner Harriet Taylor, petitioned Parliament in
1866. She presented a Ladies' Petition to her step-father John
Stuart Mill in the House of Commons. The petition argued,
'Since women are permitted to hold property they should
also be permitted to exercise all the rights which, by our
laws, the possession of property brings with it.'[308] For Taylor
the demand for suffrage was a demand for citizenship rights
to be extended to women with property and, as she made
clear, 'advanced so entirely without reference to any abstract
rights'. Richard Pankhurst, husband of Emmeline, in contrast
argued that, 'The basis of political freedom is expressed in
the great maxim of the equality of all men, of humanity, of
all human beings before the law.' He continued, 'Each
individual receives the right to vote in the character of
human being, possessing intelligence and adequate reasoning
power.' Taylor and Pankhurst were expressing a fundamental
difference between the rights of people and the rights of property — a distinction that became central to debates within
what was later to be termed first-wave feminism.

Emerging from this was a far more significant political
difference, epitomized by the disagreement over tactics, over
whether campaigners should argue for universal suffrage or
present certain women as more deserving of the vote. Those
demanding universal suffrage recognized men and women as
equals and argued that the right to have a say in how you
are governed was a natural human right. The suffragettes'
militancy was initially premised on an assumption that for

women to be taken seriously as men's equals, they needed to fight like men. The suffragists, on the other hand, argued that women were different to men and needed to prove their worth as propertied citizens before they could win the privilege of the vote. Over time, these political differences emerged between the Pankhursts, with Emmeline and daughter Christabel happy to put the campaign for the vote on hold and throw their efforts behind the First World War. Sylvia Pankhurst, on the other hand, demanded women be given the vote on the same grounds as men and wanted franchise extended to both men and women without property. Sylvia refused to support British efforts in what she considered to be an imperialist and anti-working-class conflict.

MORALLY SUPERIOR WOMEN

In America, debates about the nature of men and women in relation to each other led to the view that women were not just different but morally superior to men. This perception of moral superiority stems from the fight against slavery having been waged, in part, as a fight against patriarchy. Perhaps more significantly it comes from the origins of many women's rights campaigns in the temperance movement: women were at the forefront of calls for prohibition on the sale of alcohol. Likewise, in discussions of sexuality, men were deemed to be subject to animal appetites and the role of women was to withstand the sexual pressures placed upon them. Demands for women's rights were premised on the view that women, who were naturally caring and nurturing, could be a civilizing influence on society.

In her early years as a campaigner, Cady Stanton held the belief that men and women had similar natures and therefore deserved equality under the law. However, in 1854, despite maintaining her views on equality, she strategically argued that women were morally superior to men. 'Women's moral power ought to speak,' she argued, 'not only in the home but in the ballot box.' Giving women the vote, she claimed, would reform men through the regulation of saloons and gambling halls 'which lure our youth on to excessive indulgence and destruction'.[309] In her later years, Cady Stanton became more convinced of the existence of differences between the sexes and women's innate moral superiority. She argued that problems such as war and violence were a result of the world having been governed by the 'masculine element'. If the 'feminine element' had 'asserted itself from the beginning', she suggests, 'those governments of force and religions of damnation would have been modified long ago, mercy would have tempered justice and love banished superstition. Neither capital punishment and war nor the concept of hell could have emanated from the mother soul.'[310]

The argument that women are morally superior to men takes us a long way from Mary Wollstonecraft's view that men were the superior sex – not because of a 'masculine element' or any inherent virtues but because of the education, upbringing and opportunities society afforded them: 'Men have increased that inferiority till women are almost sunk below the standard of rational creatures.'[311] Wollstonecraft is similarly scathing of the idea that girls are naturally more nurturing than boys, 'The doll never excite attention,' she proclaimed, 'unless confinement allows her no alternative.' This view that men and women are born equal but created differently has been echoed by feminist writers ever since, from de Beauvoir who argued that the '"true woman" is an artificial product that civilization makes, as formerly eunuchs were made',[312] to Germaine Greer's view that 'a female is castrated and becomes feminine'.[313] However, such arguments have also sat alongside a persistent view of innate differences between the sexes and a belief that women are naturally more nurturing and empathetic.

Ultimately, it was the pragmatism and the compromise displayed by Cady Stanton and Emmeline Pankhurst that led to the vote being granted in Britain to propertied women over the age of 30 in the 1918 Representation of the People Act and the 19th Amendment to the Constitution giving women throughout America the right to vote in 1920. Although suffrage represented a significant victory, it was granted only after demands for equality between the sexes had dissipated. As Rosalind Delmar notes, the dynamics of feminist activity in the late nineteenth and early twentieth centuries moved away from a concept of equality, 'by developing much more than previously the concept of inescapable differences between the sexes, the term equal rights became filled with different contents'.[314] The struggle for 'human' rights was replaced by a demand for 'women's' rights; campaigners came to conceive of women not as lying within the generic category of 'man' but as a subgroup of humanity. It was on this assumption of fundamental difference that women argued they needed their own representatives. Such arguments reverberate in today's feminist campaigns for women to be represented on boards of directors so that businesses are less driven by machismo and in campaigns against lad culture in higher education.

The Family

The reformulation of sex differences by women's rights campaigners returns us to an old idea, one evoked by Aristotle and Rousseau, that the natural differences between men and women explain their inequality. This turns the clock back on Mill who described the subjection of women as 'a universal custom', explaining that 'everything which is usual appears natural'. It is not sufficient to explain women's oppression according to natural or biological differences; this gets in the way of understanding the social nature of inequality and the relationships between men and women.

Wollstonecraft, Mill and Cady Stanton looked beyond biology to the socialization of girls through their upbringing and schooling. But to understand why boys and girls were socialized in different ways, we need to look at men and women not as individuals but in collective relationship to each other. Frederick Engels, writing in *The Origin of the Family, Private Property and the State* in 1884, located women's oppression in the institution of the family. He argued that the role women were forced to play in the domestic sphere prevented them from fully participating in public life.

In the 1960s and into the early 1970s, feminists such as Betty Friedan and Germaine Greer argued that a combination of formal legislation and informal practices meant women were still oppressed because they were unable to participate in all aspects of society in the same way as men. Lack of access to contraception, abortion and childcare hindered women's capacity to engage in the public realm on their own terms. Engels argues that women became a class, an oppressed class with collective interests in common, with the emergence of civilization and, in particular, the monogamous marriage. Within the family, Engels explains, the husband 'is the bourgeois and the wife represents the proletariat'.[315] Germaine Greer follows through the logic of this argument: 'If women are the true proletariat, the truly oppressed majority, the revolution can only be drawn nearer by their withdrawal of support for the capitalist system.'[316]

Engels argued women's oppression began with the development of the family as an economic unit. Property became privatized, owned by the family and passed from father to son. Women, unable to inherit, became instead the man's possession. With the industrial revolution, the production of goods moved from the domestic sphere to the factory. This separated men from the daily routines of the family and, later, separated many women from economic production. This division, naturalized through religion and education, made women solely responsible for the home; a status revered by many among the middle class but experienced as an additional burden by the working-class women who still needed to earn money. It became the role of women to ensure male wage earners were sufficiently fed and cared for to enable them to continue working.

Today, we have sadly become used to viewing the family as problematic. We have become accustomed to thinking of the intimacy of family relationships as sheltering domestic violence and child abuse. This makes it is all too easy to accept the argument that marriage is the site of women's oppression. However, this is not what Engels meant. It wasn't the relationships between people, either as a couple or as a family, that were oppressive, but the way the family became organized as a private economic unit and women were made into economic dependents, cast into a specific role in relation to children and home.[317]

FREEDOM TO WORK

Gaining an accurate picture of the number of women employed before the twentieth century is complicated by the low status and informal nature of women's work. When weaving was first taken out of the home and established within factories, it was women and children who were considered best suited to operating looms. The paid work women did could be as arduous as work carried out by men, but they were nonetheless considered a cheap and easily disposable source of labour. Simone de Beauvoir reminds us of the long and ignoble history of women earning less than men even for the very same work, 'The woman worker in France, according to a study made in the years 1889—93, received only half the pay of a man for a day's work equal to that of a man.'[318]

Women are reported to have made up roughly 18 per cent of the American work force in 1900, although the real figure may have been higher.[319] In the UK at this time it is thought that up to two-thirds of women had paid work.[320] It is hard to know for certain because in the nineteenth century many working-class women were still employed in their own homes, perhaps engaged in 'piece work' such as sewing. Alternatively, they worked in other people's homes as domestic servants or for family-run farms and businesses. For middle-class women, employment options were more limited and concentrated primarily within teaching or nursing. The idea of a woman having a career rather than a job, work that might have provided intellectual satisfaction rather than just a small wage, was rare indeed.

As we saw in the first part of this book, campaigns concerned with women's rights at work are a focal point for feminism today. Paid work has become fetishized as a representation of women's social status and the source of financial, emotional and intellectual fulfilment. However, in the past, the restricted opportunities for women to work, and even the far more labour-intensive demands of housework, did not prevent a number of women from becoming involved in voluntary work and reform societies outside of the home. As Christopher Lasch reminds us, women who did not work for wages were often active outside the home in voluntary organizations that demanded much more from women than simply a little fund-raising.

THE PUBLIC SPHERE

At the dawn of the twentieth century women took an active role in civic society, sitting on committees, managing budgets and being involved in local planning decisions.[321] They created municipal life, distinct from both the private domestic sphere and the realm of business and profit, in the form of libraries, play grounds and youth clubs. This activity outside of either paid work or the home was not the preserve of middle-class women. As the sociologist Ann Oakley tells us, working-class women's political activities continued throughout the nineteenth century, 'Female chartists ran their own political unions and pursued questions of female independence, sex equality and political participation.'[322]

Voluntary work brought women into the public sphere but their domestic responsibilities did not diminish. On the contrary, as Lasch points out, voluntary work was attractive 'in part because it was easily combined with domestic responsibilities, unlike the inflexible schedules imposed by paid work.'[323] Involvement in civic society was made possible in part because child rearing wasn't seen as the labour intensive and privatized concern it is today. Even very young children were thought able to spend time unsupervised, playing outside of the home and being looked after by older siblings and extended family members. For many women, the formal boundaries between work and home, between paid work and public duty, remained blurred until well into the twentieth century. At the same time, however, society remained rigidly segregated according to sex, class and race.

THE SECOND WORLD WAR

The Second World War marked a significant turning point in women's lives. With men conscripted to fight, women were expected to take up work in all sectors including factories, mines, administration and agriculture. State-run nurseries provided some childcare and many women enjoyed the liberation and stimulation work provided; they were not, however, paid the same wages as the men whose jobs they had replaced. In the US, in 1942 the National War Labor Board urged employers to pay men and women the same for work that was comparable in quality and quantity. Unfortunately for women, employers did not heed this advice. In Scotland, Bella Keyzer, a weaver, was assigned to work in the Scottish shipyards during the Second World War where she trained as a welder. It was the trade unions that played a key role in reinforcing the message that Bella's contract was only temporary. The unions welcomed the fact that the men she worked alongside as equals earned three times as much as she did. After the war, they helped to ensure women returned to the home and 'men's jobs' went back to men. Bella had to leave welding and return to 'women's work'.[324]

After the Second World War, women in both Britain and America, especially those who were married or had children, were expected to give up their new found freedom and return to the home. Some women returned home reluctantly and fought against the closure of state-run nurseries and the loss of their jobs. Others embraced a return to the security of the domestic sphere after the disruption of the war. In the UK, child psychologist John Bowlby's work on attachment theory and the consequences of maternal deprivation helped spread the message that a woman's place was in the home with her children. In America, Betty Friedan describes the cult of domesticity that dominated American society throughout the 1950s noting that, there is no way a woman 'can even dream about herself, except as her children's mother, her husband's wife'.[325]

Women's return to the home was not simply a matter of personal choice or social convention; trade unions and even national labour laws formally restricted women's rights to work. As Alison Wolf points out, 'A marriage bar for teachers and the civil service lasted until 1945 in the UK; until 1957 for civil servants in the Netherlands, the 1960s in Australia, 1973 in Ireland.'[326] In America, this employment bar was particularly acute for black women. Women who weren't legally prevented from working often felt morally compelled to give up work when they got married or following the birth of their first child.[327] The paid employment they had enjoyed was gone and the public service roles they had played in a voluntary capacity had now been co-opted by the state or private enterprise. Women were effectively excluded from public life and, for some women for the first time, restricted to the domestic sphere. In America this sense of exclusion was exacerbated by the geographical move out to the suburbs, although, as Lasch notes, the initial impetus behind the move to the suburbs was the perceived freedom in the absence of public responsibilities and extended families.

The new model of the suburban family was initially welcomed. Escaping convention and family ties to an older generation was considered by many to be liberating. The image of the home as, to use Lasch's phrase, 'a haven in a

heartless world', with the figure of the wife and mother at the
centre, was an important means for people to cope with
world events that appeared scary and out of control and
work that was experienced as increasingly mechanized and
alienating. As Lasch notes, 'It was in the suburbs, much more
than in the city, that women became full-time mothers and
homemakers.'[328] The suburbs created the male breadwinner,
solely responsible for earning the family income, who com-
muted into the city and left behind a socially isolated, financially dependent woman whose role was valued only as
housewife and mother. This exacerbated the separation of the
public and the private spheres that first emerged with
industrialization.

Women who did continue to work outside the home at
this time met a highly segregated labour market. Right into
the 1960s, newspaper 'situations vacant' columns continued
to advertise men's and women's jobs separately. Women's
jobs could be easily spotted – they were those offered at a
considerably lower rate of pay. In America, between 1950
and 1960, women who worked full-time were paid between
59 and 64 cents, on average, for every dollar men earned.
Differentiating between women's and men's jobs made it easy
to justify paying women less; in fact, they could be paid less
for doing the exact same work only with a different job title.
Teachers, separated into schoolmasters and schoolmistresses,
could teach the same classes, the same subjects, and for the
same number of hours, but still be paid differently. Unequal
pay was all too often accepted as inevitable when relatively
few women worked outside the home and it was assumed
that women were only working for 'pin money'.

In the years immediately after the Second World War,
fewer than one-third of American women were employed
outside of the home.[329] By 1971 this figure had risen, but
only slightly to 38 per cent.[330] Working women at this time

were mainly older, unmarried and women of colour; few were pursuing careers. They bore the brunt of the sex discrimination that was rife in the workplace at that time. In contrast to today, the group missing from the labour market was the younger, white, middle-class women Betty Friedan wrote about in *The Feminine Mystique*. Friedan describes 1960s suburban housewives as suffering from 'the problem that has no name': 'Each suburban wife struggles with it alone. As she made the beds, shopped for groceries, matched slipcover material, ate peanut butter sandwiches with her children, chauffeured Cub Scouts and Brownies, lay beside her husband at night — she was afraid to ask even of herself the silent question — "Is this all?"'[331]

In Britain, the position of women changed a little sooner. Women began to re-enter the workforce in significant numbers throughout the 1960s and by 1971 53 per cent of women had paid work, although, as we have already noted, for the majority this was part-time.[332] Although employment was less rigidly structured than it was fifty years earlier, women still found that they were prevented from entering some careers or from being promoted beyond a certain level. The numbers may have been better but for many women the reality of work meant 'the worst jobs, worst wages and worst conditions'.[333]

SECOND-WAVE FEMINISM

It was in this context, with women confronting a choice between what was experienced as an increasingly stifling domesticity or a highly segregated and discriminatory workplace, that what came to be known as second-wave feminism emerged. The four decades from 1920 to 1960 are often presented as a hiatus in feminism following the success of the suffrage movement. Indeed, a visible women's movement did disappear from public prominence as the drive to get women first into work and fighting the war on the home front and then out of work and back into the home took centre stage. However, the absence of an active women's movement did not preclude the development of feminist thought. Rosalind Delmar argues that an overly strict identification of feminism with a women's movement depends on a definition of feminism as activity rather than theory. She argues this sleight of hand is also found in the use of 'first-wave' and 'second-wave' feminism to imply a seamless continuity between struggles beginning a century apart: 'The past is used to authenticate the present.'[334]

Despite the implied continuity, the context, issues and politics driving second-wave feminism were quite distinct from the preoccupations of the first wave. The presentation in the media, advertising, academia and government propaganda of the role of mother as the natural fulfilment of a woman's destiny made it seem as if the domesticity of the nuclear family had been an ever-present feature of society. In reality it represented a historically recent social phenomenon. Friedan tells us, 'The proportion of women attending college in comparison with men dropped from 47 per cent in 1920 to 35 per cent in 1958.' During this time, the age of marriage and the age at which women gave birth to their first child had both dropped. In the years after the Second World War, a well-maintained house with children in the suburbs was viewed by many young women as more aspirational than education or a career. 'A century earlier,' Friedan notes, 'women had fought for higher education; now, girls went to college to get a husband.'[335]

It would be a mistake to see the women's movement that began to take off throughout Europe and North America in the middle of the 1960s as simply a spontaneous reaction against domesticity. The political context from which it emerged is just as significant as the social position women found themselves in. The New Left, which emerged from left-wing political groups in the 1960s, defined in opposition to both the Stalinism of Eastern Europe and the resurgent capitalism of the West, expressed a growing sense of frustration with the working class at home for apparently colluding with capitalism and embracing a consumer lifestyle. The New Left became increasingly focused on the role of mass culture in sustaining capitalism and promoting the drive to suburbanization.[336] Friedan's critique of magazines, advertising and department stores for selling the myth of a purchasable domestic idyll to women was typical of this line of argument. Rather than seeing women as having positively embraced domesticity, or facing practical obstacles to any alternative lifestyle, the New Left began to see personal freedom itself as a mythical creation of the 'culture industry'. Second-wave feminism was not only influenced by this political analysis but it was started by radical women who were themselves prominent within the New Left.

It was from this social and political context that The National Organization of Women (NOW) was formed in America in 1966 and held its first national conference in 1967. As Delmar reminds us, the women's movement at this time did not label itself as feminist: feminism was simply one position that was adopted by particular groups within the movement.[337] The label second-wave feminism was first used in a 1968 *New York Times* article by Martha Weinman Lear covering NOW and its activities. It was quickly adopted by a women's rights movement rapidly growing throughout North America and Western Europe. Although the label stressed historical continuities with campaigns for women's rights and played down the links to left-wing politics, the ideas that

drove second-wave feminism continued to be firmly grounded
in the ideology of the New Left.

SEXUAL EQUALITY

The demand of second-wave feminism was for sexual equality – for women to have the same economic, social and political rights as men. A key aim was to complete the drive
begun by an earlier generation of feminists for formal equality before the law. Many legal changes had already been
introduced, or were in the process of being introduced, before
the emergence of the women's liberation movement at the
end of the 1960s. In America, the Equal Pay Act was passed
in 1963 and made it illegal for employers to pay men and
women differently for the same work. In 1964, sexual
discrimination became illegal under Title VII of the Civil
Rights Act. The Act made it unlawful for an employer to 'fail
or refuse to hire or to discharge any individual, or otherwise
to discriminate against any individual with respect to his
compensation, terms, conditions, or privileges of employment, because of such individual's race, color, religion, sex,
or national origin'.[338] In America in the 1960s, it was the
civil rights movement that represented the most significant
demand for social change and many of the legal developments that women benefitted from developed out of a
broader expansion of civil rights.

In 1972, the first black American woman to be elected to
congress, Shirley Chisholm, won the Democratic Party's nom-
ination for President, becoming the first black candidate
to run for president and the first woman to represent the
Democratic Party. Chisholm proudly identified with second
wave feminism; her campaign slogan was 'unbought and
unbossed', the title of her autobiography released two years

previously. Her candidacy provided a focal point for the women's liberation movement but her campaign was underfunded and her principles considered too radical for people at the time. Chisholm later remarked that she experienced more discrimination for being a woman than for being black. Nonetheless, the women's liberation movement emerged into a climate receptive to social change and within the space of a couple of years it became established throughout North America and much of Western Europe.

In Britain too, the passing, if not always the enactment, of equalities legislation coincided with the emergence of the women's movement rather than being brought about directly by it. The Abortion Act was passed in 1967 and the Equal Pay Act in 1970, although it did not come into force until 1975. In the intervening period employers often sought to move women into different roles or to make them redundant altogether, making it easier for them to ignore new legislation and argue that men and women were doing different jobs. This incentivized an even more rigid division between men's and women's work.

The inadequacy of legal changes helped expose the fact that changing the law wasn't enough in and of itself to bring about gender equality. Women didn't just need to be treated exactly the same as men; they also needed additional rights and protections. NOW's key demands were for Title VII of the Civil Rights Act to be enforced; the establishment of a nationwide network of childcare centres and for childcare expenses to be tax deductible for working parents. NOW also campaigned for maternity benefits and a guaranteed right to return to a job and reform of divorce laws.[339] In Britain, the first national women's liberation conference, held in 1970, set out four key demands: for equal pay; equal education and opportunity; 24-hour nurseries and free contraception and abortion on demand.

A conference manifesto explains the perceived causes of women's oppression at this time: 'We are commercially exploited by advertisements, television and press, legally we often have only the status of children. We are brought up to feel inadequate and educated to narrower horizons than men. This is our specific oppression as women.'[340] We can see here the New Left's focus on culture and the media sitting along-side legal and practical demands for change. This dichotomy was to manifest itself in different priorities, for legal change on the one hand and a critique of social and cultural restraints on women on the other hand. Second-wave feminism began to develop in different directions and, much as with earlier campaigns for suffrage, this was a movement that did not take all women along with it.

THE LIMITS OF FORMAL EQUALITY

Meanwhile, the push for new legal rights for women continued. In the US, court cases in 1970 and 1974 ruled that work did not have to be strictly identical but just 'substantially equal' to warrant equal pay and that 'the going market rate' could not be used to justify paying women less. In 1973 a landmark decision by the Supreme Court in the case of *Roe v. Wade* disallowed state and federal restrictions on abortion, making the procedure legal, for women who could access and afford it, up to the point at which the foetus was considered to be viable outside of the womb. A religious and socially conservative movement began to form in opposition to such developments, laying the groundwork for a later culture war between feminists and the political right.

British women won limited reproductive rights six years before their American counterparts, but they needed to wait until the passing of the 1975 Sex Discrimination Act before they were able to apply for almost any job they wanted.[341] Finally, Bella Keyzer, who we met earlier, was able to return to welding 30 years after the end of the Second World War and when she did she saw her weekly wage jump from £27 to £73.[342] For Bella and many other women like her, legislation helped expose where women were being paid less than men for doing the same work and allowed women the freedom to apply for better paying jobs that had previously been denied them. It opened up new career possibilities for girls yet to enter employment.

Unfortunately, changing employment and pay legislation only went so far in closing the gender pay gap. The long history of a gender-segregated labour market meant that cultural attitudes about 'men's work' and 'women's jobs' had become entrenched. This hit women in unskilled jobs the hardest; women 'manual workers' were 'paid at rates little more than half of those for men in similar jobs'.[343] Another reason why legislation only had a limited impact upon the pay gap was because women were still expected to be primarily responsible for home and children. Taking time away from work followed by a part-time return meant that women were often starting from scratch after years away from work rather than returning to the jobs they held before having children. All women, whatever their level of education, found they were left with low-paid and unskilled jobs rather than careers. As we saw in Chapter Three, the legacy of this inequality continues to play out today.

WAGES FOR HOUSEWORK

Awarding men and women equal status within the law was an important move for women's rights, as were additional legal provisions for access to maternity leave and abortion services. But such developments revealed that legal changes alone could not bring an end to women's oppression. This prompted feminists to look beyond the public sphere into the private realm for the source of sexual inequality. Ann Oakley, exploring the role and experiences of the housewife, argued the source of women's oppression lay within their role as wives and mothers and subsequent financial dependency upon their husbands. In many ways this can be seen as a continuation of a line of thinking begun by Engels a century earlier. However, whereas Engels located women's oppression within the institution of the family and not the relationships between people, for Oakley this line is less clear cut. The emerging theory of patriarchy meant that women's oppression within the family was often understood as emanating from the marital relationship between husband and wife.

One solution to this form of oppression was to bring women — and their particular struggles — out of the private sphere and into the public domain. In part this meant a focus on getting women into the workplace, but it also prompted a discussion about the financial value of domestic labour. The activist Selma James was a key proponent of 'wages for housework'. Although it made for a popular slogan, such campaigns never really got off the ground because the private and personal nature of housework and the emotion inherent within caring for a family made putting a price on domestic labour not only impossible but, to many people, distasteful too.

BLURRING PUBLIC AND PRIVATE

The post-war nuclear family had been marked by a strong boundary between public and private, perhaps best symbolized by the picket fence, the net curtains at the window, or the traditional maxim that an Englishman's home is his castle. In an earlier era the house would have been the site of work as well as sustenance and would have been open to extended family members as well as neighbours. But this did not challenge the autonomy of the householder or subject the family to scrutiny from those outside of a closed circle. In the 1970s, the private sphere became so significant for feminists because it was understood not just as a way of organizing society and relationships but also as an ideological means of shaping an individual's consciousness. According to this understanding, bringing about changes in the private sphere and personal relationships would alter the way individuals looked at the world. In turn, this would help bring about social change, rather than, as an earlier generation of Marxists would have had it, the other way around.

The determination to bring discussion of the private sphere into the public realm became a central tenet of second-wave feminism and marks one way in which it is quite distinct from previous iterations. Kate Millett's 1969 work *Sexual Politics* was lauded for bringing the most intimate aspect of personal relationships into the public domain: 'he fucks her as woman, as subject, as chattel'.[344] Sex was no longer the sole source of a woman's fulfilment, as 1950s American housewives were taught to believe. But neither was it a relationship between men and women as equals. As Millett explains, sex was a paradigm for the exercise of men's power over women; the personal had become political.

Carol Hanisch used the phrase 'the personal is political' in a 1969 article in which she discussed the importance of bringing personal, subjective experiences into the public domain. This focus on subjectivity, on an individual's emotional response and personal understanding, came to dominate left-wing thinking in the 1960s. It was a reaction against the totalizing 'grand narratives' that were assumed to have led to

Stalinism on the one hand and fascism on the other. Introducing subjectivity was thought to expand the political realm. Millett argued for a rejection politics as the 'narrow and exclusive world of meetings, chairmen and parties' in favour of a view of politics as 'power-structured relationships, arrangements whereby one group of persons is controlled by another', with sex as the primary mechanism for control.[345] The sociologist Jennie Bristow suggests that this shift to the personal realm became a 'generational subjectivity forged less by relationship with grand narratives and more by a sensibility that the project of history making lay within personal action and experience'.[346]

The project of making the personal political, the aim of consciousness raising groups, was inherently problematic, in that it aimed to create a collective outlook through the sharing of private experiences. But such a focus on the individual revealed only the essential differences at the heart of every woman's private experiences. The middle-class mother with a twice weekly home-help and all modern conveniences faced different problems to the working-class woman who combined looking after her children with shifts in the local factory. The only shared experience was to be found in personal relationships with men. This led to the location of women's oppression within men's collective interests and male behaviour; women's inferior social status was as a result of the patriarchy exercising power.

Patriarchy took a material form; to Millett it was evident in 'the military, industry, technology, universities, science, political office, and finance – in short, every avenue of power within society, including the coercive force of the police, is entirely in male hands'.[347] But more than this, patriarchy became seen as a framework for making sense of women's oppression; the ideology of patriarchy not only shaped relationships between the sexes but formed individual consciousness from the moment of birth, through the family, education, and into the work-place, able to exercise complete control over its subjects. Patriarchal rule was so successful for being able to pass itself off as entirely natural.

Yet feminism needed to go further to explain why, even after consciousness raising, the domestic sphere, and particularly the role of mother, was not experienced by all women as oppressive. Indeed, not all women looked at their husbands going out to work with envy and some had been only too pleased to leave behind tedious and exhausting jobs for the status of mother. In response, Millet describes patriarchal power as 'the most persuasive ideology of our culture' because of its operation primarily through 'interior colonization'.[348] This notion, that patriarchy turned women into willing collaborators in their own oppression, became a significant assertion of second-wave feminism.

A key feature of this interior colonization was, as Oakley explains, the widespread acceptance of the myth that 'femininity and domesticity are equated'.[349] Feminists explored how sexual politics operated through consent coerced at the point of the 'socialization' of both sexes into 'basic patriarchal polities with regard to temperament, role and status'.[350] Girls were, in other words, socialized from childhood to see their future role as wives, homemakers and mothers. As all other ambitions were educated out of them, the fulfilment of their destiny, however inevitable, appeared to be a matter of personal choice.

THE PATRIARCHY

The foundation of second-wave feminism in the politics of experience led to renewed focus on the role of language, images, music, toys, fashion and entertainment to shape a specifically female consciousness and acceptance of subservience. The patriarchal notion of women as secondary to men was thought to be written into every aspect of culture, altering the relationships between the sexes and the very identity of individual men and women. This turn towards culture was perceived as a radical move because it challenged the way in which society was organized. Instead of demanding legal changes so that women could compete as equals in a game designed and operated by men, feminists demanded instead a new way of organizing society along more feminine lines. Rather than women being held to masculine standards and judged by a masculine norm, they argued the norms had to change.

Where an earlier generation of feminists demanded rights so women could reach their true potential as the equals of men, second-wave feminism argued that while women were forced to emulate men they would be permanently judged as inferior. In practice this meant that, as Oakley makes clear, 'Unless the gender role system itself, together with its economic base, is questioned, what women gain in the way of rights is too easily put to the service of men.'[351] The rejection of a masculine norm was taken up by Germaine Greer in *The Female Eunuch*: 'If women understand by emancipation the adoption of the masculine role then we are lost indeed.'[352] She argued that sexual equality, rather than being something to aspire towards, was actually 'an utterly conservative aim', because in taking 'the male status quo as the condition to which women aspire' a woman 'finds herself in an alien and repellent world which changes her fundamentally even as she is struggling to exert the smallest influence on it'.[353] The rejection of a masculine norm was ultimately a rejection of sexual equality in favour of celebrating differences between men and women. Here, second-wave feminists come to share

Elizabeth Cady Stanton's argument that women were not just different but morally superior to men.

Despite the best efforts of socialists to insert a critique of capitalism and the bourgeois family into feminism, the totalizing theory of patriarchy left little room to account for the impact of social class in structuring society and impacting upon experiences and relationships. Some argued that social class was irrelevant to understanding the position of women who were often outside of the workplace and dependent upon first fathers and then husbands for their social position. Millett went further and argued that, under patriarchy, the concept of class was a mere distraction, designed to 'set one woman against another'.[354]

By the mid-1970s, women had achieved some significant legal victories that saw their position in society transformed from what it had been a century earlier. Second-wave feminism's recognition that these legal changes were not in themselves enough to bring about women's liberation was a significant insight. The exploration of the role played by the family, the workplace, relationships and culture in the socialization of men and women and the naturalization of sexual differences also represented an important political understanding. However, the blurring of the private and the public and with it an attempt to focus on women's subjective experiences proved more problematic; the rejection of a 'masculine norm', leading inevitably to a celebration of women's difference, places feminism in a bind.

CONCLUSIONS

Feminism, with its demand for women's liberation, consciousness raising workshops and apocryphal tales of bra burning, burst upon a suburban and conservative society and shook it to the core. Or at least, that's as legend would have it. Certainly, the idea that patriarchal power was exercised in the home gave once private issues a public airing and helped expose the continued nature of women's oppression. In casting a new focus on women's personal experiences and intimate relationships, feminism drew attention to reproductive rights, childcare and housework. However, while campaigns for sexual equality aimed, at least in theory, to improve life for everyone, pitching men as the cause of women's problems eroded the possibility of men and women finding common cause. But challenges to tradition and to the universalism inherent within a concept of such as equal rights were already well underway before feminism's second incarnation.

Despite resistance from those who felt their position to be most threatened, feminism in the 1970s was less revolutionary than is sometimes portrayed and, in many ways, it met a receptive political climate. It was precisely because second-wave feminism emerged into a period when an older set of values was already being discredited that it had such a profound impact. The Enlightenment notions of instrumental reason, scientific progress and mankind's domination over nature were thought to have contributed to the horrors of the Second World War; the obsession with taxonomy, eugenics and man's domination over man were assumed to lead logically and ultimately to the holocaust. Feminism's further challenge to a patriarchal social order pushed at an open door.

In the 1970s, traditional values were being called into question but a new sense of purpose, a new driving force to shape society and institutions such as government, education, trade unions, the workplace and the family, had yet to be consolidated. Feminism provided a moral framework to fill this void not by defeating old arguments so much as through articulating alternative values that matched the needs of an economic system beginning to decline. Whereas the golden age of capitalism, the long post-war boom, called for physical labour, competitiveness, intellectual risk taking and demanded the emotional separation of workers from mechanized and alienating production processes, the recession of the early 1970s called for an acceptance of the limits to economic growth, an emphasis on leisure rather than work and on consumption rather than production. The emerging economic climate required people to be customer focused, empathetic and environmentally conscious. These new values found their clearest expression within a feminism that emphasized women's essential differences to men, and celebrated their caring maternalism and apparent closeness to nature.

The challenge to feminism at this time came primarily from those with something to lose, not only from men of all social classes who perceived their livelihoods and social position to be under threat but also from more socially conservative women. The American religious right, which became increasingly influential throughout the 1970s, emphasized traditional family values and opposition to abortion. However, significant challenges to second-wave feminism emerged from within the women's movement itself and this will provide the focus for the next chapter.

CHAPTER NINE

THE PERSONAL IS POLITICAL

As we saw in the previous chapter, feminism is often contradictory. On one hand, there is an assumption that men and women are equal and potentially, with different socialization than today, the same. On the other hand, there is a celebration of women as different from men, with specifically feminine values that make them more nurturing and caring. On one hand, there is a focus on women's individual achievements in education and in the workplace; on the other, an assumption that women are collaborative, a sisterhood. There is a focus on gender, exploring what it means to be a woman, and at the same time a desire to move beyond gender altogether, or, most recently, define it as a fluid concept that is more to do with how a person feels than their biology. It is argued that women are a class with interests in common but there is also recognition that women's experiences vary according to their age, race, social class, disability and sexuality. Many of these contradictions were present in the earliest incarnations of the women's movement. From the 1970s, particularly with the working out of the second-wave mantra that the personal is political, these tensions came ever more to the fore.

Today, campaigners and theorists alike tell us there is not one feminism but instead there are many different forms of feminism: from radical to liberal feminism, black feminism to lesbian feminism, from intersectional to the derogatory 'white' feminism. It seems the particular label is all important: it does more than just describe a political position; it speaks to a woman's sense of identity. Many of these different feminisms have emerged not through campaigning and reshaping political allegiances but through academic debates within universities. Higher education has become the primary site for the development of feminist theory and ideas generated in the conference hall and seminar room overflow and influence the practice and discussion of feminism outside of the academy. This chapter explores how the feminisms that emerged in the 1970s have influenced current thinking about intersectionality and identity politics, leading to third- and fourth-wave feminism.

WOMEN IN THE ACADEMY

In Britain, the number of women students entering higher education grew steadily in the decades after the Second World War and by the late 1960s women comprised a significant proportion of postgraduate students, researchers, academics and senior administrators. In America, for reasons discussed in the first part of this book, an increase in the number of women students only really began to occur in the early 1970s. In 1972, Title IX of the Education Amendments Act was passed, which protected students from discrimination on the basis of sex in educational programs that receive federal financial assistance and in 1974 the Women's

Educational Equity Act (WEEA) was enacted. Such legislation no doubt accelerated the pace of change, but women were, by this point, already entering even the once most carefully guarded bastions of male academic privilege.

The increase in the number of women in universities at the same time as feminism was becoming increasingly influential brought the women's liberation movement into higher education. However, this development was certainly not welcomed with open arms. Male-dominated universities were steeped in tradition and many scholars, particularly within the humanities, saw their role as conserving a national cultural heritage. The presence of women was considered a threat to academic standards, the standing of the university and the intellectual life of the nation. It was only when admitting women was considered to be in the best interests of the university that practice began to shift. Although institutions were slow to change, a younger generation of academics had already begun to question not just who should go to university but what should be taught and why. This was most explicit in the new field of sociology of education where the role of universities in credentializing the cultural capital of the upper class as objectively superior knowledge and thereby reproducing a social elite became widely discussed.

The questioning of academic tradition that began in the 1960s was not prompted by feminism so much as the growing challenge to Enlightenment values epitomized by the discrediting of positivism, an approach to research that suggested people and society could be understood according to logical scientific principles. Critical theorists, such as Frankfurt School scholars like Theodor Adorno, Max Horkheimer and Jurgen Habermas, became increasingly influential within the humanities and called for culture, and especially literature, to be understood in relation to the social, political and ideological context in which it was produced.

Cultural knowledge, according to this understanding, was simply a reflection of the power relations that gave rise to it; the purpose of study became to expose the way in which the culture industry colluded in maintaining the capitalist status quo. While critics of positivism challenged the possibility of knowledge bringing people closer to truth and the desirability of objectivity in research, critical theorists likewise argued truth was an illusory reflection of power.[355] When scholarship became separated from Enlightenment values such as truth, objectivity and rationality, it was left hollowed out and in search of a purpose. This made it receptive to feminist thought.

A MALE-DOMINATED CURRICULUM

The impact of the women's liberation movement was first felt in universities as a challenge to the content of the curriculum. Women questioned the composition of the canon in literature and demanded greater representation for women writers. There was a move to uncover 'forgotten' women whose work was argued to be of an equivalent quality to men's but had not been recognized. This prompted a useful discussion about literary quality, the taken-for-granted nature of the canon and the role of higher education in preserving a national cultural heritage. This initial demand for female equality was a challenge to institutions to 'fulfil the promises of liberal education'.[356] Outside of academia, second-wave feminism's focus on the role of the private sphere in sustaining women's oppression led to a demand for social science disciplines to give greater prominence to topics such as marriage, housework and family relationships, sexuality and mental health.[357] This questioning of the curriculum was useful and led to a broadening of the scope of subjects such as sociology.

Many established academics were reluctant to embrace change and tinkering with the curriculum could only go so far in bringing about the changes feminists wanted to see within higher education. For this reason, Women's Studies developed outside of traditional disciplines. It began at Cornell University in 1969 and quickly spread to other universities throughout America in the 1970s and Britain in the 1980s. Developing outside of established disciplinary practice gave those involved in Women's Studies much more freedom to investigate not just new topics but also new research methods.

ACADEMIC FEMINISM

Feminists within universities brought the second-wave lesson that the personal is political to the heart of academic work. This went beyond seeking greater representation for women or broadening the range of topics covered and prompted a far more fundamental questioning of what counted as knowledge and whose knowledge was being legitimized within the university. Feminist scholars influenced by critical theory argued that existing assumptions about knowledge presented a masculine standard as universal and patriarchal power relations as fixed and natural: or, as feminist scholars point out, 'malestream understandings and knowledge constructions may well be hegemonic'.[358] This view developed within an intellectual climate that was already beginning to question whether the aspiration of scholarship towards truth and objectivity was either possible or desirable.

Feminist scholars argued that aiming for objectivity in research and judgement was little more than a mask for presenting masculine beliefs, values and assumptions as universal. According to this line of argument, women's interests were best served not by better, or more objective research, but by abandoning false claims to objectivity and neutrality altogether. Instead, feminists argued for a new epistemology that would position researchers as gendered 'situated knowers', where both what is known and, significantly, the way it is known, 'reflects the situation or perspective of the knower'.[359] This emphasis on standpoint brings a new subjectivity to academic work. Not only does it help bring women's experiences to the fore but, of far more consequence for the nature of scholarship, it positions truth as dependent upon context and an individual's perspective. Claims of objectivity, truth and neutrality come to be rejected as simply reflections of power relations.

Understanding truth as multiple and perspectival calls for research methods that can get to the heart of personal experiences and understandings. This led to a new emphasis on qualitative research methods and, in particular, a search for methods that could upend the power relationship that existed between researcher and subject. Interviews became less structured and more an opportunity for academics to 'give voice' to groups whose experiences were previously not considered worthy of academic study. Narrative, life history and biographical research methods became recognized as important means of allowing women to tell their own stories. Recognizing the subjective element in research was not an impetus to transcending it; objectivity was seen as a masculine contrivance. Instead, giving voice or story-telling became an end in itself. This shift towards the subjective in the classroom led to the development of pedagogical approaches that mimicked the consciousness raising groups taking off outside the academy. Students were asked to recount their personal experiences, feelings and emotions and were, in turn, taught that these subjective states were of more significance than objective analysis of data.

The assumption that claims to objectivity were a mask to conceal patriarchal power led to the belief, shared with critical theorists, that all knowledge was ideology and all culture essentially political. As such, literature was viewed as a reflection of the 'perspectives and ideals of its creators'.[360] According to this way of thinking, work by men dominated the canon not because it was intellectually superior but because it matched the ideological prejudices of those responsible for constructing the school exam syllabus and the university curriculum. This called into question not just the content of the canon but the view that some works of literature could be judged to be qualitatively better than others. What was needed were multiple canons so that women's work could be valued in its own terms rather than according to masculine standards. A feminist canon would not be any less political, it was argued, but would amplify previously marginalized voices. In the style of Millet's *Sexual Politics*, texts were judged to be valuable not on the basis of their literary merit but for the lessons they could offer readers about the workings of patriarchy.

Feminism's challenge to traditional bodies of knowledge and the drive to legitimize the study of new topics and new authors, new research methods and new approaches to pedagogy meant that educational goals easily became blurred with more explicitly political aims. Indeed, attempts to separate education from politics were considered disingenuous. Feminism's strength lay in its candour; it did not make false claims to neutrality: it aimed to expose 'the deep power relationships between men and women'.[361] One feminist scholar describes the goal of Women's Studies as being 'to challenge political ideas, to transform women's positions in social and public life, questioning their confinement to the family'.[362]

FEMINISM AND POST-MODERNISM

A feminism that questioned objectivity and truth claims sat comfortably alongside a turn towards post-modernism within the academy. Both had 'uncovered the political power of the academy and of knowledge claims'.[363] Both shared a disdain for the Enlightenment notion of universalism. The American philosopher and gender theorist Judith Butler argues: 'I tend to conceive of the claim of "universality" in exclusively negative and exclusionary terms.'[364] Whereas the rationality of the Enlightenment demanded a separation of ideas and self, under the influence of feminism this gave way to the view that such a separation was anathema to good research which situated the researcher, and her emotional responses, firmly within the research.

The argument that all knowledge is a reflection of its originator challenges the view that men and women make sense of the world in the same way. Instead, feminists contend, ways of knowing are gender specific and men and women make sense of the world in different ways, their subjective experiences leading them to different understandings. The assumption that women have a 'specifically gendered consciousness'[365] positions them firmly within a subjective and emotional domain. The quantitative, rational and logical are rejected as outdated and inherently disingenuous. As Daphne Patai and Noretta Koertge explain in *Professing Feminism*, 'Logic, the analysis of arguments, quantitative reasoning, objective evaluation of evidence, fair minded consideration of opposing views – modes of thinking central to intellectual life – were dismissed as masculinist contrivances that served only to demean and oppress women.'[366]

Academic feminists argue that not only do men and women have different life experiences but, more significantly, the qualitative and subjective way in which they experience the world is different too. There is no common or objective reality, shared by men and women alike. Instead, women's understandings and interpretations of the world lead them to a different reality, though one that is forever destined to be expressed in what Australian feminist Dale Spender refers to as 'manmade language'. Spender argues women need to 'reclaim language' in order to rediscover their own knowledge. 'Feminism,' she contends, 'refers to the alternative meanings put forward by feminists.'[367] As socialist feminist Lynne Segal wryly observes, this takes us a long way from tackling the practical obstacles women encountered on the road to equality. Instead, women's oppression becomes reduced to the expression of a set of ideas.

It was a short leap from arguing that men and women had different ways of understanding the world to arguing that women's ways of knowing were superior. Radical feminists such as Adrienne Rich claim that women's bodies, the monthly menstrual cycle and the ability to give birth and feed a baby, bring them closer to nature than men. Others argue that patriarchal social relations which privilege men prevent them from having an unbiased view of reality. Women's experiences of subordination, on the other hand, give them an understanding more grounded in sensitivity to the emotional realm. Sandra Harding argues a 'feminist vantage point' is 'more illuminating than any existing vantage point'.[368] Women, having experienced reproductive as well as productive labour, are able to develop 'a more objective viewpoint than men who have more restricted experience and more to gain from hiding the truth'.[369]

In locating claims for intellectual insight within women's experiences of subordination, feminist scholars were drawing a direct link between oppression and access to knowledge. Women's status as 'situated knowers' is celebrated in comparison to those who seek knowledge 'ruled by phallogocentrism' and 'disembodied vision'. Instead, feminist researchers 'seek those ruled by partial sight and limited voice' in order to access 'the connections and unexpected openings situated knowledge makes possible'.[370] It is women's status as victims of patriarchy that affords them superior insight: oppression leads women to develop a superior value system and more finely tuned sense of morality. Sandra Lee Bartky describes feminist consciousness as a 'consciousness of victimization'.[371] By this logic, the most victimized sections of society are those with the best understandings of the world.

Establishing a link between intellectual insight and oppression paves the way for more oppressed groups to trump the claims of feminist scholars in a process of identity-driven one-upmanship. As a result, feminist scholars become committed to maintaining women's status as victims and with every social and political advance made they are forced to seek out new sites of inequality. Patai and Koertge argue that such logic indicates 'women who do not feel crippled by sexism must "learn" that in fact they were − and are − victims of this cultural offense'.[372]

LANGUAGE CONSTRUCTS GENDER

The post-modern view of language as shaping not just interpretations of reality but reality itself led to the major intellectual assertion of academic feminism that gender itself is a social construction. The separation of gender from sex came to dominate feminist scholarship in the late 1980s and early 1990s. Christina Hoff Sommers notes, 'the "sex/gender system" became the "controlling insight" of academic feminism' and, once made visible, 'we can see it everywhere'.[373] Literature and language were implicated in the social construction of gender. Butler explores the idea of gender as a 'performance' in her 1990 book *Gender Trouble* in which she argues that the whole notion of biological sex difference 'is a discursive formation that acts as a naturalized foundation for the nature/culture distinction and the strategies of domination that the distinction supports'.[374]

Butler questions the existence of a binary concept of 'natural' sex preceding and underpinning an 'artificial' gender. Rather than being a fixed category, whether socially or naturally determined, Butler sees gender as a fluid concept that is defined only in relation to what it is not: 'a complexity whose totality is permanently deferred'.[375] Just as gender cannot be counterposed to sex, neither can man be counterposed to woman. Butler wants to move away from 'the presumption of a binary gender system' which she considers 'implicitly retains the belief in a mimetic relation of gender to sex whereby gender mirrors sex or is otherwise restricted by it'.[376] She argues, 'There is no gender identity behind the expressions of gender.' To this end, Butler sees gender as 'always a doing' rather than a fixed position. The consequences of this argument are explored in Chapter Ten.

Academic feminism holds two opposing positions. We are told that women experience the world differently to men and, furthermore, this experience of subordination affords them superior insight. At the same time, we are told that the category 'woman' is a social construction and individual understandings vary according to perspective. This subjective turn leads inevitably to the realization that women have little in common with each other. Not only is there no shared identity grounded in biology; what's more, women's understandings vary according to their social class, political outlook, race and sexuality. This raised a problem for feminism. Mitchell and Oakley explain: 'If woman cannot be fixed as an identity beyond the biological female, neither can feminism have a unified definition.'[377] Attempts at resolving the tension between the privileging of the subjective and the goal of representing the collective interests of all women absorbed feminists throughout the 1970s and 1980s.

The recognition that women's experiences are diverse effectively ends the possibility of one united women's movement. In reality, feminism has always been divided between those who argue for sexual equality (labelled by Hoff Sommers as 'equity' feminists) and those who emphasize women's differences from men ('gender' feminists). Campaigns for suffrage and reproductive rights successfully masked such differences: legislation could allow for the realization of equality or it could permit women's superior feminine virtues to improve society. Feminism had never represented a coherent ideological approach to understanding society but by the end of the 1970s it could no longer even pretend to have this goal.

FEMINISM DIVIDED

Differences emerged first between liberal, socialist and radical feminism, each claiming different causes of women's oppression and promoting alternative solutions.[378] Although this splintering appeared to be new, in many ways the labels simply made explicit differences that had been present within the women's movement from its inception. Whereas liberal feminism promoted rights for the individual woman within an existing capitalist society, socialist feminists looked at the collective oppression experienced by women and argued sexual equality could only be achieved within a society organized according to socialist principles. Radical feminism positions gender rather than social class as the key divide within society; it 'celebrates women's superior virtue and spirituality and decries "male" violence and technology'.[379]

For feminists in the late 1970s and early 1980s, definitions became all important. But the more feminism was defined in relation to women's personal experiences, the more multiple it became. Some, such as Rosalind Delmar, expressed frustration with this fracturing: 'instead of internal dialogue there is a naming of the parts: there are radical feminists, socialist feminists, Marxist feminists, lesbian separatists, women of colour, and so on.'[380] However, with the privileging of subjectivity, this separation appeared unstoppable.

In the 1980s, the same accusation developed force from those within and outside of the women's movement. Liberal, radical and socialist feminism alike were charged with presenting the experiences of white, Western women as universal and failing to account for the additional disadvantages faced by women outside of this narrow elite.[381] As Nancy Cott explains, 'Only women holding culturally hegemonic values and positions — that is, in the United States, women who are white, heterosexual, middle class, politically mid-stream — have the privilege (or deception) of seeing their condition as that of "woman" and glossing over their other characteristics.'[382]

Traditional feminism was criticized for being unable to explain the experience of imperialism in the oppression of women in the less developed world or the combined impact of sexism and racism encountered by black women in the West. In *An Open Letter to Mary Daly*, Audre Lorde noted that 'beyond sisterhood is still racism'. 'The oppression of women knows no ethnic nor racial boundaries,' she argued, 'but that does not mean that it is identical within those boundaries. Nor do the reservoirs of our ancient power know these boundaries, either. To deal with one without even alluding to the other is to distort our commonality as well as our difference.'[383] Black feminists forged a movement that would recognize both race and class as feminist issues which intersected with gender to compound oppression.

Within universities, the subjective turn initially left largely unanswered the question of how and why people experienced the world in different ways. The political theorist Iris Marion Young suggests that 'a person's particular sense of history, understanding of social relations and personal possibilities, her or his mode of reasoning, values, and expressive styles are constituted at least partly by her or his group identity'.[384] This focus on group identity risks a return to the view that women all experience the world in the same way; Young's answer was to expand both the range and the number of groups to which individuals could belong.

The academic climate that was receptive to feminism also welcomed new ideas about race, and critical race theory emerged first in the field of legal scholarship. Critical race theory challenged traditional approaches to legal scholarship, in particular, the liberal notion of civil rights. It critiqued liberalism for presenting racism as an aberration rather than a 'normal' state of society under white hegemony. This 'normality' occurs because, as one critical race theorist puts it, 'Whites have been the primary beneficiaries of civil rights legislation.'[385] Critical race theory and feminism share an assumption that the lived experience of subordination can best be uncovered through centring the subjective and privileging personal narratives in academic research. In addition, the rejection of objectivity leads, in both instances, to avowedly political aims.[386]

INTERSECTIONALITY

The focus on lived experience assumes only black people can ever have 'experiential knowledge' of racism. Just as feminism asserts that men and women do not share a common perception of reality, likewise critical race theory assumes that black and white people have no shared reality either. One critical race theorist notes that towards the end of the 1980s, 'Scholars of color within the left began to ask their white colleagues to examine their own racism and to develop oppositional critiques not just to dominant conceptions of race and racism but to the treatment of race within the left as well.'[387] The positioning of race and gender as mutually exclusive categories, particularly when no account was taken of social class, created 'complex problems of exclusion and distortion for women of color'.[388] The solution, proposed by critical race theorists, was to present 'racism not as isolated instances of conscious bigoted decision making or prejudiced practice, but as larger, systemic, structural, and cultural, as deeply psychological and socially ingrained'.[389]

The term intersectionality was coined by the African American critical legal scholar Kimberlé Crenshaw to articulate the 'dual vulnerability' experienced by women of colour. 'On the simplest level,' Crenshaw tells us, 'an intersectional framework uncovers how the dual positioning of women of color as women and as members of a subordinated racial group bears upon violence committed against us.'[390] She initially conceived of intersectionality as a provisional means of combining politics with post-modern theory. Its political expediency lay in its explanation of how 'political and representational practices relating to race and gender interrelate'.[391] Crenshaw distinguishes structural intersectionality, 'the material consequences of the interaction of these multiple hierarchies in the lives of women of color', from representational intersectionality, or the way that race and gender images 'converge to create unique and specific narratives deemed appropriate for women of color'.[392] The combined impact of structural and representational intersectionality was often the 'erasing women of color'.[393]

The theory of intersectionality has been taken on board by scholars and activists looking to explore not just intersections of gender, race and class, but also sexuality, age and ability. Not all of these features of a person's identity are necessarily permanent; some might be temporary or transient states. What's important is not that these intersections are simply added together but instead that they combine with and constitute each other.[394] In this way, intersectional feminism maintains a focus on women while at the same time practising its key assertion that women are not a homogenous group. Intersectional feminists argue that disabled women, transwomen, black women, working class and LGBTQ women not only experience the world in different ways but, more significantly, face multiple layers of intersecting oppression.

The popular website *Everyday Feminism* explains the attraction of intersectionality as 'a frame that recognizes the multiple aspects of identity that enrich our lives and experiences and that compound and complicate oppressions and marginalizations'. Although women can no longer be considered a homogenous group, and there is no concept of universal rights to strive for, all women can locate themselves within this prism of oppression; everyone has multiple aspects of identity. Indeed, the primacy of identity means that for intersectional feminists, unlike radical feminists, identifying as a woman is distinct from and more important than the biological status of being female (or cis-gendered). Crucially, feminism that is not intersectional stands accused of ignoring 'women's overlapping identities – including race, class, ethnicity, religion and sexual orientation' and how they 'impact the way they experience oppression and discrimination'.[395] With this we return to the concept of 'spirit murder' and, in order to prevent this, the practice of intersectional feminism becomes most preoccupied with the act of listening.

Just as with feminism, the premise of intersectionality means it can never provide a solution to the problems it asks us to observe. In its emphasis on the personal, lived experience of oppression, it constructs a barrier, an intersectional framework that prevents people transcending their experiences or campaigning for the liberation of those who are not like them. Instead, all those outside of a particular intersection can do is listen, all the while constructing their own framework of overlapping oppressions. There are no collective aspirations or shared political goals that unite all women. There is no common humanity or 'sisterhood' but neither is there the rugged individual of liberalism. Instead, as academic Helen Pluckrose explores, there is the group, and it is group identity that becomes all important.[396] Intersectionality holds no promise of liberation from group membership towards membership of the shared category 'human'.

THE PROBLEM WITH INTERSECTIONALITY

Group identity obliterates individuality in the assumption not only that all members share a common experience and wish to label themselves accordingly but also that they share a political outlook. In focusing on the group, intersectionality elides key differences between people; and biology once again becomes the defining feature of a person and a causal explanation for their social status. This follows logically from Catharine Mackinnon's 1979 assertion that 'white males have long been advantaged precisely on racial and sexual grounds, differentially favoured in employment and education *because* they were white and male. To intervene to alter this balance of advantage is not discrimination in reverse, but

a chance for equal consideration for the first time.'[397] This is
an argument for equality that entrenches the biological differences between people as insurmountable; it gives rise to the
popular demand that people — particularly white men —
need to 'check their privilege' before speaking, or in other
words, to shut up. Dialogue across separate intersectional
frameworks becomes impossible.

MacKinnon makes clear the connection between 'maleness' and power. As Daphne Patai notes, if men are always
powerful, '"Victims" by contrast, are always innocent and by
definition weak.'[398] This points to a further problem of intersectional feminism: in defining people according to multiple
measures of oppression it sets in place a hierarchy, where
some identities are judged more worthy of recognition than
others. The insult of 'white feminism' is attached to non-
intersectional feminism that, in the words of one writer,
'really only helps white people'. 'White feminism', its critics
argue, overlooks class, race and sexuality and assumes 'that
women being equal means that all women face identical
struggles, regardless of racial identity'.[399] Here we see the
limitations of intersectional feminism made clear: it demands
not just ideological but biological purity and thereby returns
us to outdated and prejudiced beliefs in naturalized differences. It ties people into a victimhood associated with group
identity; it undervalues both the universal human experience
and, at the same time, individual freedom and autonomy.

Intersectional feminism arose when the differences between
women became more prominent than the common experience
of womanhood. In order for feminism to survive it needed to
find a way that could account for differences at the same time
as presenting a specifically gendered experience of oppression.
Feminism succeeded through first finding a common enemy
for women: not in men individually but in male psychology,
masculinity, exercised through patriarchy and expressed in

culture. Then, in intersectionality, feminism found a way to see women as a collective with interests in common while simultaneously acknowledging overlapping aspects of their identity that could combine and compound oppression in different ways. However, some women, even those who consider themselves to be feminists, refuse to buy into this narrative of female oppression and to locate themselves within an intersectional framework. The only way intersectional feminism can account for this is to argue against a link between sex and gender. This has the additional advantage of expanding the category of women to encompass men who identify as women.

An opposition emerges between intersectional feminism and white feminism based not on identity so much as viewpoint which, in turn, sets in place a policing of women's speech. When the Nigerian writer Chimamanda Ngozi Adichie commented that transwomen had not had the same life experiences as women who were born female she came in for criticism from feminists who sought to defend the intersectional orthodoxy.[400] Her previously elevated position within intersectional feminism, premised upon her being a woman, black and from a developing country, was hastily rescinded.

THIRD-WAVE FEMINISM

Since Kimberlé Crenshaw's 1989 article, 'Demarginalizing the intersection of race and sex',[401] the working out of ideas around intersectionality within the academy has been reflected in the broader feminist movement outside of universities. New thinking in feminism began to coalesce around the label 'third wave' in the late 1980s and early 1990s. Rebecca Walker, the daughter of author Alice Walker, is credited with having coined the term third-wave feminism in a 1992 essay that ends with the declaration: 'I am not a post-feminism feminist. I am the Third Wave.'[402]

Walker's essay, written when she was 22 years old, explores the continued need for feminism in the face of what she describes as a backlash against the movement: 'The backlash against U.S. women is real. As the misconception of equality between the sexes becomes more ubiquitous, so does the attempt to restrict the boundaries of women's personal and political power.' Furthermore, Walker spells out her frustration with the civil rights movement: 'When will progressive black men prioritize my rights and well-being? When will they stop talking so damn much about 'the race' as if it revolved exclusively around them?'[403] The early 1990s saw an increase in work reflecting on the relationship between gender and race as overlapping sources of oppression. A 1994 anthology, *The Third Wave: Feminist Perspectives on Racism* was typical in focusing upon strategies for challenging racism from a feminist perspective and, in particular, giving voice to women of colour.

Walker recognized a need for both feminism and the civil rights movement, but as a young, non-heterosexual woman of colour, she argued that neither spoke to the specificity of her experiences. As a result, she launched an activist collective called Third Wave:

> *Third Wave is a member-driven multiracial, multi-cultural, multi-sexuality national non-profit organization devoted to feminist and youth activism for change. Rather than focusing on specific goals to bring about legal change for the benefit of individuals, Third Wave aimed primarily to be inclusive; By using our experiences as a starting point we can create a diverse community and cultivate a meaningful response.*[404]

Third-wave feminism begins from two quite disingenuous assumptions. Firstly, it assumes that earlier incarnations of feminism had nothing to say about the experiences of black women. But this is not true: in America the original women's movement emerged out of and worked closely alongside campaigns for abolition. As Raquel Rosario Sanchez, writing on *Feminist Current* explains, 'The women's rights movement has existed for over a century, and extends across countries and time periods. It is not accurate to assume that until the term 'intersectional feminism' came along in the U.S., the women's movement cared only about the needs and concerns of white, Western, upper-class women.'[405] The second misconception, apparent in the name 'third wave', is that there was a distinct break between the different schools of feminist thought. Just as the notion of a hiatus between first- and second-wave feminism is a myth premised on the equation of feminism with a women's movement, likewise there is no gap in feminist activity or theory between the second and third wave.

Feminism did not grind to a halt in the 1980s. It continued; most prominently in radical feminist campaigns against pornography led by Dworkin and MacKinnon in the US and in socialist feminism in the UK. Lesbian feminism and black feminism also became well established in this decade. Within the academy, as we have seen, feminism's meeting with postmodernism led to a focus on culture and the workings of language. Feminism in the 1980s became far more fragmented and by the end of the decade it was difficult to talk of a coherent feminist movement but this certainly did not mean that feminist thought was on pause.

BACKLASH MYTHS

Third-wave feminists, as we see with Walker, often describe themselves as responding to a perceived backlash against feminism. Susan Faludi, in her 1992 book *Backlash*, argues that by the end of the 1980s there was a sense of women's gains being reversed. She suggests that what was making women unhappy was not, as was being suggested at the time, equality, but the rising pressure to halt that nascent equality. There is indeed some truth in the notion of a backlash to feminism at this time. Criticisms came in particular from a socially conservative religious right which saw feminism as a threat to the traditional patriarchal family. Faludi notes, 'The most recent round of backlash first surfaced in the late 1970s on the fringes, among the evangelical right. ... By the mid-eighties, as resistance to women's rights acquired political and social acceptability, it passed into popular culture.'[406] These ideas were taken on board by Conservative politicians in the UK who campaigned around 'back to basics' family values and an American Republican party that made political capital out of opposition to abortion. There was a perception in some sections of the media at this time that feminism had served its purpose — that women had equal rights because they were able to go out to work and university and could, at least in theory, compete with men on a level playing field.

However, the backlash Faludi describes was taking place at the same time as women were continuing to make significant inroads into education, work and politics. Feminist ideas were becoming far more influential than ever before and gaining widespread acceptance among the labour movement, major political parties, national governments and within the management of institutions such as schools and colleges. In many ways the backlash can be seen as a response to this success; for the first time feminism is perceived as a serious threat to the status quo.

Third-wave feminism may appear to be a response to a backlash but in many ways this presentation is misleading. It overstates the opposition to feminism and downplays the successes women were achieving. Third-wave feminism can itself be seen as a backlash against earlier incarnations of second-wave feminism that placed a priority on legal equality and stood accused of working only in the interests of white, middle class, heterosexual and able-bodied women. This appears most clearly in third-wave feminism's vocal rejection of 'liberal' feminists like Katie Roiphe, Camille Paglia and Christina Hoff Sommers who argued that women were not the victims radical feminism considered them to be.

A GENERATIONAL CONSCIOUSNESS

Third-wave feminism prioritized the experiences of young, non-heterosexual women, women of colour, working-class women and transwomen. However, in creating space for the experiences of different groups of women, third-wave feminism built upon many of the ideas that had been established by later second-wave feminists, in particular the centrality of subjectivity and personal experience. Third-wave feminism does not, therefore, mark a clean break from an older feminism, but it does develop a distinct generational consciousness, perhaps expressed most succinctly in the title of a 2001 anthology edited by Barbara Findlen: *Listen Up: Voices from the Next Feminist Generation*.

The editors of *Third Wave Agenda* similarly describe themselves as, 'gathering the voices of young activists struggling to come to terms with the historical specificity of our feminisms and with the times in which we came of age (the late 1970s through the late 1980s)'.[407] Here, the term 'third wave' is used quite specifically to refer to women born between 1963 and 1973; elsewhere it correlates more loosely to Generation X. Some consider third-wave feminism to have been superseded by a fourth wave while others still use the term third wave seemingly as a synonym for 'young people's feminism'.

Many self-professed third-wave writers are quick to stress the specificity of their generational experience in relation to feminism. They argue they grew up with, to use Hoff Sommer's terms, 'equity feminism', a view that women and men were equal, but then, at college, 'got victim feminism' along with post-structuralism. Rather than opting for one or the other, third-wave feminists set out to create 'a feminism that strategically combines elements of these feminisms, along with black feminism, working-class feminism, pro-sex feminism, and so on'.[408] Elsewhere the generational experience is expressed in relation to the labour market. For early second-wave feminists getting a job was considered to be a conscious choice involving a rejection of domesticity and therefore a feminist act; for younger women, on the other hand, work is a financial necessity and not a choice. However, it is argued that although the vast majority of women work nowadays, the jobs they have are primarily low paid and insecure.

The mass movement of women into work that occurred between second- and third-wave feminism has shifted attention away from the position of women in the home and the source of women's oppression as lying within the financial dependency and drudgery of the housewife role. The third-wave focus on youth meant that the particular issues concerning older women and mothers were often overlooked. Instead oppression came to be seen more as a result of culture and personal relationships – again, ideas that started to develop under second-wave feminism. The separation between the realms of political activism and cultural production was contested and culture came to be seen as inherently political.[409] Sexual politics became a key feature of the culture wars. According to this way of thinking, craft, art, music, even fashion and make-up were interpreted as forms of political expression. Women were considered to be divided less by social class and more by the lifestyle choices they made.

Third-wave feminism shared with second wave a focus on power as played out in relations between men and women but whereas for an earlier generation this translated into a critique of capitalism, now capitalism became seen as just one among many of the factors contributing to women's oppression. The focus on patriarchy became more dominant as a source of subjugation experienced by women in common and distinct from men. In this way second- and third-wave feminism share an exclusive focus on women: it is women's rights that are promoted, not human rights.

WOMAN AS OBJECT AND SUBJECT

The move from second- to third-wave feminism consolidates the idea of women not just as object of feminism but as the subject of feminism too. With the privileging of the subjective that emerged from within the academy, third-wave feminism comes to be ever more closely associated with a gender specific way of thinking and of experiencing the world. To be a third-wave feminist is not just to advocate for women's rights but to have a particular consciousness emerging from gendered experience. It is argued that third-wave feminism involves, 'the development of modes of thinking that can come to terms with the multiple, constantly shifting bases of oppression in relation to the multiple, interpenetrating axes of identity'.[410] But when the development of these modes of thinking is made contingent upon a lived experience of oppression then it is an accomplishment only some can achieve.

Whereas Simone de Beauvoir described feminists as women or men who fight to change the position of women, by the mid-1980s feminism had become a 'gender-specific' way of thinking created by, for, and on behalf of, women. As Rosalind Delmar notes, perceiving of women as both subject and object, 'can produce a circular, self-confirming rhetoric and a hermetic closure of thought. The feminine subject becomes trapped by the dynamics of self-reflectivity within the narcissism of the mirror image.'[411] The product of this narcissistic self-reflection can be seen in writing by third-wave feminists that 'relies on personal anecdote for definitional and argumentative strategies'.[412] In the second wave, feminism became associated with the women's movement; in the third-wave feminism came to be identified with women: to be a woman was to be a feminist and to oppose feminism — or at least one dominant idea of it — was to be anti-women.

The combined focus on both subjectivity and inclusion in third-wave feminism throws up problems for political activity when the lived experiences and the political interests of group members are disparate. Bell hooks, a leading light in third-wave feminism discusses one solution, 'Rather than thinking we would come together as "women" in an identity-based bonding, we might be drawn together rather by a commonality of feeling.'[413] This focus on feeling and emotion explains why facts about women's lives have little impact upon the view that women are victims. The existence of the pay gap and rape culture has become an article of faith that feminists 'feel' to be true. The emphasis on shared emotional responses shapes the third-wave approach to activism and theorizing through personal anecdote and collaboration. Rather than formulating specific campaign objectives which may exclude some members, feminist praxis, 'a political position in which "knowledge" is not simply defined as "knowledge *what*" but as "knowledge *for*"'[414] is developed through 'coalition politics'. The therapeutic ethos of the consciousness raising group is replicated and transformed into a model for political action.

The more third-wave feminism acknowledges the differences between women, the more it is forced to promote gender as the unifying category around which coalitions of those who share a 'commonality of feeling' can form. Intersectionality splinters the universality of womanhood through the need to pay deference to the complex and over-lapping oppressions experienced by working-class women, women of colour, transwomen and non-heterosexual women. The focus on the social construction of gender means that the woman is understood not as biology but as identity. Judith Butler argues, 'A new sort of feminist politics is now desirable to contest the very reifications of gender and identity, one that will take the variable construction of identity as both a methodological and normative prerequisite, if not a political goal.'[415]

The absence of a common experience does not signal the end of feminism but precisely the opposite: the more fractured and contingent womanhood becomes, the more it needs to be defended as an identity, a feeling and a way of being in the world. Third-wave feminism asks us to see 'woman' as a diverse and socially constructed category, constructed out of and in response to a common experience of gender oppression. Calling misogyny into question, or arguing that women's lives have changed for the better, not only challenges the need for feminism but is perceived as an attack upon what it means to identify as a woman.

A determination both to see and make sense of the world through a prism of gender escalates the antagonisms between the sexes feminism once sought to overcome. Lasch argues that this preoccupation with gender simplistically reduces every issue to opposition between men and women. As such, it 'tends to coarsen our sensibilities rather than to refine them. It replaces historical explanation with formulas, rips ideas out of context and often strengthens the very stereotypes it seeks to discredit'.[416] In reducing the totality of human experience to a never ending gender war in which men are perpetually called to account for their role in the oppression of women, third-wave feminism also challenges the concept of individual autonomy.

Judith Butler is critical of an earlier incarnation of feminist theory and literature that 'has assumed that there is a "doer" behind the deed'.[417] In Butler's view there are no autonomous actors, no 'doers', simply identities constructed through the cultural script of oppressing or being oppressed. The second-wave aspiration for sexual equality, which viewed women as capable of participating in the world on the same basis as men, is abandoned for a view of women as fragile, not doers but done to, acted upon, and all the while, internalizing the patriarchal ideology that sustains their own oppression. What it means to be a woman returns us once more to an experience of victimization.

FOURTH-WAVE FEMINISM

The legacy of third-wave feminism is that every issue today, from education to pay, from children's toys and clothes to workplace dress codes, statues, banknotes and literature is viewed through a prism of gender. For all the promotion of gender fluidity, gender neutral bathrooms and school uniforms, 'pink stinks' and 'let toys be toys' initiatives, it seems that gender is more entrenched as a way of dividing up and making sense of the world than ever before. Success for one gender, most often men, is presented as being at the expense of the other, usually women. This creates a need to remind women that they are victims of patriarchy and of men in particular; as one feminist writer puts it: 'Whenever we talk about patriarchy, either in general or in any particular element, we need to bear in mind that the main problem is men: men's choices, men's ways of seeing and treating women.'[418] In this way, feminism sets men and women in opposition to one another.

There is little consensus as to whether or not feminism has entered a fourth wave. In a 2009 interview with the *New York Times*, the prominent feminist journalist Jessica Valenti suggested that a fourth-wave feminism was emerging online, through social media and blogs. Valenti goes on to reinforce the idea of a 'wave' as a generational consciousness: 'I know people who are considered third-wave feminists who are 20 years older than me,' she claims.[419] The feminist website *Bustle* defines fourth-wave feminism as founded upon the 'queering of gender and sexuality based binaries'. It is sex positive, trans-inclusive, anti-misandrist, body positive and digitally driven.[420] This list of defining features reveals fourth-wave feminism to be less a coherent ideology or a political response to a particular issue and more a branch of identity politics. Indeed, identity politics is expressed most clearly and concretely today in feminism.

Just as third-wave feminism did not mark a complete break from second-wave feminism but instead emerged out of and developed some of its key ideas, so too, in turn, has fourth-wave feminism emerged from the third wave. In particular, fourth-wave feminism owes much to the third-wave concept of intersectionality. For fourth-wave feminists it is the intersecting oppressions that forge a person's identity that are all important. Gender is the most important of these characteristics, but it is fluid, constructed and based more upon innate feelings than biology. Although we can find the roots of today's fourth-wave feminism in the third wave, the influence of identity politics marks a distinct break from the feminism that existed prior to the 1970s that was developed within the context of a binary political opposition between left and right.

Whereas older feminists had a view that men and women could be equal or that all women shared experiences in common, this has now disappeared completely. Whereas second-wave feminists emphasized the biological experience of being a woman, fourth-wave feminism encompasses anyone, male or female, who identifies as a woman. While second-wave feminists argued female biology led to superior understandings, and greater insight emerged from the experience of subordination, fourth-wave feminists afford the transwoman an elevated status. The more oppressed features a person identifies with, the more, it seems, others have to learn from them.

The bind of fourth-wave feminism is that identity, particularly identities that are fragile constructs or premised on an experience of oppression, need to be defended with vigilance. Threats to identity are everywhere, most especially in culture and images. In the summer of 2013 British campaigners drew attention to an economic injustice: not the financial disparities between rich and poor but the lack of women represented on banknotes. In 2015 there were similar complaints that the new British passport design featured just two women. In the US, activists have demanded more statues of women in New York's Central Park. In London a campaign against an advertisement featuring a woman in a bikini posing the question, 'Are you beach body ready?' led to the successful removal of billboard posters in summer 2016. The focus on words and images, more than actions or material inequalities, comes in part because genuine inequalities between the sexes are few and far between while there remains an overarching assumption that words and images create the reality we all inhabit.

The impact of such campaigns is to make people ever more defined by their gender, sexuality and skin colour. The act of embodying characteristics that a previous generation of activists sought to surpass becomes all consuming. Rather than a celebration of gender and sexual fluidity, of the endless possibilities for people to transform and make themselves anew, the obsessive desire for affirmation means people come to see themselves as 'born this way' – even though what they are born with is a mental rather than physical state – and bravely playing out a pre-determined script in the face of an increasingly intolerant society. This leads only to the proliferation of more identities seeking confirmation. The most effective way for any identity group to gain recognition is to stake a claim to victimhood and to present themselves as increasingly vulnerable and fragile.

THE END OF CLASS POLITICS

Identity politics effectively marks the end of class politics. Whereas previous generations of activists made sense of the world through competing class interests, in the context of identity politics, social class becomes reconceived as just another identity, a badge to be worn, signified through cultural choices around food, clothes and television programmes as much as through job or income.

Feminists have never agreed on the relationship between class and gender. In 1973, the sociologist Anthony Giddens maintained, 'female workers are largely peripheral to the class system'.[421] It was assumed that the location of women's oppression within the home situated them outside of a formal relationship to social class. On the other hand, Ann Oakley wrote a few years later that, 'class inequality and gender inequality coexist'.[422] Some feminists argue that social class is used as a means of dividing women and denying their collective experience while others claim that women themselves constitute a class. This is to assume that women have more in common with each other than they do with any man; a view expressed by the Canadian feminist Meghan Murphy: 'What patriarchy does is to create a dominant group (men) that holds systemic, individual power over an oppressed group (women), creating a system wherein sexism keeps women, as a class, in a vulnerable and subordinate position.'[423]

Today, at the same time as some feminists present women as a class with interests in common, others criticize the concept of social class because it doesn't divide women enough. Social class, they argue, ignores the intersections of race, gender, sexuality and (dis)ability that make some women's lives more difficult than others. As DiDi Delgado, a poet and activist notes: 'I think working class is a misnomer, since work is no indication of any shared socio-economic status. An undocumented sex worker, for example, and a white housewife trying to get her Etsy Store off the ground don't have much in common. Saying both are working class does a lot to alleviate the conscience of those in positions of privilege.' She explains, 'Terms like working class often erase intersections of oppression and replace them with a fictional shared experience.'[424]

When working class is defined so broadly as to encompass anyone who works, it does indeed become meaningless. However, there are certainly still differences in the experiences of women who are in unskilled, insecure and low-paid employment and those who are in better paid and more secure, professional occupations. It tends to be middle-class feminists who lead privileged lives and have the time to seek out prejudice and inequality who are the main drivers of today's feminism. But this is rarely acknowledged as the focus on race, gender, disability, sexuality and myriad other identity signifiers distract from the significance of class.

Whereas a focus on social class spoke to a political project that moved beyond the individual to forge solidarities that went beyond race, gender and sexuality, identity politics abandons such universal objectives. Instead, focus is turned only upon the self in a narcissistic act of definition. Rather than looking out on the world, identity politics demands we look inwards. Rather than forging solidarity with others, we demand recognition for ourselves, for what makes us special. A focus on identity speaks to exhaustion with politics and a cynicism about humanity.

CONCLUSIONS

Online and in the mainstream media, feminism appears to be more dominant than ever before. But feminism today means something quite different from in the past. The focus placed on the private sphere moved second-wave feminism away from legal and practical obstacles women faced to achieving equality with men. In turn, it found both a common problem all women could unite around: patriarchy and male behaviour and at the same time the experiences of women became splintered. A women's movement gave way to radical, socialist, black and lesbian feminisms. Rather than a demand for equality, feminism now places women's disparate identities to the fore and becomes an insistence that difference be recognized.

Today's identity-driven, fourth wave, or intersectional feminism fills the vacuum left by the death of traditional, left versus right, social class—based politics. Whereas the politics of a previous era could, at best, unite disparate people around universal demands, identity politics can only ever speak to the particular interests of a select group. For today's feminists, this group is people who identify as women; it is a club for people who share the same emotional responses, tastes, political perspectives and lifestyle. The final chapter of this book takes up the consequences of this move, exploring the impact of feminism on what it means to be a woman today.

CHAPTER TEN

BEING A WOMAN

For today's feminists, the personal is no longer political. Identity politics supersedes and reinvents the political as it has been traditionally understood. Throughout most of the twentieth century, politics meant competing ideologies and perspectives: communism versus capitalism; left versus right. Political views were not simply reducible to demography; politics was an attempt to win people over to a set of ideas. There was an assumption that political gains, such as civil rights, could extend to more than a narrow section of society and be of universal benefit.

Feminism has always had a problematic relationship with politics because it spoke to the particular interests of women or, more often than not, a small proportion of middle-class women, rather than the collective interests of everyone in society. The best feminist arguments, such as those advanced by Mary Wollstonecraft, John Stuart Mill, Sylvia Pankhurst and Simone De Beauvoir, transcended the specific interests of some women to explore how sexual equality could benefit men as well as women or working-class people of every nationality. Today, expressions of universalism are derided as, at best, outdated and at worst as irredeemably elitist, racist, sexist and homophobic. Forget the political: the personal is now all there is.

Today's feminists speak 'as a woman', or, even more narrowly, 'as a woman of colour' or 'as a bisexual woman'. Fourth-wave feminism finds a comfortable home within the inherent narcissism of identity politics. It demands recognition for who people are rather than the moral or intellectual superiority of their arguments. This chapter explores the intersection of identity politics with feminism and how this plays out in relation to the question of what it means to be a woman.

THE FEMALE BODY

In meetings, newspaper columns and social media biographies, the fashion for prefacing statements with the now ritualized 'speaking as a ....' comes from a belief that knowledge derives from personal experience. Today, it is often assumed that only black people can understand racism and only women can ever truly understand misogyny because they are the only people to have had relevant lived experiences. Furthermore, because only certain people are afforded special insight, only they can speak on these issues: everyone else must shut up and listen. By this account, the thought of winning people over to a political viewpoint is futile: men can never understand women's experiences; a white person can never become black. The aim of identity politics is not to propose an alternative vision of society that improves life for everyone but rather to define group identity and police its boundaries.

Attempts at defining what it means to be a woman in an era of identity politics have led to an obsession with female body parts and bodily functions. What has been labelled 'gross out feminism' aims at 'normalizing' women through a focus on their bodies. One proponent claims the intention is 'to provide a kind of shock therapy to those still harbouring the notion that women don't have bodily functions, trapped gas, or insubordinate periods'.[425] As a result of this taboo-busting imperative, Chinese swimmer Fu Yuanhui was celebrated for telling the world's media that she underperformed in the 2016 Olympic relay event because she had her period during the race.[426] Likewise, activist and runner Kiran Ghandi decided not to use sanitary protection when she began her period before the 2016 London marathon but to 'free bleed' instead. She argued that 'by establishing a norm of period-shaming, [male-preferring] societies effectively prevent the ability to bond over an experience that 50% of us in the human population share monthly'.[427] Both women — although we can note Ghandi's careful avoidance of the word — have been heralded for their bravery.

DISCUSSING VAGINAS

For all the talk of taboo-busting, few body parts are as publicly discussed nowadays as the vagina. Shops now sell lip balm for vaginas 'because your other lips get chapped too'; cosmetic surgeons market a 'face' lift for the vagina and vulva. Celebrities like Gwyneth Paltrow and Khloe Kardashian have well-publicized beauty routines for their vaginas. There is a call to establish a vagina museum because, argues the 25-year-old founder, 'We don't talk about vaginas enough' and women need help to 'learn about consent and their health'. Following the election of Donald Trump as US President, the vagina became a symbol of political protest. Trump's inauguration was followed by women's marches in major

international cities; protesters wore hand-knitted pink hats
with pussy ears as a reminder of Trump's decade-old 'grab
them by the pussy' remark. Letters written to denounce
Trump's attack on women's access to contraception and abortion were delivered to the White House in a giant vulva-
shaped papier mâché model.

If fourth-wave feminism is best considered an offshoot of
identity politics then the vagina has become its symbol. Just
as social class has come to be seen as a matter of personal
taste and cultural preferences in relation to food, clothing,
television programmes and newspaper choices so being a
feminist is expressed through attitudes, values and tastes as
much as through any political position. Celebrating female
biology is considered a way to empower women in relation
to their own bodies; it's the most basic marker of group identity. Simply possessing a vagina is not enough: it needs to be
discussed, written about, modelled and performed to ensure
membership of a today's feminist clique.

One problem with this focus on the vagina is that it effectively reduces women to their body parts. In the run up to the
2016 US Presidential election there was much discussion
about the rights and wrongs of women 'voting with their
vaginas' with some feminists proudly declaring, 'I am voting
with my vagina.'[428] Interviewed on *The Late Show*, actor
Cate Blanchett was asked, 'What is your moral compass?
Where does kindness and humanity sit in a brutal world?'
Blanchett didn't miss a beat in replying: 'In my vagina'.[429]
Mocking men for thinking with their genitals has long been
an in-joke among women but now it seems some women are
keen to do just this and proudly tell the world about it.

For a previous generation of feminists being defined by
their anatomy was something they vehemently fought against.
As a political symbol, the vagina is meaningless: it's simply
a body part. The logic of taboo-busting is that it should be

treated as a body part like any other, not afforded some mythical status. The obsession with the vagina has taken off
because identity politics demands groups share common
features yet women themselves are divided by politics, race,
social class, sexuality, age and disability. Possessing a vagina
becomes one thing women have in common. The focus on
bodily functions also represents the loss of any boundary
between public and the private. Free bleeding represents an
extreme act of making the private public.

Yet feminism today is full of contradictions. On the one
hand it reduces women to their biology yet, at the very same
time, it seeks to expand gender categories to encompass
people who do not identify with the sex they were born into.
Not every woman has a vagina, we are reminded, and likewise, not everyone with a vagina identifies as a woman.
Sometimes the contradiction between celebrating women's
bodies and defining womanhood as no more than an innate
feeling is recognized and challenged: pussy-themed anti-
Trump protests have been criticized for excluding transwomen. At other times, the contradictions are glossed over.
The founder of the vagina museum argues, 'A woman can be
whoever she wants to be no matter what's in her pants.
Women deserve more respect than being defined by what's in
their pants.'[430] The obvious question as to why there should
then be an entire museum dedicated to what women have in
their pants is avoided.

There was a time when talking about women's bodies was
so taboo that some women did not seek medical help for problems 'from the waist down'. In *Out of the Doll's House*,
Angela Holdsworth notes, 'Edwardian women were shy of
talking about their bodies. Some of this embarrassment
rubbed off on their children and grandchildren, extending a
veil of silence on feminine matters well into the second half of
the century.'[431] Feminists in the 1960s and 1970s fought to

challenge such taboos but at the same time they argued
women were more than just their body parts. Today, it can
seem as if the public discussion of vaginas, vulvas and periods
is simply to allow modern feminists to be applauded for their
bravery in saying the words out loud.

ESSENTIAL DIFFERENCES

Simone De Beauvoir, writing in her 1949 book, *The Second
Sex,* considered the role of the body in allowing people to
make sense of the world: 'In girls, as in boys, the body is first
of all the radiation of a subjectivity, the instrument that
makes possible the comprehension of the world: it is through
the eyes, the hands, that children apprehend the universe, and
not through the sexual parts.'[432] The obsession with the
vagina, and most specifically whether you need to possess
one in order to be a woman, speaks to confusion about what
it means to be a woman today. De Beauvoir's famous claim
that 'one is not born, but rather becomes, a woman'[433] is
not, as it is often misinterpreted today, a denial of biological
differences between males and females. To De Beauvoir,
women are more than 'merely the human beings arbitrarily
designated by the word *woman*'.[434] She argues the differences between men and women are perhaps 'superficial' or
'destined to disappear' but 'what is certain is that they do
most obviously exist'.[435]

Unlike De Beauvoir, it can seem as if few feminists nowadays accept that neither biology nor socialization alone can
account for what it means to be a woman. Today, there is a
celebration of women's bodies and an attempt to define
women according to biology at the very same time as an
assumption that sex is irrelevant and gender is entirely socially
constructed.

THE INVENTION OF GENDER[436]

The separation De Beauvoir makes between being born female and becoming a woman hints at the 'invention' of gender which occurred just a few years after publication of *The Second Sex*. The psychologist John Money was, in 1955, the first to draw a distinction between biological sex, or the physical attributes that distinguish male and female, and gender — the behaviour and roles that a person experiences and expresses. Before this time the word 'sex' was used to describe a person's physical body and their sense of identity without any distinction being made between the two. The word 'gender' became popularized in the 1970s when feminists began to debate the rigid categories of social roles for men and women.[437]

Neither De Beauvoir nor those who first defined gender sought to deny the underlying biological reality of a person's sex. Indeed, the body, as a physical entity, fascinates the existentialist De Beauvoir who argues that the existence of a female body precedes the essence of a woman but the way in which this biological fact was enacted was socially determined. As Germaine Greer later explained: 'Female is essence and feminine social construct.'[438] Later gender theorists go a step further and deny the existence of a biological female that exists concurrently with a socially constructed woman. Judith Butler is critical of the idea that 'there is a natural or biological female who is subsequently transformed into a socially subordinate "woman", with the consequence that "sex" is to "nature" or "the raw" as gender is to culture or "the cooked"'. She argues that this 'is a discursive formation that acts as a naturalized foundation for the nature/culture distinction and the strategies of domination that the distinction supports'.[439]

Today, sex has, it seems, been rejected by many feminists as an outdated and biologically deterministic category. Gender, as a social construct, has come to dominate thinking: it is assumed that society socializes people into thinking and behaving in a particular way according to the sex they are assigned at birth. This has led to a questioning of the rigid binary categories of male and female, man and woman. Gender is conceived not as a fixed category, but fluid and not binary but multiple. According to this view, the act of dividing people into one of two categories is an entirely arbitrary imposition, an act of symbolic violence conducted at the moment of birth.

Children are taught by parents, friends and teachers that some gendered lifestyle choices are appropriate for them while others are not. Such lessons, often played out imperceptibly, are said to form the 'structural and symbolic roots' of the 'gendered and "gentle" violence that underpin processes of female socialization'.[440] As socially constructed gender can never be assumed, Facebook now famously offers 72 gender options for people to choose from, students declare their preferred gender pronouns to lecturers and classmates, and even some very young children have come to consider themselves transgender.[441]

FEELING LIKE A WOMAN

Not everyone goes so far as to deny the significance of biology; some argue, with De Beauvoir, that society and biology interact: 'It is more than plausible to suggest that experience plays a significant role in our hormone levels and the way our brains develop, including after puberty.'[442] Certainly it is the case that psychological tests, presented as uncovering 'natural' neurological differences between the sexes, are influenced by the prior assumptions of participants of what is expected of them.[443] For example, as psychologists Nancy Eisenberg and Randy Lennon discovered back in 1983, when women are told that a study is measuring empathy they appear to have an empathetic advantage over men. When this isn't obviously the focus of the research, this difference disappears. In other words, women act out the gendered expectations they think the researchers hold of them and moderate how they want to appear to others.[444]

The differences that do exist between the sexes are most likely a combination of nature and nurture, of the biological and social interacting with each other. We are unlikely ever to be able to determine the exact balance between the two because babies are born into an already-existing world that comes with ready-made attitudes and assumptions about gender. A person may be able to accept or reject their socialization but they cannot avoid it altogether. As Fine puts it: 'Everything we do — be it maths, chess, child care, or driving — we do with a mind that is exquisitely sensitive to the social environment around it.'[445]

Often today it is argued that gender is less to do with biology and more to do with an innate feeling that individuals determine for themselves and then seek to bring their physical biology into line with their 'true' gender identity. The concept of gender fluidity emerges from a therapeutic and relativistic culture. People are told that their feelings are of preeminent importance and they should accept no constraints: they can be whoever they want to be. More narcissistic is the demand that everyone else they encounter should deny biological reality and refer to people in whatever way they dictate. The assumption that gender is fluid leads to a proliferation in gender options. People can identify as 'pangender', 'polygender' or 'agender'.

Gender fluidity is attractive to feminists because it holds out the hope of abolishing gender as a category and with it all the constraints and restrictions gender places upon people's lives. However, rather than transcending gender, the notion of fluidity has the opposite effect: it simply entrenches people in different boxes. The political philosopher Rebecca Reilly Cooper argues that in order for gender not to be oppressive there would need to be 'as many possible gender identities as there are humans on the planet'.[446] When gender is considered to be based on nothing other than an innate feeling, the onus is on individuals to determine for themselves what these feelings are, embody them and enact them in public. When there can be no recourse to either biology or social convention, gender is nothing more than a lifestyle choice performed through fashion, music, make-up and hair styles.

PERFORMING GENDER

Judith Butler, as we have seen, argues gender is 'always a doing' and as such is located not in culture, biology or society but in performance. Butler's proviso that this performance is 'not a doing by a subject who might be said to pre-exist the deed' turns De Beauvoir's existentialism upside down: rather than a person, De Beauvoir's self-determining woman, acting out femininity, it is the action, the act of performance that creates the gendered subject. She argues: 'There is no gender identity behind the expressions of gender; that identity is per-formatively constituted by the very "expressions" that are said to be its results.'[447] This assertion has become widely accepted by fourth-wave feminist activists and gender theorists within the academy. The authors of *Gendering Women* write, 'We are constantly and actively doing and performing, creating and recreating our gender identities.'[448]

For Butler, gender is chiefly performed through sexuality. She asks: 'How do certain sexual practices compel the question: what is a woman, what is a man?'[449] In this way, Butler comes to agree with an earlier generation of feminists such as Dworkin and MacKinnon in her argument that it is heterosexuality that positions women as subordinate to men. Indeed, for Butler, 'to have a gender means to have entered already into a heterosexual relationship of subordination': it is through the performance of heterosexuality that women become lesser than men. Her answer to the question 'what is a woman?' is a being who performs a submissive position within a heterosexual framework.

Butler's argument that heterosexuality has become 'naturalized', even 'compulsory' has its roots in Adrienne Rich's 1980 work *Compulsory Heterosexuality and Lesbian Existence*. Butler suggests it is the policing of heterosexuality that regulates gender as a binary construct and relegates women to a subordinate position in society. According to this view, 'sexual harassment is the paradigmatic allegory for the production of gender'.[450] It is through the act of harassment that 'a person is "made" into a certain gender'. Men become domineering, aggressive and masculine; women become submissive, passive and feminine. The current preoccupation with sexual harassment and rape culture, particularly on university campuses, shows the extent to which this view has become accepted.

Butler's focus on sexual harassment shows how the notion of gender as a performance takes us a long way from the thinking of both Wollstonecraft and De Beauvoir. All three challenge a biological understanding of femininity as natural to womanhood and ask us to look at the role of childhood, education, the family and the workplace in creating gender differences as we have traditionally come to understand them. De Beauvoir claims, 'Every female human being is not

necessarily a woman; to be so considered she must share in
that mysterious and threatened reality known as femininity.'[451] The crucial phrase here is 'she must share'. De
Beauvoir suggests that females play an active part in constructing themselves as women. She criticizes women who
practice 'bad faith' and refuse to accept responsibility for
their lives. But whereas for De Beauvoir women actively participate in their gendered behaviour, for Butler there is no
such agent able to do the constructing. Instead of a woman
performing gender and 'making' herself, Butler's woman is
'made' through a performance she is coerced into.

De Beauvoir's privileging of a woman's individual agency
in determining her destiny is a retort to biological constructions of womanhood: 'It is not nature that defines woman; it
is she who defines herself by dealing with nature on her own
account in her emotional life.'[452] Yet today this privileging of
agency presents an equivalent challenge to the argument that
women are made by society. Of course, De Beauvoir was not
blind to the difficulties women faced in assuming responsibility for their own destiny: a woman is 'treated like a live doll
and refused liberty' she decried, 'thus a vicious circle is
formed; for the less she exercises her freedom to understand,
to grasp and discover the world about her, the less resources
will she find within herself, the less will she dare to affirm
herself as subject.'[453] However, De Beauvoir stresses the
choices a woman does have, 'I believe that she has the power
to choose between the assertion of her transcendence and her
alienation as object.' For Butler, on the other hand, women
are constructed through being acted upon and done to rather
than through a performance they actively participate in
themselves.

Butler's rejection of any connection between biology and
gender and with it a rejection of male and female as binary
opposites can appear, on the surface, to be liberating. People

are now freed from the supposedly oppressive tyrannies of biology and society. We no longer have to comply with convention or fit into neat categories: we can identify with any point on a gender spectrum. As a result we see an increase in the number of people, including children, identifying as transgender, born (or cis-) men who identify as women and cis-women who identify as men. However, this fluidity comes at a price. Unlike for feminists such as De Beauvoir and Greer, for whom the shift from sex to gender emphasized a woman's agency, Butler's de-biologizing of gender renders women passive; there is no 'they' prior to the sexual performance. Butler's women may not be biologically female but in return they must spend time gazing inwards, ascertaining the 'innate feeling' and bringing this in line with their self-declared identity and preferred pronouns.

TRANSWOMEN

When gender is performed through heterosexuality, and in particular through the experience of sexual harassment, being a woman becomes intrinsically bound up with the experience of victimhood. By this token, those who have suffered most embody womanhood most completely. Transwomen have struggled to reconcile the contradiction between their innate gender identity and the sex they were assigned at birth. They then face a unique set of challenges when they are forced to confront a heteronormative society that is gendered along a rigid binary axis. By this account, transwomen suffer more than women who find a neat correlation between the gender they identify with and the sex they were assigned at birth. Transwomen suffer in performing womanhood, and inhabit the props of feminine clothing, make-up, speech patterns and gestures traditionally associated with 'born' women. For this reason transwomen are often celebrated. In 2015, Caitlyn Jenner, formerly Olympic athlete and television presenter Bruce Jenner, was named Glamour magazine's woman of the year.[454] It can seem as if the people who do womanhood most successfully today are women who used to be men.

Some feminists have criticized the elevation of transgender women. In the UK, radio presenter and journalist Jenni Murray and in the US, author Chimamanda Ngozi Adichie have both hit the headlines for arguing that transwomen are not 'real' women because they have not experienced childhood and formative experiences that born women go through. In some ways this is a brave attempt at cutting through the current gender relativism and injecting badly needed reality into debates that risk losing all grounding. However, both Murray and Adichie premised their declarations of 'real' womanhood upon an experience of suffering and disadvantage. Ultimately we are being asked to choose: 'who has struggled most?' When 'real' womanhood boils down to a greater experience of suffering then it is hardly an inspiring proposition.

NEW GENDER ORTHODOXIES

In contrast to Wollstonecraft's desire to liberate women from the stifling social conventions that left them intellectually impoverished and irrational, Butler imposes a new gender tyranny. We may be able to define ourselves in a multitude of different ways but our life's work becomes thinking about our feelings towards our body and researching our gender identity. The further we move away from any connection between sex and either biology or society, the more individuals require public affirmation that they are who they say they are. It is no longer enough to be a woman, you need recognition from other people that this is, indeed, who you are and you need to have your gendered performances confirmed in the public arena. It is for this reason that dress and public lavatories have become such important issues. Through such mundane features of life, gender is performed, asserted and publicly endorsed.

The performance of gender becomes an ongoing process of self-construction. This traps us within ourselves: our happiness, our sense of who we are, hinges on our ability to assert our identity. A far more radical and progressive message comes from De Beauvoir who declared: 'I am interested in the fortunes of the individual as defined not in terms of happiness but in terms of liberty.'[455] There is little positive, progressive or experimental about the current obsession with gender-fluidity. It rapidly becomes as restrictive as old ideas about sex and gender.

Today, anyone can be a woman. Yet there appears to be little that is liberating about this freedom from biology. Instead, new orthodoxies entrench conservative attitudes about the 'correct' behaviour and appearance for those who identify as boys or girls. We have no more tomboys or effeminate men; instead we have transgender children. The stereotypes that a previous generation of feminist campaigners fought against are once more being rigidly reinforced. No man goes to the trouble of hormone therapy and gender reassignment surgery in order to dress and act in a gender neutral fashion. Instead, pretty dresses and an old-fashioned stereotypical femininity make a return.

REPRODUCTIVE RIGHTS

Gender fluidity is supposed to be a radical move to end restrictive binaries and sexist stereotyping. Unfortunately it ends up creating new boxes for people to slot themselves into; it reinforces sexist stereotypes and it ramps up the need for the policing of language and behaviour. Perhaps worse than any of this, when gender becomes separated from sex, the need for women to have access to abortion, contraception and pre- and post-natal healthcare is problematized.

Women share the experience of and potential for reproduction: put simply, men do not get pregnant. For women to live as full members of society they need access to contraception, abortion and maternity services in a way that men, even those who consider themselves to be transwomen, never will. Campaigns that demand maternity nurses and abortion providers stop referring to 'pregnant women' and talk instead of 'pregnant people' or change breast feeding to 'chest feeding' trivialize women's specific needs. It becomes harder to argue for medical and healthcare provision for women when the category of woman has to incorporate men who, not only have no need for such services, but see their promotion as an existential threat.

The limited rights to abortion women won in the 1960s and 1970s represented a significant victory in allowing women to act as autonomous citizens and engage fully in the public domain. However, such victories were only ever partial and particularly under Trump's presidency cannot be taken for granted. Trump's global 'gagging order' prevents abortion services being provided or publicized for women in countries receiving medical aid or funding from the US government. There has been some kickback against this but Trump can single out abortion in this way because previous administrations, not just in the US but in the UK too, have placed abortion outside of the provision of mainstream healthcare.

In America, the pro-life lobby is ascendant while in the UK abortion continues to be restricted by outdated legislation.

Everywhere, access to abortion services is dependent upon political whims rather than medical provision. For too long abortion has been presented not just as a routine medical intervention but as a special, morally dubious procedure requiring women to argue they are physically or mentally at risk if they proceed with a pregnancy. This is a demand that women who want to decide for themselves whether or to continue with a pregnancy must present themselves as vulnerable and incapable rather than strong, competent and in control of their own lives. Abortion cannot be publicly celebrated as a positive decision even if that is how it is experienced privately by an individual woman.

Today's feminists who view gender as nothing more than an innate feeling, a fluid and socially constructed category, are not in a strong position to argue for women's reproductive rights. Similarly, a feminism that encourages all women to consider themselves as victims at home, at work and in the street renders it more difficult to project a view of women as strong, capable and rational. Vulnerable women get sympathy and special protections: they do not get rights. To defend abortion rights today, we need to win the argument that women are autonomous beings with a right to determine the course of their own lives. We need to argue for 'bodily integrity' or, as Ann Furedi writes in *The Moral Case for Abortion*, 'The belief that our bodies are our own for us to control and that, providing we cause no harm to others, no one may interfere with us without our consent.'[456] We can only make these arguments if we see people as capable of deciding for themselves how best to run their own lives and what should happen to their own bodies.

A defence of abortion requires making the case that women can and should be able to decide for themselves whether or not to continue with a pregnancy. For the second-wave feminists who campaigned for the legalization of abortion, a woman's ability to control her own body was both a practical and symbolic sign of her freedom and her ability to determine the course of her life for herself. Today, as Jennie Bristow argues, 'women's ability to "choose" motherhood is presented as coming with the responsibility to plan it in minute detail, and the obligation to submit their bodies and personal lives to surveillance and regulation, for the sake of their "unborn children".'[457] As we explored in Chapter Four, women who choose to become mothers are increasingly expected to subjugate their own lives to the demands of intensive parenting.

MORE TO LIFE THAN THIS....

The obsession with gender identity speaks to a desire, particularly evident among young people, to mark themselves out as different, more radical and more interesting, than other people and especially older generations. It suggests dissatisfaction with the world as it has traditionally been organized according to conventional gender roles, with a promised future of employment, relationships and parenting. The major gains of feminism – sexual liberation and equality in education and work – expose new frustrations. Equality, at school, in the office and in the bedroom, does not in itself bring satisfaction.

Feminism helped reveal the limited potential first for housework, then parenting and employment, as they are currently constituted, to provide life with meaning and a sense of purpose. Betty Friedan described the lack of fulfilment women found in a suburban lifestyle that revolved primarily around their role as housewife as 'the problem that has no name'. In response, second-wave feminists challenged the restrictions placed on women's lives and fought for full social and economic equality. This took its clearest form in the demand for the right to work and be paid the same as men.

But the victories of the 1960s and 1970s brought to light new 'problems with no name'. Writing in *The Second Shift*, Arlie Hochschild describes Ann Myerson, a woman whose 'surface ideology was egalitarian'. We're told that Myerson, '*wanted* to feel as engaged with her career as her husband was with his. This was her view of the "proper experience" of her career. She thought she *should* love her work. She *should* think it mattered. In fact, as she confessed in a troubled tone, she didn't love her work and didn't think it mattered.'[458] The right for women to work on the same basis as men was an important feminist victory, but, in turn, for many women, it exposes the limited capacity of paid employment to provide a sense of purpose or a source of emotional or intellectual fulfilment.

Motherhood can appear to offer women an alternative and more meaningful existence than can be found in the workplace. Few things seem more important than the role of nurturing a new generation, particularly when the responsibilities of parents are elevated through a weight of policy pronouncements and expert advice. Yet this same guidance is disempowering: parents have many obligations but little authority. Raising children has become not just more intensive but also increasingly individualized; each parent alone carries the weight of determining their child's destiny. Problems of public life, such as an unproductive national economy, have become reinterpreted as individual concerns. It is assumed that to be successful and 'socially mobile' children need mothers who avoid alcohol while pregnant, breast feed, monitor their child's diet and 'screen time', and provide a range of stimulating and educational activities. As a result, the adult woman becomes submerged within the life of her child.

Katie Roiphe describes the attraction of all-consuming motherhood: 'Children are the best excuse in the world not to pursue happiness, not to live fully or take risks or attempt the work one loves. The compromises we make are justified, elevated and transfigured by the fact of children, and this can be a relief.'[459] This suggests motherhood is an act of 'bad faith', a means of self-deception. Motherhood, like employment, appears to provide individuals with a sense of purpose and fulfilment – and in important respects both do. But there remains what Judith Warner describes as a 'sense that life should have led up to more than it has. A sense that after all the hard work, for all our achievements as individuals and as a "post-feminist" generation, life should be better than this.'[460]

Young people today see little hope in careers, parenting or even intimate relationships as a source of excitement and purpose for the future. In the past, this sense of dissatisfaction might have been expressed through joining a political party or engaging in a collective protest movement. Feminism shows us the limitations of life as it is at the moment, but its current incarnation offers only a focus on the self and individual identity as solutions. The more feminism merges with identity politics, the further it leads us into a dead end and the desire for a different way of life becomes directed inwards.

CONCLUSIONS

Young people today might not have faith in their ability to change the world, but they are able to discuss periods and talk about vaginas. They might not be able to tackle issues of global poverty, climate change or war, but they can reject the sex they were assigned at birth, dress differently and insist the world recognizes their specialness.

Feminism sells moving beyond gender as a liberating act. Without having to dress, behave and act according to strict and limiting conventions, both men and women, in theory, are free just to be themselves. However, the celebration of identity as an end in itself leads to a gender fluidity that, far from being experienced as liberating, comes with its own rigid instructions to follow. The focus on individual identity downplays the potential for different people to come together, to find interests in common and collectively influence the future shape of society. It prevents people engaging in the very activities that provide life with meaning.

At times, such as with the anti-Trump women's march or Black Lives Matter demonstrations, protest appears to take a collective form once more. But these protests are restricted to group members and often demand little more than public affirmation of suffering endured. Intersectional feminism has become reduced to one more competing demand for recognition among others. Today's feminism appears to offer a clear values framework emanating from an assumed championing of the oppressed but it comes with a moralistic authoritarianism and is destined to play out in a gender war without winners.

CHAPTER ELEVEN

CONCLUSIONS

DO WE STILL NEED FEMINISM?

It's now 100 years since a proportion of British women won the right to vote for the first time. As this book has shown, women's lives have transformed beyond all recognition since this time. Even a few decades ago, women were unable to start a business, take out a credit card or own their own home without their husband's permission. Women were, in living memory, prevented from applying for the same jobs as men, being paid the same as men for the same work and keeping their jobs once pregnant. Unmarried women couldn't get the contraceptive pill and abortion was illegal. The freedom and opportunities available to young women today would have been unimaginable to their great-grandparents.

LIFE IS DIFFERENT TODAY

But the transformation in women's lives has not been even. Some – particularly younger, middle class and, in the US especially, white – women's lives have changed far more fundamentally than others. Similarly, change has been far more dramatic in some areas of life. At school and university, girls have not just caught up with boys but are now leaving them far behind; while at home, even though men are more involved, it is often women who still take on board most of the responsibility for housework and childcare. The legacy of historical disadvantage continues to play out, especially for older women, while the expectations of previous generations still have an impact upon children today.

Women's lives have changed but this progress has not occurred while the rest of the world has remained set in aspic. Men's lives have changed too. A society that once rewarded attributes such as physical and mental strength, competitiveness, courage, independence and assertiveness, no longer exists. School, work and even home life are all very different to a century ago and success today means meeting new criteria. In many walks of life, women today are doing better than men but according to different standards and expectations than in the past.

Feminism encourages us to score successes according to gender but this is a zero-sum game. Success for men in one area of life does not spell disaster for women and likewise, women's gains are not necessarily made at the expense of men. Women do not lead their lives in isolation from men; they have brothers, partners and sons. Women and men live, grow-up and work alongside each other. The universal aspiration for a better life is best achieved through men and women working alongside each other rather than seeing each other as bitter rivals.

FEMINISM HAS CHANGED TOO

Just as society has changed, so too has feminism. The issues highlighted by today's fourth wave, intersectional feminism are very different to the demands of the suffragettes and many of the second-wave feminists of the 1960s and 1970s. There has never been a 'golden age' of feminism. Intrinsic to the demand for 'women's rights' is a challenge to a far more progressive idea of human rights. However, among the earliest feminists there was recognition that liberation for women meant liberation for men too. Men could never be truly free while women were still oppressed. This feminism was less about pitching men and women in opposition to one another and more about realizing universal aspirations for liberty and equality.

In a previous era, even when feminism didn't have explicitly universal aspirations, it promoted a view of women as strong, independent and rational, as capable of enjoying freedom, and all the challenges that came with it, as men. Sexual liberation was demanded as well as equal pay because there was a belief that women could do anything men could do. The women's movement of the 1960s and 1970s was a powerful political force that continued the battles for sexual equality started by the suffragettes of a previous era.

Feminism has come a long way since this time. Today's feminism, ascendant precisely as women can no longer be said to be oppressed in any meaningful sense, has become detached from the reality of many women's lives. Rather than celebrating women's successes, the search for 'everyday sexism' turns up a range of increasingly banal new offences for us to worry about. We're told that song lyrics, advertising billboards, the characters in children's story books, baby clothes, workplace dress codes and the very words we use make the world a hostile place for women.

Rather than a demand for equality, today's feminism is a plea for recognition. Recent high-profile campaigns have focused on the lack of representation of women on banknotes, statues and traffic light symbols; and the gender balance of contributors to comedy panel shows, political debates and boards of directors. Feminism has become distant from the lives of women who have never felt oppressed by a bank note (only, perhaps, the lack of one) or felt unable to cross a road because the light shows an image of a green man.

Today's feminist campaigns present a view of women as vulnerable rather than strong. Campaigns against skinny models in advertisements, for example, send a message that all women are at risk of developing eating disorders if they see a beautiful but undernourished woman. When many women are faring better than men in school and at work, the message that women are victims flies in the face of reality. Worse, it risks turning back the clock on previous feminist victories.

ENFORCING A FEMINIST ETIQUETTE

Once, women fought for the freedom to engage in public life as equals to men and female students conspired to be rid of chaperones. Uninvited comments from men were considered a small price to pay for independence. The right to risk harassment meant women were finally equal to men and many aspired to answer back with uninvited comments of their own. Today, in contrast, the message from feminism that women are vulnerable results in calls for special protections to guard them from men. The assumption is that women can't be expected to handle public life in the raw.

When women, especially younger women today, are equal to men in every meaningful regard, feminism becomes reinvented as distinctly values-laden and moralistic. Its primary concern is to modify the behaviour of men and women who fall foul of feminist-approved ways for people to interact, speak and even, it seems, think. The fun and feistiness of yesteryear's 'girl power' has been replaced by an authoritarian exercise in policing language, attitudes and behaviour. Enforcing a feminist etiquette comes at the expense of our freedom and independence.

Today's feminism, preoccupied with the concerns of a small and elite group of women, cannot account for the experiences of older or working-class women. Yet it is all too ready to appropriate the disadvantages faced by these women to support claims for special privileges for the already successful. But these privileges come at a huge cost.

Young women today are told that schools, universities and the workplace are threatening and intimidating not by patriarchal fathers wanting to keep them at home but by trendy feminist campaigners. The frequent repetition of claims that women are victimized by men may have unintended consequences. In 2015, Girl Guiding UK found that 75 per cent of girls and young women said anxiety about potentially experiencing sexual harassment affects their lives in some way.[461] A 2016 survey suggested that 41 per cent of young women expect to face discrimination at work.[462] These young women had not faced harassment or discrimination: their anxiety was around what might, potentially, happen to them in the future. It may be the fear of sexual harassment, more than the reality, that is holding women back today. If so, women now need liberating from feminism.

If women are to continue to live as equals to men and play a full role in forging the world for future generations, they need to throw off the shackles of feminism. Feminism's presentation of women as victims of a dominant and rapacious masculinity, on the one hand, and faceless patriarchal forces, on the other, does neither women nor men any favours. It's time for us to rehabilitate a word popular among feminists in the 1960s: liberation. For women and men to be truly free and able to realize their full potential today, we all need to be liberated from feminism and the gender wars.

ENDNOTES

1. Topping (2017).
2. Adams (2016).
3. Turner (2017).
4. Leach (2016).
5. Turner (2015).
6. Ratcliffe (2013).
7. U.S. Department of Education, National Center for Education Statistics (2016).
8. Department for Education, National Statistics (2015).
9. Busby (2016).
10. California Department of Education (2016).
11. Gershenson (2016).
12. *Ibid.*
13. Daubney (2016).
14. Woodfield and Thomas (2012).
15. Perry (2016).
16. *Ibid.*
17. U.S. Bureau of Labor Statistics (2015).
18. Read (2016).
19. National Education Association (2011).
20. Daubney (2016).
21. See the University of Edinburgh: Educated Pass.
22. Palejwala (2015).
23. Fine (2012), p. xix.
24. Fine (2012), p. 136.

25. Fine (2012), p. xxvi.
26. Fine (2012), p. 178.
27. Pine (2001), p. 12.
28. Hoff Sommers (2013), p. 35.
29. Rosin (2013), p. 86.
30. Hoff Sommers (2013), p. 41.
31. Shepherd (2010).
32. Davis (2017).
33. Furedi (2016b).
34. Makel, Wai, Peairs, and Putallaz (2016).
35. Leake (2016).
36. Didau (2016).
37. Conversation with author (28 November 2016).
38. Mitchell (1986), p. 45.
39. Hillman and Robinson (2016).
40. Hoff Sommers (2013), p. 36.
41. Niemtus (2016).
42. Raffray (2014).
43. National Union of Teachers (2017).
44. True Tube (2017).
45. Brighton and Hove Equality and Anti-Bullying School Strategy Group (2017).
46. Issadore (2015).
47. Bell (2015).
48. Pierre (2017).
49. Arnett (2014).
50. Institute of Physics (2012).
51. HESA (2014).
52. Equality Challenge Unit website.
53. Conversation with author (23 February 2017).
54. Catalyst (2016).
55. Court (1995).
56. Office for National Statistics (2016a, 2016b).
57. United States Department of Labor (2015).

58. U.S. Department of Labor (2017a, 2017b, 2017c).

59. Status of Women in the States (2017).

60. Catalyst (2016).

61. United States Department of Labor (2017a, 2017b, 2017c).

62. Department for Professional Employees (2017).

63. Office for National Statistics (2013).

64. Office for National Statistics (2015).

65. Veterinary Woman (2015).

66. Hillman and Robinson (2016).

67. Marshall (1982), p. 47.

68. Catalyst (2016).

69. Miller and Alderman (2014).

70. United States Department of Labor (2017a, 2017b, 2017c).

71. Miller (2017).

72. Rivers and Barnett (2016).

73. Bennett (2016).

74. Jeapes (2016).

75. Pryce (2015), p. 44.

76. Rankin (2015).

77. Bennett (2016), p. 11.

78. Pryce (2015).

79. Brearley (2016).

80. Wolf (2013), p. xv.

81. Morris (2016).

82. Wolf (2013), p. 9.

83. Williams (2016a, 2016b, 2016c).

84. The 3% Movement (2016).

85. Cory and Stirling (2015).

86. Wang, Parker, and Taylor (2013).

87. Moss (2015).

88. Atler (2015).

89. Barrett (2016).

90. Wolf (2013), p. 34.
91. Wolf (2013), p. 26.
92. Office for National Statistics (2016a, 2016b).
93. Wolf (2013), p. 241.
94. Cliff (2014).
95. The Fawcett Society. *The Gender Pay Gap*.
96. The Fawcett Society. *Equal Pay Day*.
97. Wolf (2016).
98. Mason and Treanor (2015).
99. Smothers (2016).
100. Smith (2015).
101. Gettell (2016).
102. GirlTalkHQ (2014).
103. Mayer (2016).
104. O'Brien (2015).
105. Allen (2016a).
106. Hoff Sommers (2012).
107. Maybin (2016).
108. Allen (2016a).
109. Office for National Statistics (2016a, 2016b).
110. Press Association (2015).
111. Belfield, Cribb, Hood, and Joyce (2017).
112. Catalyst (2016).
113. *Ibid.*
114. Maybin (2016).
115. Office for National Statistics (2016a, 2016b).
116. *Ibid.*
117. Packham (2015).
118. Belfield et al. (2017).
119. Friedman, Laurison, and Macmillan (2017).
120. Swinford (2015).
121. Grove (2016a).
122. Grove (2016b).
123. Costa Dias, Elming, and Joyce (2016).

124. *Ibid.*
125. Wolf (2013), p. 49.
126. Office for National Statistics (2013).
127. Slaughter (2012).
128. Oakley (1990), p. 61.
129. Marshall (1982), p. 9.
130. Kenny (1979).
131. Marshall (1982), p. 42.
132. Marshall (1982), p. 48.
133. Stone-Lee (2005).
134. Slaughter (2012).
135. Rivers and Barnett (2015), p. 199.
136. Lyonette and Crompton (2015).
137. Slaughter (2012).
138. Rosin (2013), p. 221.
139. Rosin (2013), p. 224.
140. Kenny (1979), p. 17.
141. Lee (2014), p. 3.
142. Lee (2009), p. 109.
143. Lee (2014), p. 7.
144. NHS Choices (2016).
145. NHS Choices (2017).
146. Downey (2017).
147. Roiphe (2013).
148. Schiller (2016).
149. Phillips (2017), p. 170.
150. Faircloth (2014), p. 26.
151. Conversation with author (8 January 2017).
152. Macvarish (2016), p. 2.
153. Macvarish (2016), p. 5.
154. Biddulph (2017).
155. Bristow (2009), p. 50.
156. Greer (2012), p. 110.
157. Warner (2006), p. 55.

158. Pryce (2015).

159. Rosin (2013), p. 195.

160. Shriver (2010), p. xi.

161. Khomami (2016).

162. Leftly (2017).

163. Laville (2016).

164. Hunt (2016).

165. Cooper (2016).

166. Phillips (2017), p. 103.

167. Violence Against Women (2016).

168. http://www.shiftingsands.org.uk/

169. Bentham (2017).

170. Williams (2017).

171. Moore (2017).

172. Press Association (2016).

173. http://www.lennyletter.com/

174. https://everydaysexism.com/

175. February 19th 2017.

176. Livingston (2017).

177. Paul (2015).

178. Parker (2016).

179. Soave (2016).

180. Students for Life of America (2016).

181. O'Brien (2016).

182. *Ibid.*

183. Stanley (2014).

184. McIntyre (2014).

185. Greer (2007), p. 81.

186. Quinn (2015).

187. Penny (2014).

188. Flaherty (2014).

189. Moore (2016).

190. Millett (1999), p. 55.

191. Hynde (2015), p. 119.

192. See https://books.google.com/ngrams/graph?content=
victim&case_insensitive=on&year_start=1800&year_
end=2017&corpus=15&smoothing=7&share=&
direct_url=t4%3B%2Cvictim%3B%2Cc0%3B%
2Cs0%3B%3Bvictim%3B%2Cc0%3B%3BVictim%
3B%2Cc0

193. Edelman (2015).

194. See Williams (2016b).

195. Cosslett (2016).

196. Oakley (1981), p. 68.

197. Beauvoir, de (1997), p. 378.

198. In Thorpe (2016).

199. Lorde (1988).

200. Ahmed (2014).

201. Thorpe (2016).

202. Tran (2016) '.

203. Thorpe (2016).

204. Ahmed (2014).

205. Wolf (2013), p. 152.

206. Hynde (2015).

207. Wolf (2013), p. xiii.

208. Hynde (2015), p. 39.

209. Kenny (2015).

210. Millett (1999), p. 20.

211. Dworkin (2007), p. 91.

212. Roiphe (1994), p. 12.

213. Roiphe (1994), p. 15.

214. Mackinnon (1979), p. xi.

215. Mackinnon (1979), p. 26.

216. Patai (1998), p. 79.

217. Mackinnon (1979), p. 55.

218. Mackinnon (1979), p. 35.

219. Mackinnon (1979), p. 28.

220. Mackinnon (1979), p. 101.

221. Citizens Advice (2017).

222. *Ibid.*

223. Trades Union Congress (2016).

224. Butler (2014).

225. Morgan (1978).

226. Kaminer (1992).

227. *Ibid.*

228. Dworkin (2007), p. 21.

229. Patai (1998), p. 130.

230. Patai (1998), p. 117.

231. Strossen (2000), p. 33.

232. Strossen (2000), p. 39.

233. Campbell (1988), p. 72.

234. Campbell (1988), p. 78.

235. McElroy (2016).

236. Solnit (2014), p. 121.

237. McElroy (2016).

238. Gittos (2015), p. 22.

239. Gittos (2015), p. 24.

240. Reece (2013).

241. Gittos (2015).

242. Levin (2016).

243. MacKinnon (1989), p. 245.

244. Patai (1998), p. 69.

245. Roiphe (1994), p. 9.

246. Washington Post-Kaiser Family Foundation (2015).

247. Stanton (2014).

248. Krebs et al. (2007).

249. Schow (2014).

250. Krebs and Lindquist (2014).

251. National Union of Students (2011).

252. Hoff Sommers (2014).

253. Gershman (2016).

254. Suk Gersen (2014).

255. Roiphe (1994), p. 80.
256. Gianini (2016).
257. Strossen (2000), p. 20.
258. Tarzia (2015), p. 115.
259. Solnit (2014), p. 24.
260. Tarzia (2015), p. 121.
261. Solnit (2014), p. 6.
262. Matsuda et al. (1993), p. 1.
263. Matsuda et al. (1993), p. 24.
264. Desanctis (2017).
265. Furedi (2017).
266. Shibley (2016), p. 42.
267. Shibley (2016), p. 72.
268. Shibley (2016), p. 84.
269. Twenge, Sherman, and Wells (2017).
270. Kuperberg and Padgett (2017).
271. *Ibid.*
272. DiDomizio (2016).
273. Bromwich (2016).
274. Allen (2016b).
275. Greer (2007), p. 112.
276. Kipnis (2015).
277. In Segal (1987), p. 18.
278. Segal (1987), p. ix.
279. Hoff Sommers (2013), p. 4.
280. New (2014).
281. Silverman, Ough, and Dennis (2013).
282. Ticoll-Ramirez (2016).
283. Jackson, Dempster, and Pollard (2015).
284. Jackson et al. (2015).
285. Temple (2013).
286. Alcorn (2016).
287. Hughes (2016).
288. Lasch (1997), p. 139.

289. Rousseau (1991).

290. Wollstonecraft (1996), p. 13.

291. Wollstonecraft (1996).

292. Wollstonecraft (1996), p. 9.

293. Banner (1980), p. 8.

294. In Engels (1994), p. 50.

295. Engels (1994), p. 57.

296. Mill (1869).

297. Oakley (1981), p. 1.

298. Banner (1980), p. 40.

299. Lasch (1997), p. 83.

300. Truth (1851).

301. Lewis (2017).

302. Mill (1869), p. 14.

303. Friedan (2010), p. 67.

304. Astin and Hirsch (1978).

305. Robinson (2010), p. 66.

306. Evans (2016).

307. Oakley (1981), p. 11.

308. In Delmar (1986).

309. Banner (1980), p. 80.

310. Lasch (1997), p. 82.

311. Wollstonecraft (1996), p. 34.

312. Beauvoir, de (1997), p. 428.

313. Greer (2012), p. 78.

314. Delmar (1986), p. 21.

315. Engels (1994), p. 65.

316. Greer (2012), p. 25.

317. Bristow (2008).

318. Beauvoir, de (1997), p. 147.

319. Department for Professional Employees (2017).

320. Hudson (2011).

321. Lasch (1997), p. 96.

322. Oakley (1981), p. 9.

323. Lasch (1997), p. 102.

324. Holdsworth (1988), p. 82.

325. Friedan (2010).

326. Wolf (2013), p. 4.

327. U.S. Bureau of Labor Statistics (2015).

328. Lasch (1997), p. 105.

329. Friedan (2010), p. 7.

330. U.S. Bureau of Labor Statistics (2015).

331. Friedan (2010), p. 5.

332. Office for National Statistics (2016a, 2016b).

333. Marshall (1982).

334. Delmar (1986), p. 23.

335. Friedan (2010), p. 6.

336. Williams (2016a, 2016b, 2016c), p. 138.

337. Delmar (1986), p. 11.

338. Napikoski (2017).

339. Napikoski (2016).

340. In Oakley (1981), p. 30.

341. Holdsworth (1988), p. 82.

342. Holdsworth (1988), p. 82.

343. Marshall (1982), p. 56.

344. Millett (1999), p. 21.

345. Millett (1999), p. 23.

346. Bristow (2015), p. 56.

347. Millett (1999), p. 25.

348. *Ibid.*

349. Oakley (1990), p. 156.

350. Millett (1999), p. 26.

351. Oakley (1981), p. 16.

352. Greer (2012), p. 130.

353. Greer (2007), p. 384.

354. Millett (1999), p. 38.

355. For a fuller discussion of this issue, see Williams (2016a, 2016b, 2016c) Chapter 6, 'The Impact of Feminism'.

356. Solomon (1985), p. 188.

357. Nicholson (1990), p. 4.

358. Clisby and Holdsworth (2016), p. 4.

359. Clisby and Holdsworth (2016), p. 4.

360. Nicholson (1990), p. 3.

361. David (2004), p. 103.

362. David (2004), p. 106.

363. Nicholson (1990), p. 5.

364. Butler (2006), p. xviii.

365. Crowley and Himmelweit (1995), p. 5.

366. Patai and Koertge (2003), pp. xiii/xiv.

367. In Segal (1987), p. 23.

368. In Nicholson (1990), p. 7.

369. Crowley and Himmelweit (1995), p. 4.

370. Harraway (1988), pp. 590–592 in Clisby and Holdsworth (2016), p. 4.

371. Bartky (1975).

372. Patai and Koertge (2003), p. 77.

373. Hoff Sommers (1995), p. 26.

374. Butler (2006), p. 50.

375. Butler (2006), p. 22.

376. Butler (2006), p 9.

377. Mitchell and Oakley (1986).

378. Acker (1987).

379. Segal (1987) 3.

380. Delmar (1986), p. 9.

381. See Acker (1987).

382. Cott (1986), p. 58.

383. Lorde (1979).

384. Assiter (2016), p. 49.

385. Ladson-Billings (1998).

386. Lawrence, Matsuda, Delgado, and Crenshaw (1993), p. 3.

387. Lawrence et al. (1993), p. 5.

388. Crenshaw (1993), p. 112.
389. Lawrence et al. (1993), p. 5.
390. Crenshaw (1993), p. 112.
391. Crenshaw (1993), p. 112.
392. Crenshaw (1993), p. 116.
393. Crenshaw (1993), p. 115.
394. Assiter (2016), p. 51.
395. Dastagir (2017).
396. Pluckrose (2017).
397. Mackinnon (1979), p. 119.
398. Patai (1998), p. 37.
399. McClousky (2015).
400. Sanchez (2017).
401. Crenshaw (1989).
402. Walker (1992).
403. *Ibid*.
404. Heywood and Drake (1997), p. 7.
405. Sanchez (2017).
406. Faludi (1992), p. 13.
407. Heywood and Drake (1997), p. 2.
408. Heywood and Drake (1997), p. 3.
409. Heywood and Drake (1997), p. 52.
410. Heywood and Drake (1997), p. 3.
411. Delmar (1986), p. 27.
412. Heywood and Drake (1997), p. 2.
413. Heywood and Drake (1997), p. 50.
414. Stanley (1990), p. 12 in Clisby and Holdsworth (2016), p. 3.
415. Butler (2006), p. 8.
416. Lasch (1997), p. 144.
417. Butler (2006), p. 34.
418. Wishnant (2015), p. 3.
419. Solomon (2009).
420. Sollee (2015).

421. Oakley (1981), p. 281.
422. Oakley (1981), p. 281.
423. Murphy (2015), p. 17.
424. Delgado (2017).
425. Strimpel (2016).
426. Phillips (2016b).
427. Sanghani (2015b).
428. Harding (2015).
429. Brill (2017).
430. Gander (2017).
431. Holdsworth (1988), p. 88.
432. Beauvoir, de (1997), p. 295.
433. Beauvoir, de (1997), p. 295.
434. Beauvoir, de (1997), p. 14.
435. Beauvoir, de (1997), p. 15.
436. Much of the following section is reproduced from a 2016 essay I wrote for *Spiked-Online*, 'The Prison-House of Gender' and is reprinted here with permission.
437. Garbacik (2013), p. 13.
438. Greer (2007), p. 294.
439. Butler (2006), p. 50.
440. Clisby and Holdsworth (2016), p. 117.
441. Phillips (2016a).
442. Garbacik (2013), p. 21.
443. Garbacik (2013), p. 23.
444. Garbacik (2013), p. 21.
445. Fine (2012), p. 39.
446. Reilly-Cooper (2016).
447. Butler (2006), p. 34.
448. Clisby and Holdsworth (2016), p. 58.
449. Butler (2006), p. xi.
450. Butler (2006), p. xiii.
451. Beauvoir, de (1997), p. 13.

452. Beauvoir, de (1997), p. 69.

453. Beauvoir, de (1997), p. 308.

454. Bayley (2015).

455. Beauvoir, de (1997), p. 29.

456. Furedi (2016a).

457. Bristow (2017).

458. Hochschild and Machung (1990), p. 16.

459. Roiphe (2013).

460. Warner (2006), p. 53.

461. Girlguiding (2015), p. 19.

462. Inman (2016).

BIBLIOGRAPHY

Acker, S. (1987). Feminist theory and the study of gender and education. *International Review of Education*, *33*(4), 419–435.

Adams, R. (2016). Brighton College alters uniform code to accommodate transgender pupils. *The Guardian*, January 20.

Ahmed, S. (2014). Self-care as warfare. *Feminist Killjoys*, August 25. Retrieved from https://feministkilljoys.com/2014/08/25/selfcare-as-warfare/. Accessed on May 6, 2017.

Alcorn, C. L. (2016). How millennials in the workplace are turning peer mentoring on its head. *Fortune*, July 26. Retrieved from http://fortune.com/2016/07/26/reverse-mentoring-target-unitedhealth/. Accessed on May 5, 2017.

Allen, K. (2016a). Gender pay gap: Women earn £300,000 less than men over working life. *The Guardian*, March 7.

Allen, S. (2016b). The unsexy truth about millennials: They're poor. *Daily Beast*, August 6. Retrieved from http://www.thedailybeast.com/articles/2016/08/05/the-unsexy-truth-about-millennials-they-re-poor.html. Accessed on May 7, 2017.

Arnett, G. (2014). A-level results 2014: The full breakdown. *The Guardian*, August 14.

Assiter, A. (2016). Why universalism? *Feminist Dissent*, *2016*(1), 35–63.

Astin, H., & Hirsch, W. (1978). *The higher education of women: Essays in honor of Rosemary Park*. New York, NY: Praeger.

Atler, C. (2015). Here's the history of the battle for equal pay for American women. *Time*, April 14.

Banner, L. W. (1980). *Elizabeth Cady Stanton a radical for woman's rights*. Boston, MA: Little, Brown and Company.

Barrett, E. (2016). The true heroes of Grunwick. *Spiked-Online*. Retrieved from http://www.spiked-online.com/news-ite/article/the-true-heroes-of-grunwick/19105#.WH83fFOLTX4. Accessed on April 27.

Bartky, S. L. (1975). Towards a phenomenology of feminist consciousness. *Social Theory and Practice*, 3(4), 425–439.

Bayley, L. (2015). Caitlyn Jenner won big at Glamour's Woman of The Year Awards. *Glamour*, November 10.

Beauvoir de, S. (1997). *The second sex*. London: Vintage Books.

Belfield, C., Cribb, J., Hood, A., & Joyce, R. (2017). *Two decades of income inequality in Britain: The role of wages, household earnings and redistribution*. IFS Working Paper W17/01. The Institute for Fiscal Studies.

Bell, D. (2015). We must stop indoctrinating boys in feminist ideology. *The Telegraph*, July 20.

Bennett, J. (2016). *Feminist fight club: An office survival manual for a sexist workplace*. London: Penguin Random House.

Bentham, M. (2017). Doctor cleared over FGM says women should be free to have intimate surgery. *Evening Standard*, February 28.

Biddulph, S. (2017). The goal is a strong woman. *The Sunday Times*, April 16.

Bourdieu, P., & Passeron, J.-C. (2000). *Reproduction in education, society and culture*. London: Sage Publications.

Brearley, J. (2016). Maternity discrimination is pushing women out of work — and it's time to shout about it. *The Telegraph*, March 23.

Brighton and Hove Equality and Anti-Bullying School Strategy Group. (2017). *A brief guide to challenging sexist and sexual language and bullying*. Retrieved from http://brightonandhovelscb.org.uk/wp-content/uploads/Challenging_sexist_language.pdf. Accessed April 26, 2017.

Brill, K. (2017). Cate Blanchet locates her moral compass in her vagina. *Vanity Fair*, March 8, 2017.

Bristow, J. (2008). Why we need a parents' liberation movement. *Spiked-Online*, June 27. Retrieved from http://www.spiked-online.com/review_of_books/article/5386#.WRLq7vkrLX4. Accessed on May 10, 2017.

Bristow, J. (2009). *Standing up to supernanny*. Exeter: Societas.

Bristow, J. (2015). *Baby boomers and generational conflict*. London: Palgrave Macmillan.

Bristow, J. (2017). Policing pregnancy: The new attack on women's autonomy. *Spiked-Online*. Retrieved from http://www.spiked-online.com/newsite/article/policing-pregnancy-the-new-attack-on-womens-autonomy/19765#.WRLpp_krLX4. Accessed on May 10, 2017.

Bromwich, J. E. (2016). Some millennials are not having sex: But a vast majority are. *New York Times*, August 4.

Busby, E. (2016). GCSE results: Gender gap widens as girls pull further ahead. *Times Educational Supplement*, August 25.

Butler, B. (2014). The story behind that '10 hours of walking in NYC' viral street harassment video. *The Washington Post*, October 29.

Butler, J. (2006). *Gender trouble*. New York, NY: Routledge Classics.

California Department of Education. (2016). *California Longitudinal Pupil Achievement Data System*, May.

Campbell, B. (1988). *Unofficial secrets: Child abuse – The Cleveland Case*. London: Virago.

Catalyst (2016). *Quick take: Women in the labour force in the UK*. New York, NY: Catalyst..

Citizens Advice. (2017). *Sexual harassment: What is sexual harassment?* Retrieved from https://www.citizensadvice.org.uk/law-and-courts/discrimination/what-are-the-different-types-of-discrimination/sexual-harassment/. Accessed on May 5, 2017.

Cliff, M. (2014). 'This is sexist bull****!': Potty Mouth Princesses are back in a new Christmas video … and all they want from Santa is equal pay for women. *The Daily Mail*, December 9.

Clisby, S., & Holdsworth, J. (2016). *Gendering women, identity and mental wellbeing through the lifecourse*. University of Bristol: Policy Press.

Cooper, Y. (2016). Why I'm campaigning to reclaim the internet from sexist trolls. *The Telegraph*, May 26.

Cory, G., & Stirling, A. (2015). *Who's breadwinning in Europe? A comparative analysis of maternal breadwinning in Great Britain and Germany*. London: Institute for Public Policy Research.

Cosslett, R. L. (2016). This is modern Britain — No wonder young women have PTSD. *The Guardian*, September 29.

Costa Dias, M., Elming, W., & Joyce, R. (2016). *The gender wage gap*. The Institute for Fiscal Studies.

Cott, N. (1986). Feminist theory and feminist movements: The past before us. In J. Mitchell & A. Oakley (Eds.), *What is feminism?* Oxford: Basil Blackwell.

Court, G. (1995). *Women in the labour market: Two decades of change and continuity*. Brighton: The Institute for Employment Studies.

Crenshaw, K. (1989). Demarginalizing the intersection of race and sex: A black feminist critique of antidiscrimination doctrine, feminist theory and anti-racist politics. *The University of Chicago Legal Forum, 1*(8), 139–168.

Crenshaw, K. (1993). Beyond racism and misogyny: Black feminism and 2 live crew. In M. J. Matsuda, C. R. Lawrence III, R. Delgado, & C. W. Crenshaw (Eds.), *Words that wound: Critical race theory, assaultive speech, and the First Amendment*. New Perspectives on Law, Culture & Society. Boulder, CO: Westview Press.

Crowley, H., & Himmelweit, S. (1995). *Knowing women, feminism and knowledge*. Cambridge, MA: Polity Press.

Dastagir, A. E. (2017). What is intersectional feminism? A look at the term you may be hearing a lot. *USA Today*, January 19.

Daubney, M. (2016). My son and Britain's boy crisis. *The Times*, October 15.

David, M. (2004). Feminist sociology and feminist knowledges: Contributions to higher education pedagogies and professional practices in the knowledge economy. *International Studies in Sociology of Education*, 14(2), 99–123.

Davis, N. (2017). Girls believe brilliance is a male trait, research into gender stereotypes shows. *The Guardian*, January 27.

Delgado, D. (2017). Befriending Becky: On the imperative of intersectional solidarity. *Huffington Post*, February 14. Retrieved from http://www.huffingtonpost.com/entry/befriending-becky-on-the-imperative-of-intersectional_us_58a339efe4b080bf74f04114. Accessed on May 7, 2017.

Delmar, R. (1986). What is feminism? In J. Mitchell & A. Oakley (Eds.), *What is feminism?* Oxford: Basil Blackwell..

Department for Education, National Statistics. (2015). *Phonics screening check and national curriculum assessments at key stage 1 in England.* SFR 32/2015.

Department for Professional Employees (2017). *Professional women: A gendered look at inequality in the U.S. workforce.* Factsheet 2017. Retrieved from http://dpeaflcio.org/programs-publications/issue-fact-sheets/professional-women-a-gendered-look-at-occupational-obstacles-and-opportunities/. Accessed on May 6, 2017.

Desanctis, A. (2017). Day without a woman: Fake feminism, and doomed to failure. *National Review*, March 9. Retrieved from http://www.nationalreview.com/article/445643/why-day-without-woman-strike-failed-biggest-victim-contest. Accessed on May 5, 2017.

Didau, D. (2016). What causes the gender gap in education? *The Learning Spy*, September 25. Retrieved from http://www.learningspy.co.uk/featured/gender-gap-perception-causality/. Accessed March 26, 2017.

DiDomizio, N. (2016). Millennials are having less sex because the internet is way more fun. *Mic*. Retrieved from https://mic.com/articles/150399/millennials-are-having-less-sex-because-the-internet-is-way-more-fun#.mTeIrRuKh. Accessed May 7, 2017.

Downey, A. (2017). Shop till you stop: Pregnant women can pocket £260 in shopping vouchers if they quit smoking. *The Sun*, February 15.

Dworkin, A. (2007). *Intercourse*. New York, NY: Free Press Paperbacks.

Edelman, S. (2015). Scholar: 'Grievance Feminism' crippling debate on gender politics. *The Washington Free Beacon*, June 5.

Engels, F. (1994). *The origin of the family, private property and the state*. London: Junius Publications.

Equality Challenge Unit. *Athena Swan Charter*. Retrieved from http://www.ecu.ac.uk/equality-charters/athena-swan/. Accessed on May 4.

Evans, M. (2016). Their privilege at stake: The elite pull no punches. *Times Higher Education*, October 13.

Faircloth, C. (2014). Intensive parenting. In E. Lee, J. Bristow, C. Faircloth, & J. Macvarish (Eds.), *Parenting culture studies*. London: Palgrave Macmillan.

Faludi, S. (1992). *Backlash: The undeclared war against women*. London: Vintage.

Fawcett Society, The. *Equal pay day*. Retrieved from http://www.fawcettsociety.org.uk/our-work/campaigns/equal-pay-day-2/. Accessed April 27, 2017.

Fawcett Society, The. *The gender pay gap*. Retrieved from http://www.fawcettsociety.org.uk/policy-research/the-gender-pay-gap/. Accessed on April 27, 2017.

Fine, C. (2012). *Delusions of gender*. London: Icon Books.

Flaherty, C. (2014). Law school trigger warnings. *Inside Higher Ed,* December 17. Retrieved from https://www.inside-highered.com/news/2014/12/17/harvard-law-professor-says-requests-trigger-warnings-limit-education-about-rape-law. Accessed on May 6, 2017.

Friedan, B. (2010). *The feminine mystique*. London: Penguin Modern Classics.

Friedman, S., Laurison, D., & Macmillan, L. (2017). *Social mobility, the class pay gap and intergenerational workless-ness: New insights from the Labour Force Survey*. London: Social Mobility Commission.

Furedi, A. (2016a). *The moral case for abortion*. London: Palgrave Macmillan.

Furedi, F. (2016b). Boys have internalised the stereotype that they're not supposed to like books or learning. *Times Educational Supplement*, April 23.

Furedi, F. (2017). *What's happened to the university? A sociological exploration of its infantilisation*. London: Routledge.

Gander, K. (2017). Vaginas deserve their own museum to help women learn about consent and their health, says YouTuber. *The Independent*, March 29.

Garbacik, J. (2013). *Gender and Sexuality for Beginners*. Danbury: For Beginners.

Gershenson, S. (2016). Gender gaps merit more attention than they receive, January 1. Brown Center Chalkboard. Brookings.

Gershman, J. (2016). 'Jackie' from debunked rolling stone rape story in tussle over deposition demands. *The Wall Street Journal*, March 25.

Gettell, O. (2016). Patricia Arquette on gender pay gap: 'We've reached a breaking point'. *Entertainment Weekly*, April 12.

Gianini, L. (2016). I didn't say no — But it was still rape. *Bustle*, February 9. Retrieved from https://www.bustle.com/articles/135171-i-didnt-say-no-but-it-was-still-rape. Accessed on May 5, 2017.

Girlguiding. (2015). *Girls' Attitudes Survey 2015*. London: Girlguiding.

GirlTalkHQ. (2014). *A list of reasons why Laci Green is a feminist and you should be too*, April 30. Retrieved from http://girltalkhq.com/list-reasons-laci-green-feminist/. Accessed on April 27, 2017.

Gittos, L. (2015). *Why rape culture is a dangerous myth: From Steubenville to Ched Evans*. Exeter: Imprint Academic.

Greer, G. (2007). *The whole woman*. London: Black Swan.

Greer, G. (2012). *The female eunuch*. London: Fourth Estate.

Grove, J. (2016a). Times higher education pay survey 2016. *Times Higher Education*, May 19, 2016.

Grove, J. (2016b). University of Essex hikes salaries for female professors to eliminate pay gap. *Times Higher Education*, June 2, 2016.

Harding, K. (2015). I am voting with my vagina: Hillary Clinton for president. *Dame Magazine*, April 14. Retrieved from https://www.damemagazine.com/2015/04/14/i-am-voting-my-vagina-hillary-clinton-president#sthash.lwyMoymA.dpuf. Accessed on May 10, 2017.

HESA. (2014). *Introduction: Students 2012/13*, Higher Education Statistics Agency. Retrieved from https://www.hesa.ac.uk/data-and-analysis/publications/students-2012-13/introduction. Accessed on April 15, 2017.

Heywood, L., & Drake, J. (1997). *Third wave agenda, being feminist, doing feminism*. Minnesota: University of Minnesota Press.

Hillman, N., & Robinson, N. (2016). *Boys to men: The underachievement of young men in higher education and how to start tackling it*. Report 84. Higher Education Policy Institute.

Hochschild, A., & Machung, A. (1990). *The second shift*. New York, NY: Avon Books.

Hoff Sommers, C. (1995). *Who stole feminism? How women have betrayed women*. New York, NY: Touchstone.

Hoff Sommers, C. (2012). Wage gap myth exposed — By feminists. *Huffington Post*, November 4. Retrieved from http://www.huffingtonpost.com/christina-hoff-sommers/wage-gap_b_2073804.html. Accessed April 27, 2017.

Hoff Sommers, C. (2013). *The war against boys*. New York, NY: Simon and Schuster Paperbacks.

Hoff Sommers, C. (2014). Rape culture is a 'panic where paranoia, censorship, and false accusations flourish'. *Time*, May 15.

Holdsworth, A. (1988). *Out of the doll's house*. London: BBC Books.

Hudson, P. (2011). Women's work. *BBC History*, March 29. Retrieved from http://www.bbc.co.uk/history/british/victorians/womens_work_01.shtml. Accessed on May 6, 2017.

Hughes, T. (2016). Firm where women train older men not to be sexists: Young female staff are combating the problem of out-of-touch male executives. *The Daily Mail*, April 16.

Hunt, E. (2016). Higher proportion of men than women report online abuse in survey. *The Guardian*, September 5.

Hynde, C. (2015). *Reckless*. London: Ebury Press.

Inman, P. (2016). Survey: 41% of young women expect to face discrimination at work. *The Guardian*, October 25.

Institute of Physics (2012). Physics students in UK higher education institutions. *Research and Policy*, March, Oxford.

Issadore, M. (2015). Feminism for first-graders, and other ways to support early gender equity. *Noodle*, December 1. Retrieved from https://www.noodle.com/articles/teach-feminism-in-elementary-school-with-these-tips. Accessed on May 10, 2017.

Jackson, C., Dempster, S., & Pollard, L. (2015). 'They just don't seem to really care, they just think it's cool to sit there and talk': Laddism in university teaching-learning contexts. *Educational Review*, 67(3), 300–314.

Jeapes, M. (2016). 83% of women think gender discrimination exists in the workplace. *Investors in People*, March 8.

Retrieved from https://www.investorsinpeople.com/press/83-women-think-gender-discrimination-exists-workplace. Accessed on May 4, 2017.

Kaminer, W. (1992). Feminists against the first amendment. *The Atlantic*, November.

Kenny, M. (1979). *Woman x two: How to cope with a double life*. Middlesex: Hamlyn Paperbacks.

Kenny, M. (2015). The condom train is our story, including its misguided folly. *Irish Independent*, September 28.

Khomami, N. (2016). Receptionist 'sent home from PwC for not wearing high heels'. *The Guardian*, May 11.

Kipnis, L. (2015). My Title IX inquisition. *The Chronicle of Higher Education*, May 29.

Krebs, C., & Lindquist, C. (2014). Setting the record straight on '1 in 5'. *Time*, December 15.

Krebs, C. P., et al. (2007). *The campus sexual assault (CSA) study*. Washington: National Institute of Justice.

Kuperberg, A., & Padgett, J. E. J. (2017). Partner meeting contexts and risky behavior in college students' other-sex and same-sex hookups. *Journal of Sex Research*, 54(1), 55–72.

Ladson-Billings, G. (1998). Just what is critical race theory and what's it doing in a nice field like education? *International Journal of Qualitative Studies in Education*, 2(1).

Lasch, C. (1991). *The culture of narcissism*. New York, NY: Norton Paperback.

Lasch, C. (1997). *Women and the common life*. London: W. W. Norton.

Laville, S. (2016). Research reveals huge scale of social media misogyny. *The Guardian*, May 26.

Lawrence, III, C. R., Matsuda, M. J., Delgado, R., & Crenshaw, K. W. (1993). Introduction. In Matsuda, et al. (Eds.), *Words that wound: Critical race theory, assaultive speech, and the First Amendment*. New Perspectives on Law, Culture & Society. Boulder, CO: Westview Press.

Leach, A. (2016). 'It's all about democracy': Inside gender neutral schools in Sweden. *The Guardian*, February 2.

Leake, J. (2016). Factor this: Women are closing the maths gap. *The Times*, November 27.

Lee, E. (2009). The normalisation of parent training. In J. Bristow (Ed.), *Standing up to supernanny*. Exeter: Imprint Academic.

Lee, E. (2014). Introduction. In E. Lee, J. Bristow, C. Faircloth, & J. Macvarish (Eds.), *Parenting culture studies*. London: Palgrave Macmillan.

Leftly, M. (2017). Tesco cuts price of women's razors so they cost the same as men's. *The Guardian*, January 1.

Levin, S. (2016). Ex-Stanford swimmer gets six months in jail and probation for sexual assault. *The Guardian*, June 2.

Lewis, F. (2017). The National Association of Colored Women: Fighting for racial justice. *Thoughtco*, February 4. Retrieved from https://www.thoughtco.com/national-associa-tion-of-colored-women-45392. Accessed on May 6, 2017.

Livingston, E. (2017). When will universities wake up to this epidemic of sexual harassment? *The Guardian*, March 7.

Lorde, A. (1979). An open letter to Mary Daly. *History is a Weapon*. Retrieved from http://www.historyisaweapon.com/

defcon1/lordeopenlettertomarydaly.html. Accessed on May 9, 2017.

Lorde, A. (1988). *A burst of light*. Ann Arbor, MI: Firebrand Books.

Lyonette, C., & Crompton, R. (2015). Sharing the load? Partners' relative earnings and the division of domestic labour. *Work, Employment and Society, 29*(1), 23–40.

MacKinnon, C. (1979). *Sexual harassment of working women*. London: Yale University Press.

MacKinnon, C. (1989). *Towards a feminist theory of the state*. Cambridge, MA: Harvard University Press.

Macvarish, J. (2016). *Neuroparenting: The expert invasion of family life*. London: Palgrave Pivot.

Makel, M. C., Wai, J., Peairs, K., & Putallaz, M. (2016). Sex differences in the right tail of cognitive abilities: An update and cross cultural extension. *Intelligence* (59), 8–15.

Marshall, K. (1982). *Real freedom*. London: Junius Publications.

Mason, R., & Treanor, J. (2015). David Cameron to force companies to disclose gender pay gaps. *The Guardian*, July 14.

Matsuda, M. (Eds.) (1993). Words that wound: Critical race theory, assaultive speech, and the First Amendment. *New Perspectives on Law, Culture & Society*. Boulder, CO: Westview Press.

Maybin, S. (2016). Four ways the gender pay gap isn't all it seems. *BBC*, August 29. Retrieved from http://www.bbc.co.uk/news/magazine-37198653. Accessed May 5, 2017.

Mayer, C. (2016). Politics is a funny business — But there's nothing funny about the failure to fix the gender pay gap. *Huffington Post*, March 23. Retrieved from http://www.huffingtonpost.co.uk/catherine-mayer/gender-pay-gap_b_9530482.html. Accessed on April 27, 2017.

McClousky, M. (2015). Here are 4 ways to navigate whiteness and feminism — Without being a white feminist. *Everyday Feminism*, June 29. Retrieved from http://everydayfeminism.com/2015/06/navigating-whiteness-feminism/. Accessed May 7, 2017.

McElroy, W. (2016). *Rape culture hysteria: Fixing the damage done to men and women*. CreateSpace Independent Publishing Platform.

McIntyre, N. (2014). I helped shut down an abortion debate between two men because my uterus isn't up for their discussion. *The Independent*, November 18.

Mill, J. S. (1869). *The subjection of women*. London: Longmans.

Miller, C. C. (2017). Why men don't want the jobs done mostly by women. *New York Times*, January 4.

Miller, C. C., & Alderman, L. (2014). Why U.S. women are leaving jobs behind. *New York Times*, December 12.

Millett, K. (1999). *Sexual politics*. London: Virago.

Mitchell, J. (1986). Reflections on twenty years of feminism. In J. Mitchell & A. Oakley (Eds.), *What is feminism?* Oxford: Basil Blackwell.

Mitchell, J., & Oakley, A. (Eds.). (1986). *What is feminism?* Oxford: Basil Blackwell.

Moore, S. (2016). Why did women vote for Trump? Because misogyny is not a male-only attribute. *The Guardian*, November 16.

Moore, S. (2017). Women in public life are now being openly bullied: How has this become normal? *The Guardian*, February 13.

Morgan, R. (1978). *Going too far: The personal chronicle of a feminist*. London: Random House.

Morris, S. (2016). UK company to introduce 'period policy' for female staff. *The Guardian*, March 2.

Moss, R. (2015). Gender pay gap reports extended to include bonuses and public sector. *Personnel Today*, October 26.

Murphy, M. (2015). I do what I want, fuck yeah!': Moving beyond a woman's choice. In M. Kiraly & M. Tyler (Eds.), *Freedom fallacy: The limits of liberal feminism*. Ballarat: Connor Court Publishing.

Napikoski, L. (2016). The second feminist wave. *Thoughtco*, March 3. Retrieved from https://www.thoughtco.com/the-second-feminist-wave-3528923. Accessed May 6, 2017.

Napikoski, L. (2017). How women became part of the Civil Rights Act. *Thoughtco*, March 25. Retrieved from https://www.thoughtco.com/women-and-the-civil-rights-act-3529477. Accessed May 6, 2017.

National Education Association. (2011). *Race against time: Educating black boys*. Focus on Blacks, February.

National Union of Students. (2011). *Hidden marks: A study of women students' experiences of harassment, stalking, violence and sexual assault*. London: National Union of Students.

National Union of Teachers. (2017). *Challenging gender stereotypes through reading*. Retrieved from https://www.teachers.org.uk/sites/default/files2014/childs-play-20pp-final-for-website_0.pdf. Accessed on April 26, 2017.

New, J. (2014). Banning frats? *Inside Higher Ed,* September 29. Retrieved from https://www.insidehighered.com/news/2014/09/30/should-colleges-ban-fraternities-and-sororities. Accessed May 7, 2017.

NHS Choices. (2016). *What is preconception care?* Retrieved from http://www.nhs.uk/chq/Pages/2594.aspx?CategoryID=54&SubCategoryID=127. Accessed on May 5, 2017.

NHS Choices. (2017). *Foods to avoid in pregnancy*. Retrieved from http://www.nhs.uk/conditions/pregnancy-and-baby/pages/foods-to-avoid-pregnant.aspx#Herbal. Accessed on May 5, 2017.

Nicholson, L. J. (1990). *Feminism/Postmodernism*. London: Routledge.

Niemtus, Z. (2016). How to teach….feminism. *The Guardian*, January 11.

O'Brien, J. (2016). Debating abortion on campus: The crisis of free speech. *Conscience*, XXXVII, No. 3.

O'Brien, S. A. (2015). 78 cents on the dollar: The facts about the gender wage gap. *CNN Money*, Retrieved from http://money.cnn.com/2015/04/13/news/economy/equal-pay-day-2015/. Accessed on April 27, 2017.

Oakley, A. (1981). *Subject women*. New York, NY: Pantheon Books.

Oakley, A. (1990). *Housewife*. London: Penguin Books.

Office for National Statistics. (2013). *Full report — Women in the labour market*, September 25.

Office for National Statistics. (2015). *Compendium participation rates in the UK — 2014 — 2. Women*, March 19.

Office for National Statistics. (2016a). *Statistical bulletin: Annual survey of hours and earnings: 2016 provisional results*. Retrieved from https://www.ons.gov.uk/employment andlabourmarket/peopleinwork/earningsandworkinghours/ bulletins/annualsurveyofhoursandearnings/2016provisional- results. Accessed April 27, 2017.

Office for National Statistics. (2016b). *Statistical bulletin: UK labour market*, September.

Packham, A. (2015). Men working in high-earning part-time roles reaches record high: Dads explain how it works for them. *Huffington Post*, November 9. Retrieved from http:// www.huffingtonpost.co.uk/2015/11/09/men-working-part- time-dads-family_n_8478862.html. Accessed May 5.

Palejwala, M. (2015). Gender differences in latent cognitive abilities in children aged 2 to 7. *Intelligence* (46), 96—108.

Parker, C. E. (2016). Occidental students protest Harvard Law Professor as commencement speaker. *The Harvard Crimson*, April 29. Retrieved from http://www.thecrimson. com/article/2016/4/29/occidental-students-criticize-kennedy/. Accessed on May 6.

Patai, D. (1998). *Heterophobia sexual harassment and the future of feminism*. Oxford: Rowman and Littlefield.

Patai, D., & Koertge, N. (2003). *Professing feminism*. New York, NY: Lexington Books.

Paul, E. (2015). Students protest Sommers' lecture. *The Oberlin Review*, April 24. Retrieved from https://oberlinreview.org/8088/news/students-protest-som-mers-lecture/. Accessed on May 5, 2017.

Penny, L. (2014). Laurie Penny on trigger warnings: What we're really talking about. *The New Statesman*, May 21.

Perry, M. (2016). Women earned majority of doctoral degrees in 2015 for 7th straight year and outnumber men in grad school 135 to 100. *AEIdeas: A Policy Blog of the American Enterprise Institute*, September 16.

Phillips, J. (2017). *Everywoman: One woman's truth about speaking the truth*. London: Hutchinson.

Phillips, M. (2016a). It's dangerous and wrong to tell all children they're gender fluid. *The Spectator*, January 30.

Phillips, T. (2016b). 'It's because I had my period': Swimmer Fu Yuanhui praised for breaking taboo. *The Guardian*, August 16.

Pierre, L. K. (2017). More evidence that sexism is a big problem in science. *Popular Science*. Retrieved from http://www.popsci.com/women-are-asked-to-review-fewer-studies-espe-cially-by-men. Accessed on May 4, 2017.

Pine, M. (2001). How exams are fixed in favour of girls. *The Spectator*, 12, January 20.

Pluckrose, H. (2017). The problem with intersectional femi-nism. *Aero Magazine*, February 15. Retrieved from https://areomagazine.com/2017/02/15/the-problem-with-intersec-tional-feminism/. Accessed on May 7, 2017.

Press Association (2015). Women in their 20s earn more than men of same age, study finds. *The Guardian*, August 29.

Press Association (2016). Mila Kunis rails against Hollywood sexism: Insulted, sidelined, paid less. *The Guardian*, November 3.

Pryce, V. (2015). *Why women need quotas*. London: Biteback Publishing.

Quinn, B. (2015). Petition urges Cardiff University to cancel Germaine Greer lecture. *The Guardian*, October 23.

Raffray, S. (2014). International Women's Day: How to empower female students in school. *The Guardian*, March 8.

Rankin, J. (2015). Fewer women leading FTSE firms than men called John. *The Guardian*, March 6.

Ratcliffe, R. (2013). The gender gap at universities: Where are all the men? *The Guardian*, January 29.

Read, C. (2016). *The lost boys*. London: Save The Children.

Reece, H. (2013). Rape myths: Is elite opinion right and popular opinion wrong? *Oxford Journal of Legal Studies*, *33*(3), 445–473.

Reilly-Cooper, R. (2016). Gender is not a spectrum. *Aeon*, June 28. Retrieved from https://aeon.co/essays/the-idea-that-gender-is-a-spectrum-is-a-new-gender-prison. Accessed on May 7, 2017.

Rivers, C., & Barnett, R. C. (2015). *The new soft war on women*. New York, NY: Penguin Random House.

Rivers, C., & Barnett, R. C. (2016). Commentary: 8 big problems for women in the workplace. *Chicago Tribune*, May 18.

Robinson, J. (2010). *Bluestockings: The remarkable story of the first women to fight for an education*. London: Penguin Books.

Roiphe, K. (1994). *The morning after, sex, fear and feminism*. London: Hamish Hamilton.

Roiphe, K. (2013). *In praise of messy lives*. Edinburgh: Canongate Books.

Rosin, H. (2013). *The end of men and the rise of women*. London: Penguin Books.

Rousseau, E. (1991). *Emile, or on education*. Middlesex: Penguin Books.

Sanchez, R. R. (2017). The third wave's tokenization of Chimamanda Ngozi Adichie is anything but intersectional. *Feminist Current*, March 20. Retrieved from http://www.feministcurrent.com/2017/03/20/third-waves-tokenization-chimamanda-ngozi-adichie-anything-intersectional/. Accessed May 7, 2017.

Sanghani, R. (2015). This woman ran the London Marathon on her period without a tampon. *The Telegraph*, August 10.

Schiller, R. (2016). The women hounded for giving birth outside the system. *The Guardian*, October 22.

Schow, A. (2014). No, 1 in 5 women have not been raped on college campuses. *Washington Examiner*, August 13.

Segal, L. (1987). *Is the future female?* London: Virago Press.

Shepherd, J. (2010). Girls think they are cleverer than boys from age four, study finds. *The Guardian*, September 1.

Shibley, R. L. (2016). *Twisting Title IX*. New York, NY: Encounter Books.

Shriver, L. (2010). Introduction. In B. Friedan (Ed.), *The feminine mystique*. London: Penguin Books.

Silverman, R., Ough, T., & Dennis, C. (2013). Oxford college rugby club relegated for drink-spiking email. *The Telegraph*, November 4.

Slaughter, A. M. (2012). Why women still can't have it all. *The Atlantic*, July/August.

Smith, N. M. (2015). Jennifer Lawrence expresses anger at Hollywood's gender pay gap. *The Guardian*, October 13.

Smothers, H. (2016). Hillary Clinton calls Donald Trump out for sexism at the first presidential debate. *Cosmopolitan*, September 27.

Soave, R. (2016). NYU cancels Milo Yiannopoulos, feared 'attacks' on Islamic and gay students, October 10. Retrieved from http://reason.com/blog/2016/10/23/nyu-cancels-milo-yiannopoulos-feared-att. Accessed on May 6.

Sollee, K. (2015). 6 things to know about 4th wave feminism. *Bustle*. Retrieved from https://www.bustle.com/articles/119524-6-things-to-know-about-4th-wave-feminism. Accessed on May 7.

Solnit, R. (2014). *Men explain things to me: And other essays*. London: Granta Books.

Solomon, B. M. (1985). *In the company of educated women*. New Haven, CT: Yale University Press.

Solomon, D. (2009). Fourth-wave feminism. *New York Times*, November 13.

Stanley, T. (2014). Oxford students shut down abortion debate: Free speech is under assault on campus. *The Telegraph*, November 19.

Stanton, J. (2014). *Lad culture & sexism survey: August–September 2014*. National Union of Students.

Status of Women in the States. (2017). *Women's labor force participation*. Retrieved from http://statusofwomendata.org/

earnings-and-the-gender-wage-gap/womens-labor-force-par-ticipation/. Accessed on April 27, 2017).

Stone-Lee, O. (2005). Thatcher's role for women. *BBC Online*, November 22. Retrieved from http://news.bbc.co.uk/1/hi/uk_politics/4435414.stm. Accessed May 5, 2017.

Strimpel, Z. (2016). Welcome to feminism's new gross out frontier. *The New Statesman*, September 29.

Strossen, N. (2000). *Defending pornography, free speech, sex, and the fight for women's rights*. New York, NY: New York University Press.

Students for Life of America. (2016). UPDATED: Catholic school hosting PP doc, uses Rosary with IUD to advertise, February 25. Retrieved from http://studentsforlife.org/catholic-school-hosting-pp-doc-uses-rosary-with-iud-to-advertise/. Accessed on May 6, 2017.

Suk Gersen, J. (2014). The trouble with teaching rape law. *The New Yorker*, December 15.

Swinford, S. (2015). David Cameron clashes with business over gender pay gap. *The Telegraph*, July 14.

Tarzia, L. (2015). A fine line between pleasure and pain? On the issue of 'choosing' sexual violence. In M. Kiraly & M. Tyler (Eds.), *Freedom fallacy: The limits of liberal feminism*. Ballarat: Connor Court Publishing.

Temple, K. (2013). Lad culture on campus. *LSE Blogs*, March 8. Retrieved from http://blogs.lse.ac.uk/equityDiversityInclusion/2013/03/lad-culture-on-campus/. Accessed on May 7, 2017.

The 3% Movement. (2016). What women want: Results from our 3% community survey, March. Retrieved from http://www.3percentconf.com/sites/default/files/download-files/WhatWomenWant%20-%20Final.pdf. Accessed on May 5, 2017.

Thorpe, J. R. (2016). Why self-care is an important feminist act. *Bustle*, December 14. Retrieved from https://www.bustle.com/articles/200074-why-self-care-is-an-important-feminist-act. Accessed on May 6, 2017.

Ticoll-Ramirez, C. (2016). 'Deconstructing masculinity': Duke Men's Project aims to facilitate discussions of male privilege and patriarchy. *The Chronicle*, September 26. Retrieved from http://www.dukechronicle.com/article/2016/09/deconstructing-masculinity-duke-mens-project-aims-to-facilitate-discussions-of-male-privilege-and-patriarchy. Accessed on May 7, 2017.

Topping, A. (2017). Campaigners hail school decision to let pupils choose gender identity. *The Guardian*, February 19.

Trades Union Congress (2016). *Still just a bit of banter? Sexual harassment in the workplace in 2016*. London: Trades Union Congress.

Tran, K. (2016). 5 self-care tips for activists — 'Cause being woke shouldn't mean your spirit's broke. *Everyday Feminism*, April 17. Retrieved from http://everydayfeminism.com/2016/04/self-care-for-woke-folks/. Accessed on May 6, 2017.

True Tube. (2017). #ShoutingBack. Retrieved from https://www.truetube.co.uk/resource/shoutingback. Accessed on April 28, 2017.

Truth, S. (1851). Ain't I a woman? *Modern History Sourcebook*. Retrieved from https://sourcebooks.fordham.edu/mod/sojtruth-woman.asp. Accessed on May 6, 2017.

Turner, C. (2015). Girls do better than boys at school, despite inequality. *The Telegraph*, January 22.

Turner, C. (2017). Teach toddlers about transgender issues: National Union of Teachers say. *The Telegraph*, April 17.

Twenge, J. M., Sherman, R. A., & Wells, B. E. (2017). Sexual inactivity during young adulthood is more common among U.S. millennials and iGen: Age, period, and cohort effects on having no sexual partners after age 18. *Archives of Sexual Behavior*, 46(2), 433–440.

U.S. Bureau of Labor Statistics. (2015). *Women in the labor force: A data book*. Report 1059. December.

U.S. Department of Education, National Center for Education Statistics. (2016). *Status and trends in the education of racial and ethnic groups*. NCES 2016-007.

U.S. Department of Labor. (2015). *Latest annual data: Women of working age*. Retrieved from https://www.dol.gov/wb/stats/latest_annual_data.htm. Accessed on April 27, 2017.

U.S. Department of Labor. (2017a). *Bureau of labor statistics, labor force statistics from the current population survey*, February 8.

U.S. Department of Labor. (2017b). *Employment characteristics of families – 2016*. Bureau of Labor Statistics.

U.S. Department of Labor. (2017c). *Women's bureau: Latest annual statistics*. Retrieved from https://www.dol.gov/wb/stats/stats_data.htm. Accessed on April 27, 2017.

University of Edinburgh: Educated Pass. Retrieved from http://www.ed.ac.uk/student-recruitment/widening-participation/projects/educated-pass. Accessed on April 26, 2017.

Veterinary Woman. (2015). *Veterinary women: Past, present and future*. Retrieved from http://www.veterinarywoman.co.uk/2015/02/veterinary-women-past-present-and-future/. Accessed on April 27, 2017.

Violence Against Women (2016). FGM prevalence rates decline in Africa as victims reach 200 million worldwide. *Africa News*, February 6. Retrieved from http://www.africa-news.com/2016/02/06/fgm-prevalence-rates-decline-in-africa-as-victims-reach-200-million-worldwide//. Accessed on May 5, 2017.

Walker, R. (1992). Becoming the third wave. *Ms.*, 2(4), 39–40.

Wang, W., Parker, K., & Taylor, P. (2013). *Breadwinner moms*. Washington, D.C.: Pew Research Center.

Warner, J. (2006). *Perfect madness, motherhood in the age of anxiety*. London: Vermilion.

Washington Post-Kaiser Family Foundation (2015). Poll: One in 5 women say they have been sexually assaulted in college. *The Washington Post*, June 12.

Williams, J. (2016a). *Academic freedom in an age of conformity: Confronting the fear of knowledge*. London: Palgrave Macmillan.

Williams, J. (2016b). Saatchi's sexism row suggests feminists can't handle debate. *The Spectator*, August 2.

Williams, J. (2016B). Saatchi's sexism row suggests feminists can't handle debate. *The Spectator*, August 2.

Williams, J. (2016c). Why are rates of mental illness soaring among young women? *Quillette*, October 4. Retrieved from http://quillette.com/2016/10/04/why-are-rates-of-mental-illness-soaring-among-young-women/. Accessed on May 6, 2017.

Williams, J. (2017). The post-fact world suits feminism just fine. *The Spectator*, February 23.

Wishnant, R. (2015). Not your father's playboy, not your mother's feminist movement: Feminism in porn culture. In M. Kiraly & M. Tyler (Eds.), *Freedom fallacy: The limits of liberal feminism*. Ballarat: Connor Court Publishing.

Wolf, A. (2013). *The XX factor*. New York, NY: Crown Publishers.

Wolf, A. (2016). Theresa May is wrong about the gender gap. *The Times,* August 24.

Wollstonecraft, M. (1996). *A vindication of the rights of women*. New York, NY: Dover Publications.

Woodfield, R., & Thomas, L. (2012). *Male students: Engagement with academic and pastoral support services*. Equality Challenge Unit.

AUTHOR BIOGRAPHY

Joanna Williams is Senior Lecturer at the University of Kent and is the author of *Academic Freedom in an Age of Conformity* and *Consuming Higher Education: Why Learning Can't Be Bought*. She is education editor of the online magazine *Spiked*, a frequent contributor to *The Spectator* and has written for numerous other publications from the *Times Higher Education* to the *Erotic Review*.

INDEX